CABLE AND X-FORCE

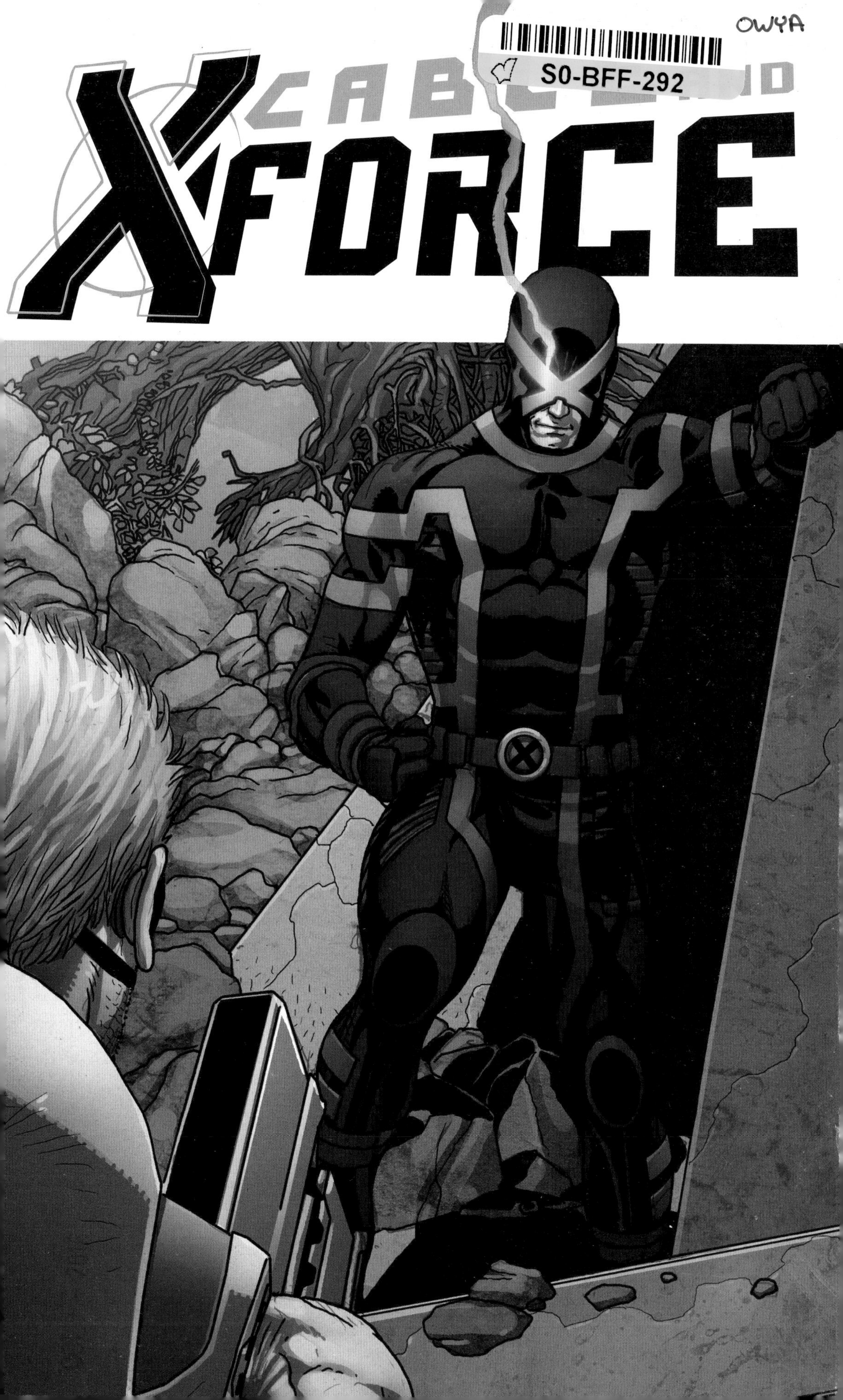

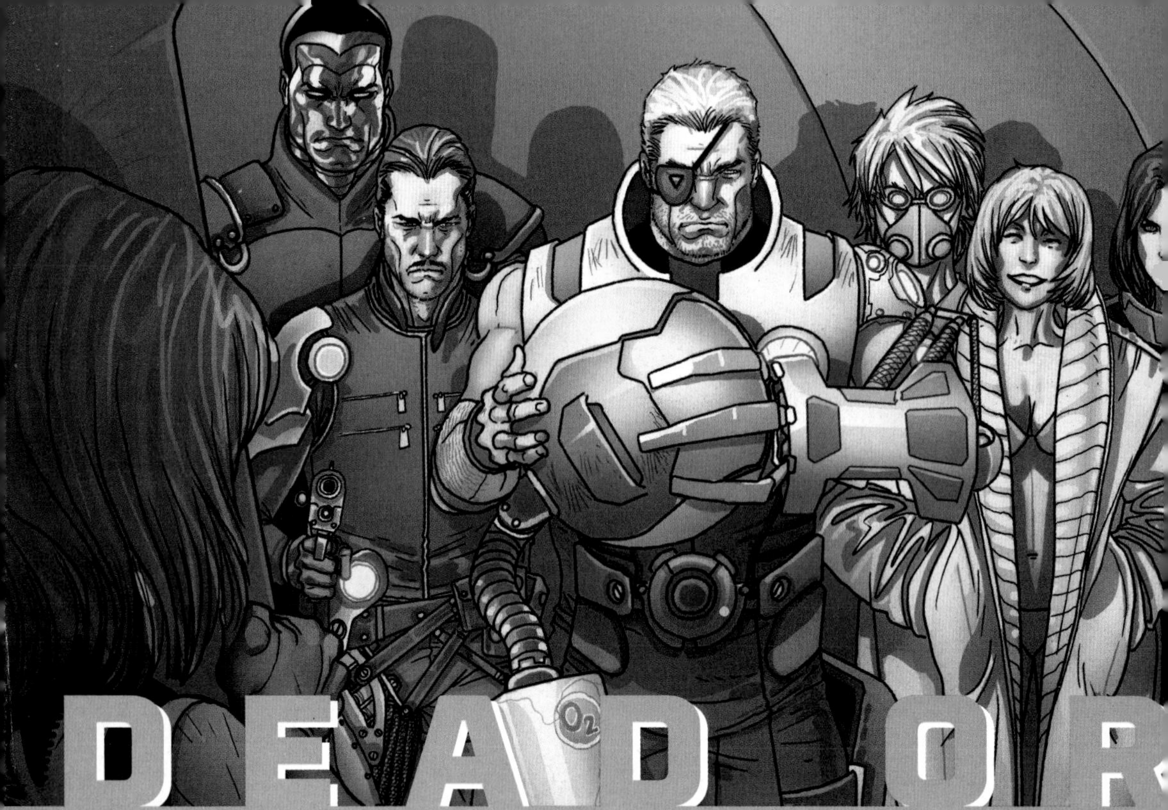

DEAD OR ALIVE

WRITERS
DENNIS HOPELESS **(#6-8)** & FRANK TIERI **(#9)**

ARTIST
SALVADOR LARROCA

COLOR ARTIST
FRANK D'ARMATA

LETTERERS
VC'S JOE SABINO & CLAYTON COWLES

COVER ART
SALVADOR LARROCA & FRANK D'ARMATA

ASSISTANT EDITOR
JENNIFER M. SMITH

ASSOCIATE EDITOR
JORDAN D. WHITE

EDITORS
NICK LOWE & DANIEL KETCHUM

COLLECTION EDITOR: **CORY LEVINE** • ASSISTANT EDITORS: **ALEX STARBUCK & NELSON RIBEIRO**
EDITORS, SPECIAL PROJECTS: **JENNIFER GRÜNWALD & MARK D. BEAZLEY**
SENIOR EDITOR, SPECIAL PROJECTS: **JEFF YOUNGQUIST**
SVP OF PRINT & DIGITAL PUBLISHING SALES: **DAVID GABRIEL** • BOOK DESIGN: **JEFF POWELL**

EDITOR IN CHIEF: **AXEL ALONSO** • CHIEF CREATIVE OFFICER: **JOE QUESADA**
PUBLISHER: **DAN BUCKLEY** • EXECUTIVE PRODUCER: **ALAN FINE**

CABLE AND X-FORCE VOL. 2: DEAD OR ALIVE. Contains material originally published in magazine form as CABLE AND X-FORCE #6-9. First printing 2013. ISBN# 978-0-7851-6691-7. Publishe by MARVEL WORLDWIDE, INC., a subsidiary of MARVEL ENTERTAINMENT, LLC. OFFICE OF PUBLICATION: 135 West 50th Street, New York, NY 10020. **Printe in the U.S.A.** ALAN FINE, EVP - Office of the President, Marvel Worldwide, Inc. and EVP & CMO Marvel Characters B.V.; DAN BUCKLEY, Publisher & President - Print, Animation & Digital Divisions; JO QUESADA, Chief Creative Officer; TOM BREVOORT, SVP of Publishing; DAVID BOGART, SVP of Operations & Procurement, Publishing; C.B. CEBULSKI, SVP of Creator & Content Development; DAVI GABRIEL, SVP of Print & Digital Publishing Sales; JIM O'KEEFE, VP of Operations & Logistics; DAN CARR, Executive Director of Publishing Technology; SUSAN CRESPI, Editorial Operations Manage ALEX MORALES, Publishing Operations Manager; STAN LEE, Chairman Emeritus. For information regarding advertising in Marvel Comics or on Marvel.com, please contact Niza Disla, Director of Marve Partnerships, at ndisla@marvel.com. For Marvel subscription inquiries, please call 800-217-9158. **Manufactured between 9/6/2013 and 10/14/2013 by QUAD/GRAPHICS, VERSAILLES, KY, USA**

10 9 8 7 6 5 4 3 2 1

CABLE AND X-FORCE

FORGE DOMINO COLOSSUS CABLE DR. NEMESIS

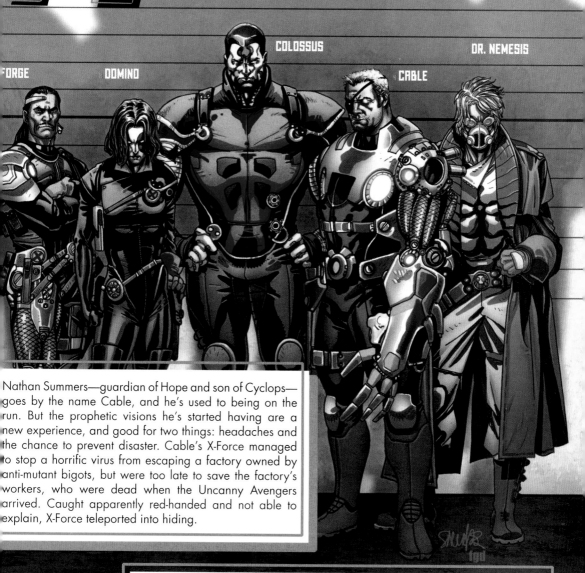

Nathan Summers—guardian of Hope and son of Cyclops—goes by the name Cable, and he's used to being on the run. But the prophetic visions he's started having are a new experience, and good for two things: headaches and the chance to prevent disaster. Cable's X-Force managed to stop a horrific virus from escaping a factory owned by anti-mutant bigots, but were too late to save the factory's workers, who were dead when the Uncanny Avengers arrived. Caught apparently red-handed and not able to explain, X-Force teleported into hiding.

Laying low in Mexico, Colossus took a break from his guilt over being one of the Phoenix Five to spend a night with Domino, and then turned himself over to the authorities. Meanwhile, Cable had a new vision, and convinced the remainder of his team, Domino, Forge, and Dr. Nemesis, to join him on a spaceship heist.

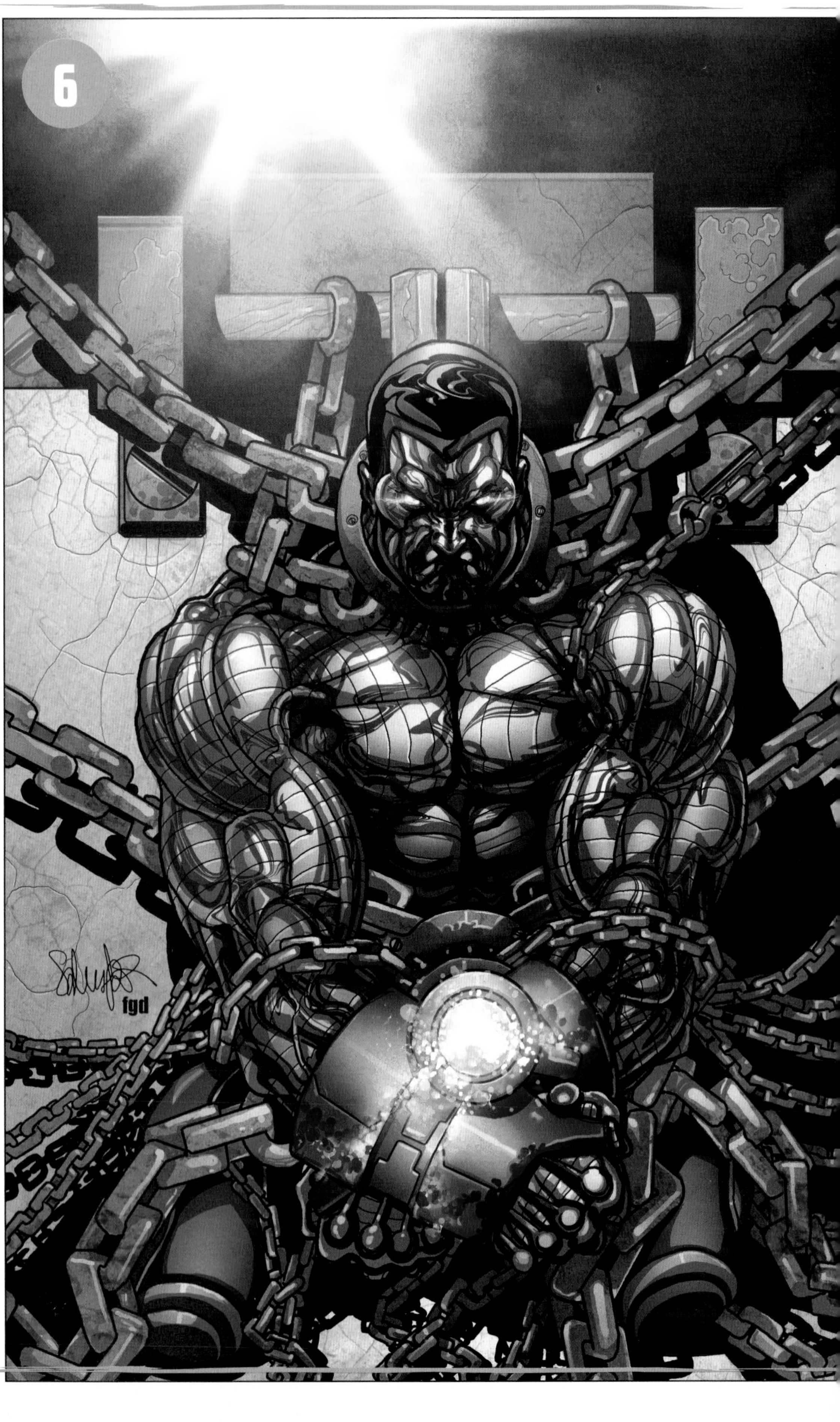
6
fgd

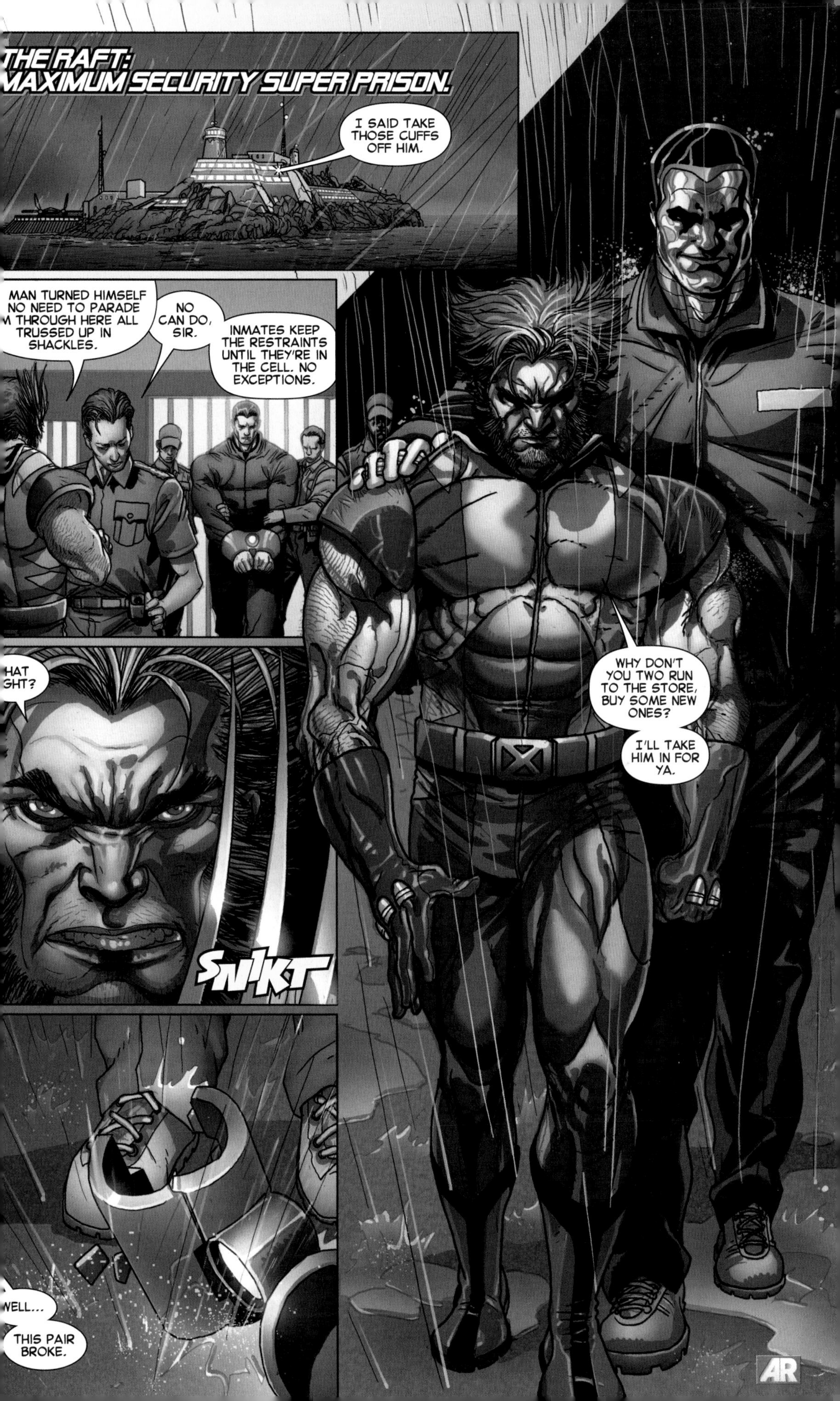
THE RAFT: MAXIMUM SECURITY SUPER PRISON.
I SAID TAKE THOSE CUFFS OFF HIM.
MAN TURNED HIMSELF NO NEED TO PARADE M THROUGH HERE ALL TRUSSED UP IN SHACKLES.
NO CAN DO, SIR.
INMATES KEEP THE RESTRAINTS UNTIL THEY'RE IN THE CELL. NO EXCEPTIONS.
HAT GHT?
SNIKT
WELL...
THIS PAIR BROKE.
WHY DON'T YOU TWO RUN TO THE STORE, BUY SOME NEW ONES?
I'LL TAKE HIM IN FOR YA.
AR

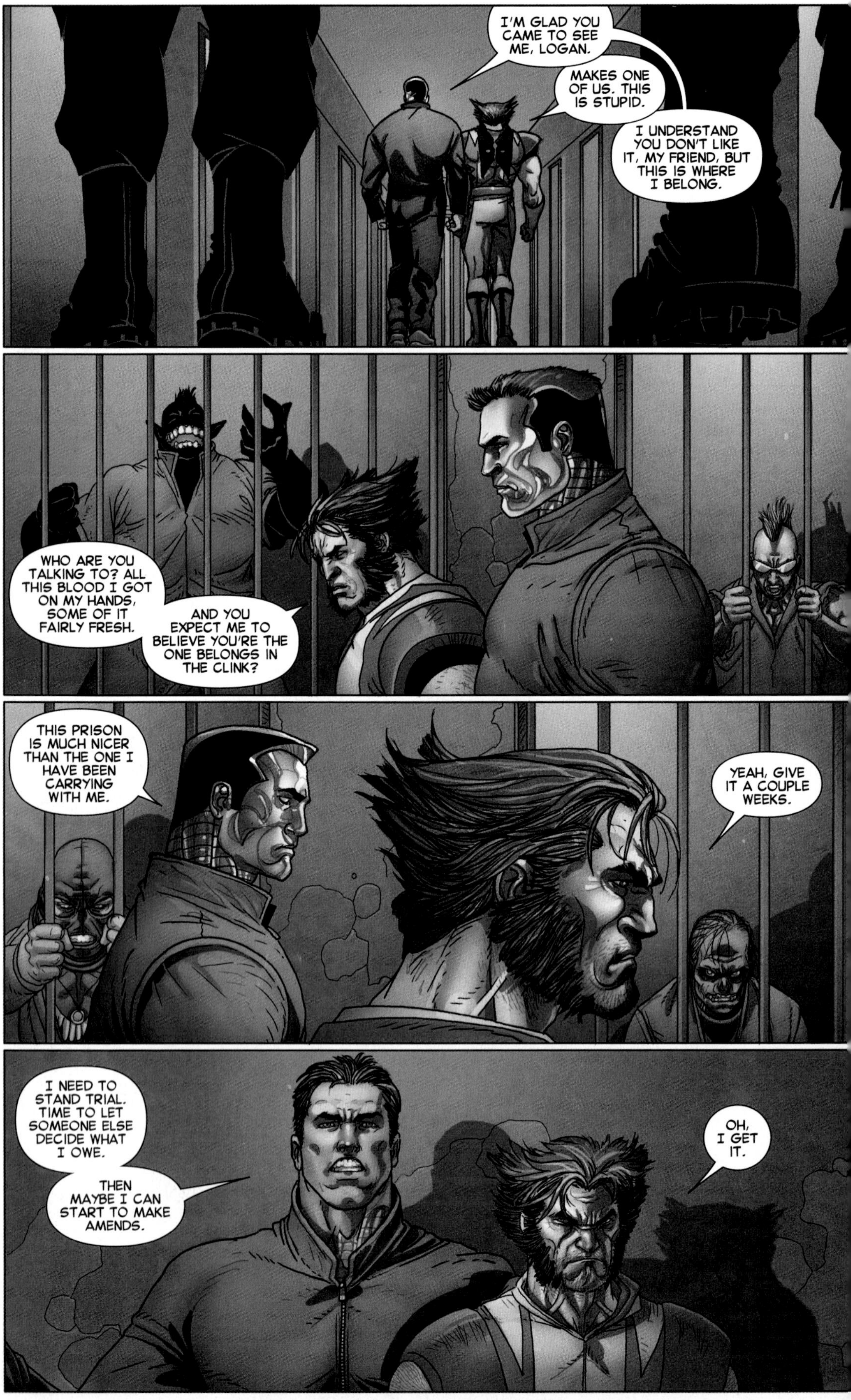

I'M GLAD YOU CAME TO SEE ME, LOGAN.
MAKES ONE OF US. THIS IS STUPID.
I UNDERSTAND YOU DON'T LIKE IT, MY FRIEND, BUT THIS IS WHERE I BELONG.
WHO ARE YOU TALKING TO? ALL THIS BLOOD I GOT ON MY HANDS, SOME OF IT FAIRLY FRESH.
AND YOU EXPECT ME TO BELIEVE YOU'RE THE ONE BELONGS IN THE CLINK?
THIS PRISON IS MUCH NICER THAN THE ONE I HAVE BEEN CARRYING WITH ME.
YEAH, GIVE IT A COUPLE WEEKS.
I NEED TO STAND TRIAL. TIME TO LET SOMEONE ELSE DECIDE WHAT I OWE.
THEN MAYBE I CAN START TO MAKE AMENDS.
OH, I GET IT.

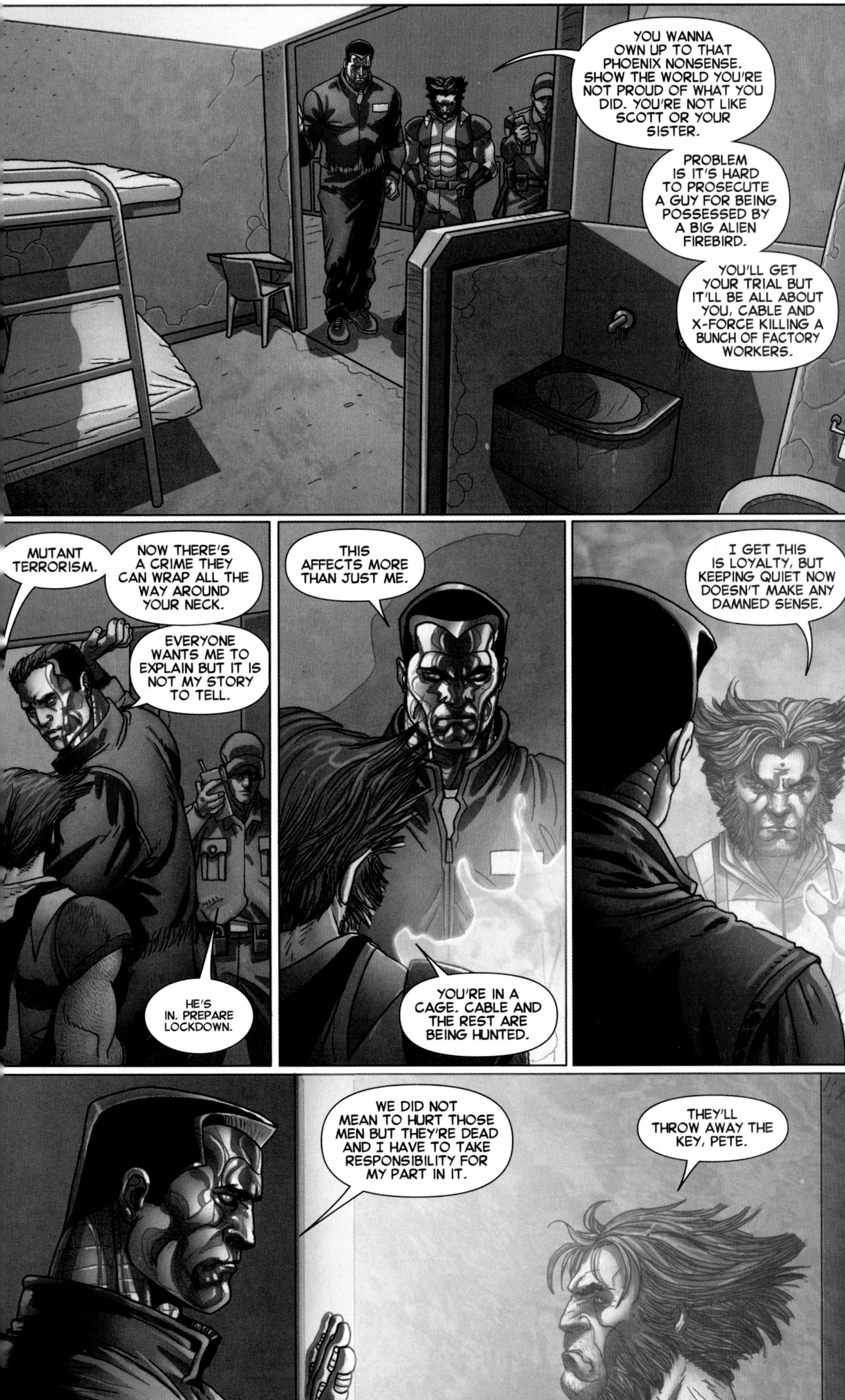
YOU WANNA OWN UP TO THAT PHOENIX NONSENSE. SHOW THE WORLD YOU'RE NOT PROUD OF WHAT YOU DID. YOU'RE NOT LIKE SCOTT OR YOUR SISTER.
PROBLEM IS IT'S HARD TO PROSECUTE A GUY FOR BEING POSSESSED BY A BIG ALIEN FIREBIRD.
YOU'LL GET YOUR TRIAL BUT IT'LL BE ALL ABOUT YOU, CABLE AND X-FORCE KILLING A BUNCH OF FACTORY WORKERS.
MUTANT TERRORISM.
NOW THERE'S A CRIME THEY CAN WRAP ALL THE WAY AROUND YOUR NECK.
EVERYONE WANTS ME TO EXPLAIN BUT IT IS NOT MY STORY TO TELL.
HE'S IN. PREPARE LOCKDOWN.
THIS AFFECTS MORE THAN JUST ME.
YOU'RE IN A CAGE. CABLE AND THE REST ARE BEING HUNTED.
I GET THIS IS LOYALTY, BUT KEEPING QUIET NOW DOESN'T MAKE ANY DAMNED SENSE.
WE DID NOT MEAN TO HURT THOSE MEN BUT THEY'RE DEAD AND I HAVE TO TAKE RESPONSIBILITY FOR MY PART IN IT.
THEY'LL THROW AWAY THE KEY, PETE.

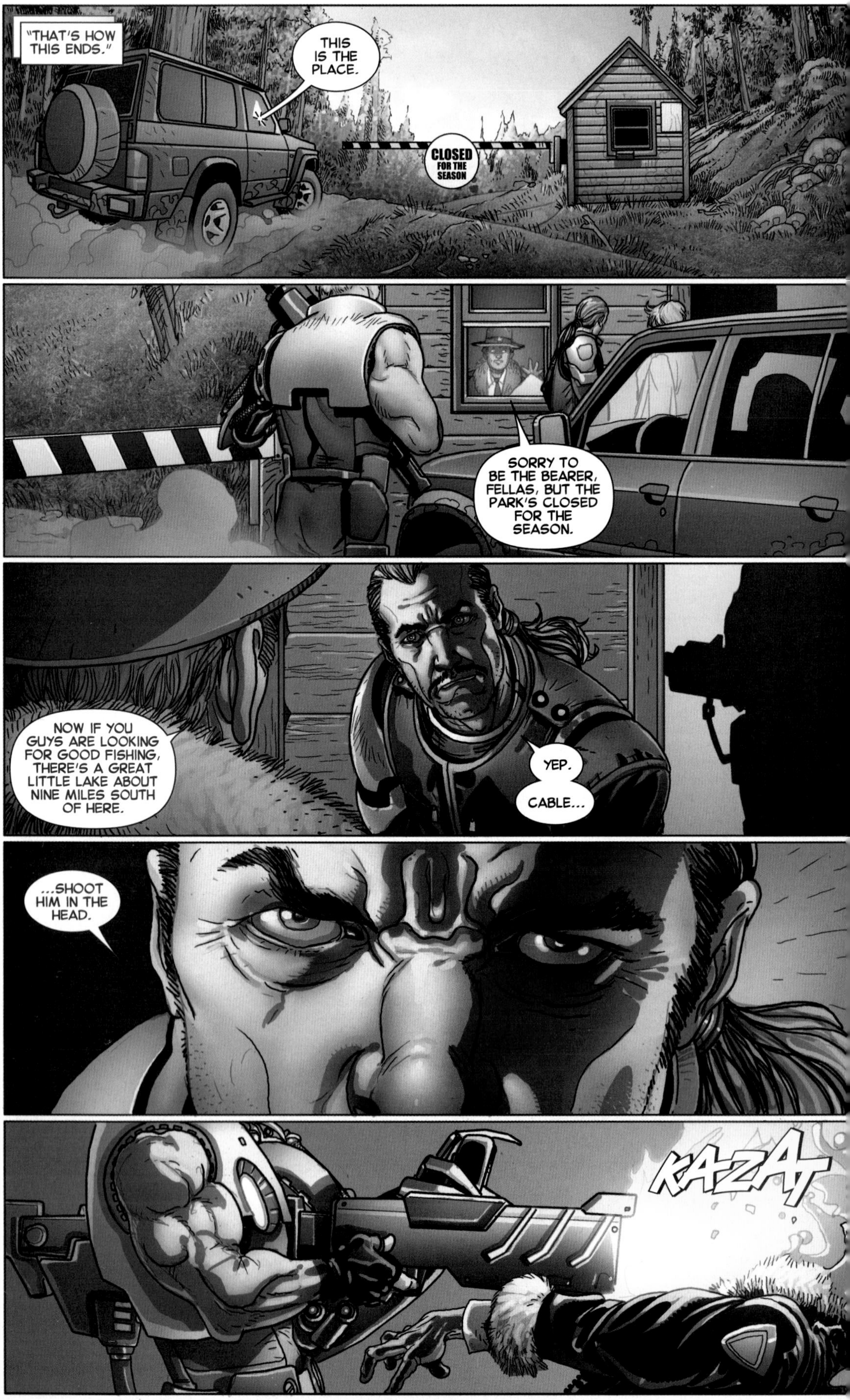
"THAT'S HOW THIS ENDS."
THIS IS THE PLACE.
CLOSED FOR THE SEASON
SORRY TO BE THE BEARER, FELLAS, BUT THE PARK'S CLOSED FOR THE SEASON.
NOW IF YOU GUYS ARE LOOKING FOR GOOD FISHING, THERE'S A GREAT LITTLE LAKE ABOUT NINE MILES SOUTH OF HERE.
YEP.
CABLE...
...SHOOT HIM IN THE HEAD.
KAZAT

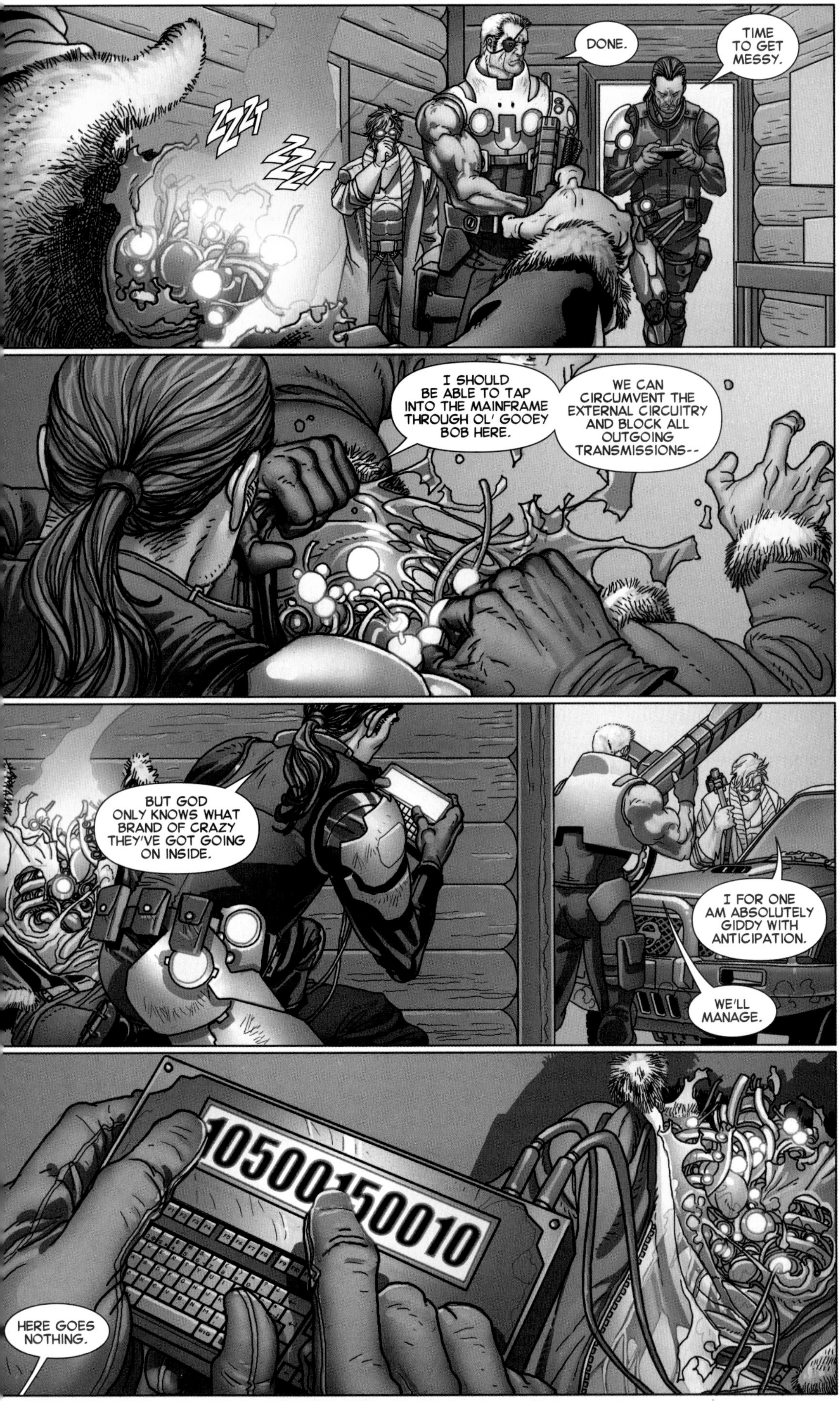
ZZZT
ZZZT
DONE.
TIME TO GET MESSY.
I SHOULD BE ABLE TO TAP INTO THE MAINFRAME THROUGH OL' GOOEY BOB HERE.
WE CAN CIRCUMVENT THE EXTERNAL CIRCUITRY AND BLOCK ALL OUTGOING TRANSMISSIONS--
BUT GOD ONLY KNOWS WHAT BRAND OF CRAZY THEY'VE GOT GOING ON INSIDE.
I FOR ONE AM ABSOLUTELY GIDDY WITH ANTICIPATION.
WE'LL MANAGE.
10500150010
HERE GOES NOTHING.

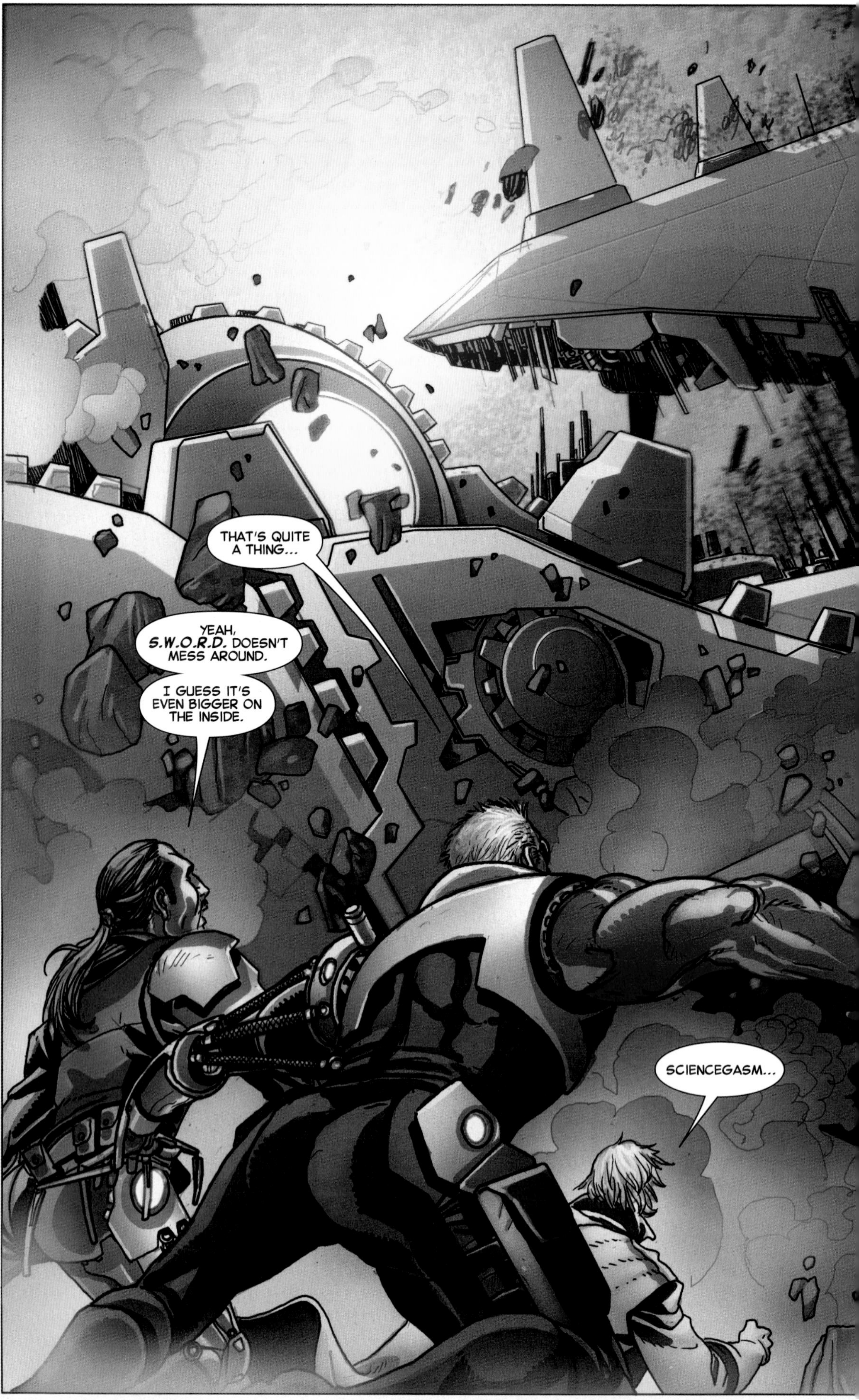
THAT'S QUITE A THING...
YEAH, S.W.O.R.D. DOESN'T MESS AROUND.
I GUESS IT'S EVEN BIGGER ON THE INSIDE.
SCIENCEGASM...

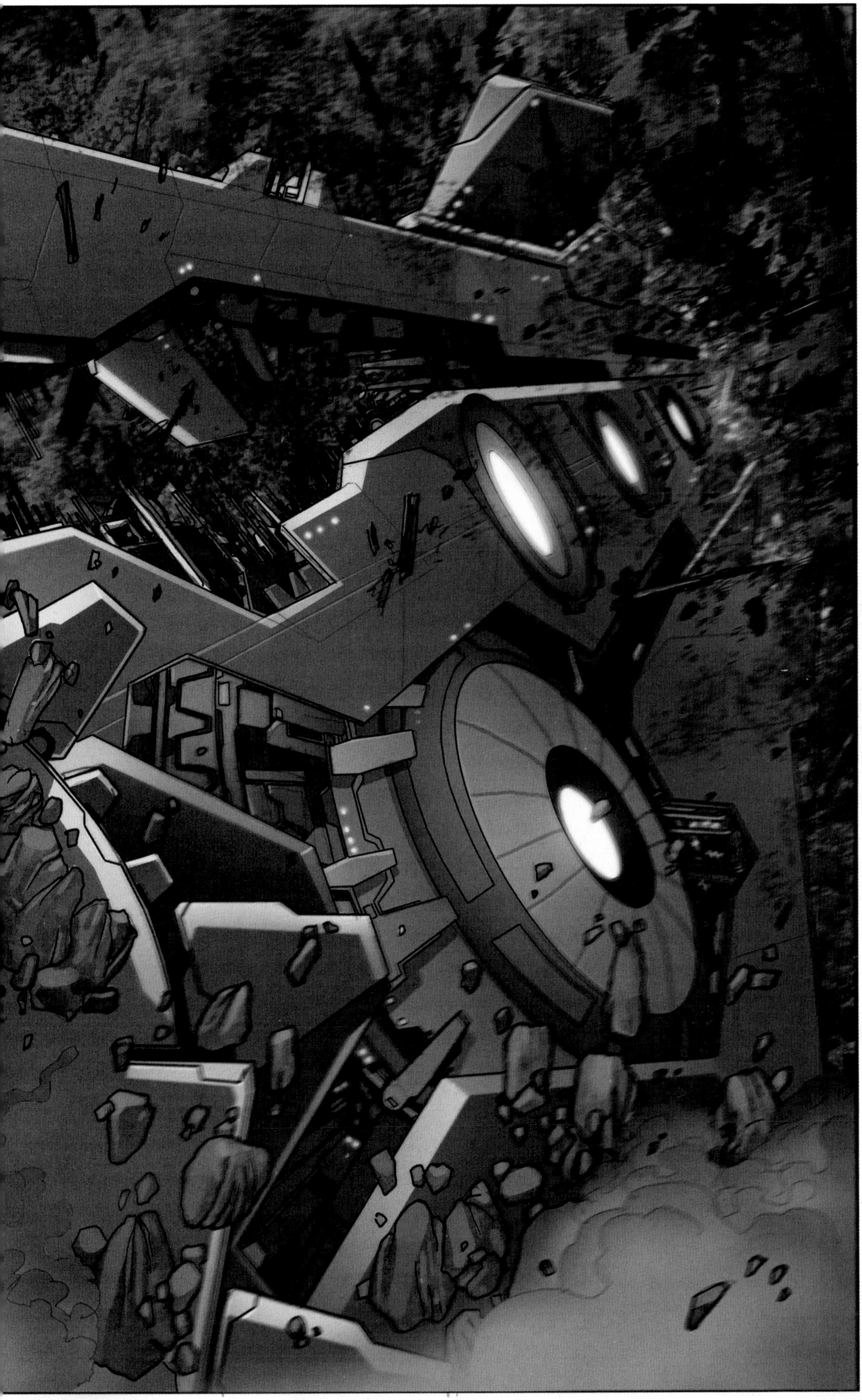

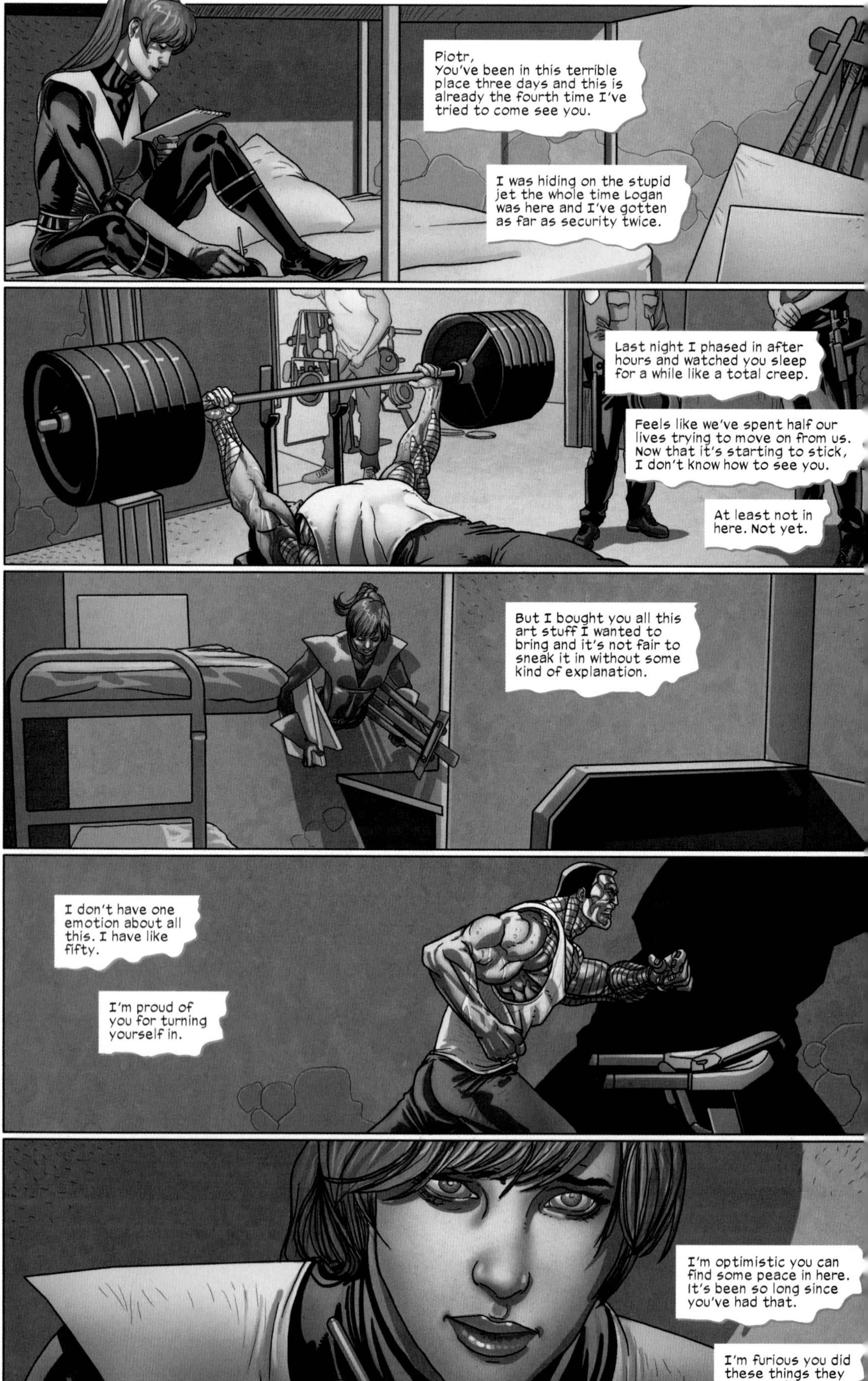
Piotr,
You've been in this terrible place three days and this is already the fourth time I've tried to come see you.
I was hiding on the stupid jet the whole time Logan was here and I've gotten as far as security twice.
Last night I phased in after hours and watched you sleep for a while like a total creep.
Feels like we've spent half our lives trying to move on from us. Now that it's starting to stick, I don't know how to see you.
At least not in here. Not yet.
But I bought you all this art stuff I wanted to bring and it's not fair to sneak it in without some kind of explanation.
I don't have one emotion about all this. I have like fifty.
I'm proud of you for turning yourself in.
I'm optimistic you can find some peace in here. It's been so long since you've had that.
I'm furious you did these things they say you did.

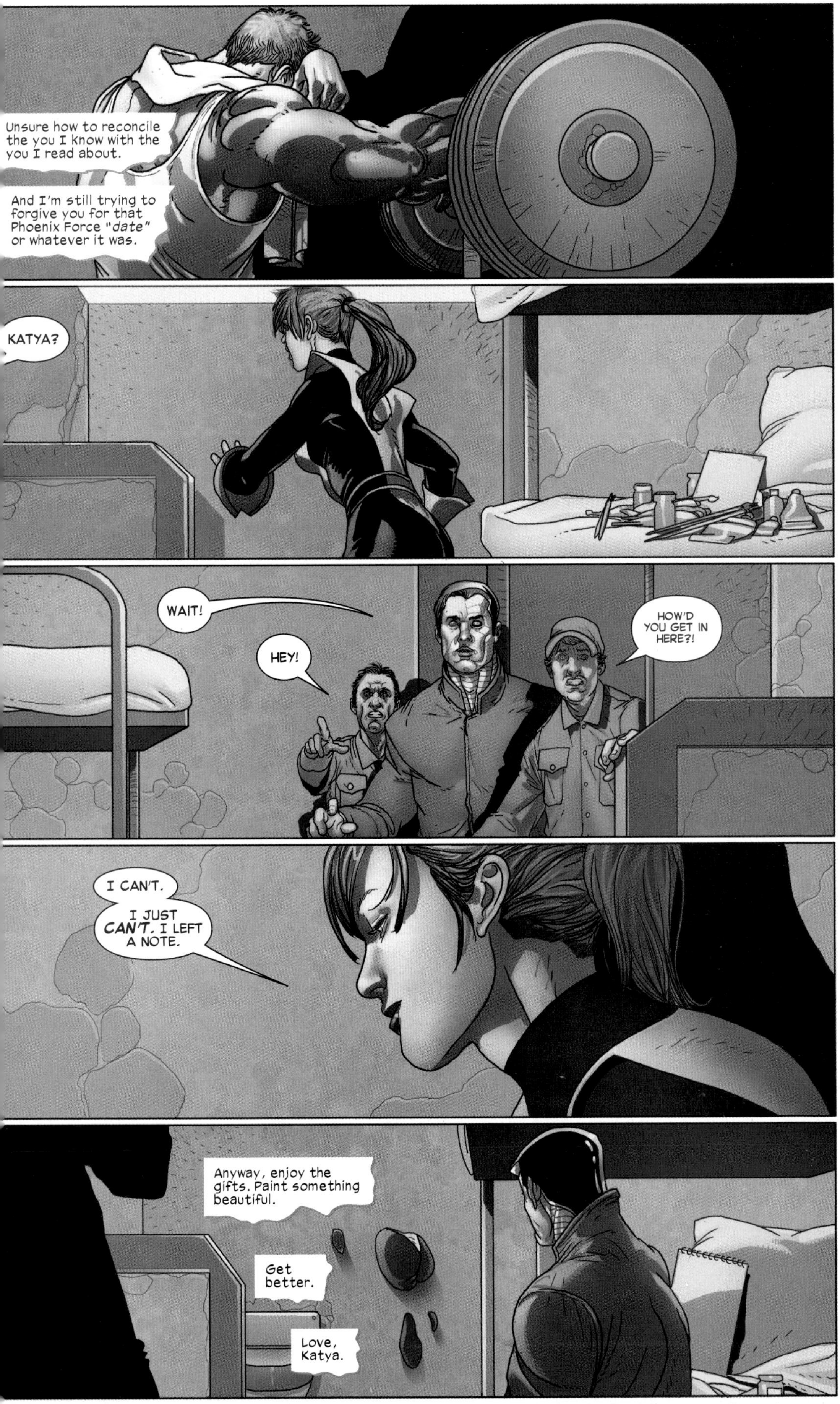
Unsure how to reconcile the you I know with the you I read about.
And I'm still trying to forgive you for that Phoenix Force "*date*" or whatever it was.
KATYA?
WAIT!
HEY!
HOW'D YOU GET IN HERE?!
I CAN'T.
I JUST *CAN'T.* I LEFT A NOTE.
Anyway, enjoy the gifts. Paint something beautiful.
Get better.
Love, Katya.

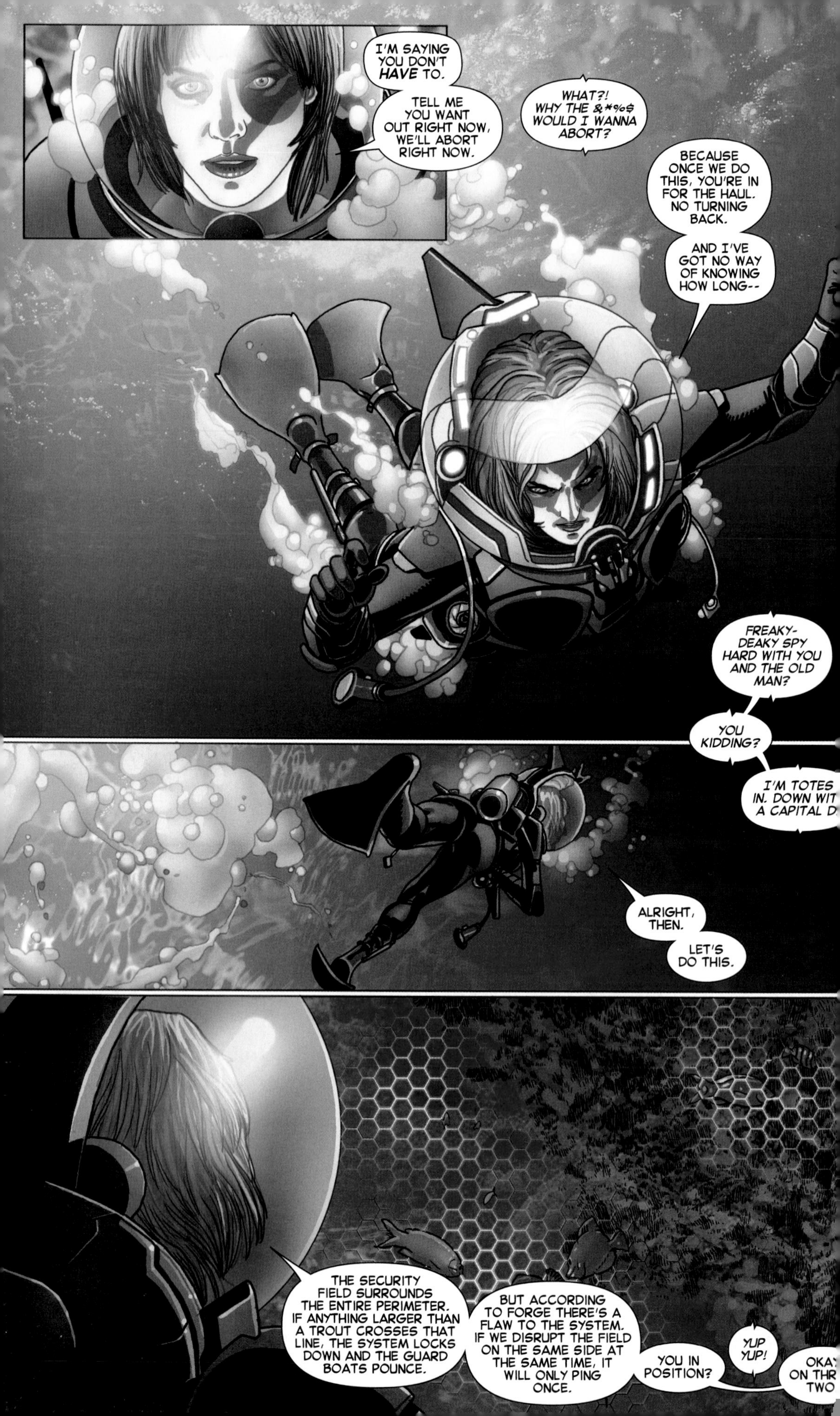
I'M SAYING YOU DON'T HAVE TO.
TELL ME YOU WANT OUT RIGHT NOW, WE'LL ABORT RIGHT NOW.
WHAT?! WHY THE &*%$ WOULD I WANNA ABORT?
BECAUSE ONCE WE DO THIS, YOU'RE IN FOR THE HAUL. NO TURNING BACK.
AND I'VE GOT NO WAY OF KNOWING HOW LONG--
FREAKY-DEAKY SPY HARD WITH YOU AND THE OLD MAN?
YOU KIDDING?
I'M TOTES IN. DOWN WIT A CAPITAL D
ALRIGHT, THEN.
LET'S DO THIS.
THE SECURITY FIELD SURROUNDS THE ENTIRE PERIMETER. IF ANYTHING LARGER THAN A TROUT CROSSES THAT LINE, THE SYSTEM LOCKS DOWN AND THE GUARD BOATS POUNCE.
BUT ACCORDING TO FORGE THERE'S A FLAW TO THE SYSTEM. IF WE DISRUPT THE FIELD ON THE SAME SIDE AT THE SAME TIME, IT WILL ONLY PING ONCE.
YOU IN POSITION?
YUP YUP!
OKA ON THR TWO

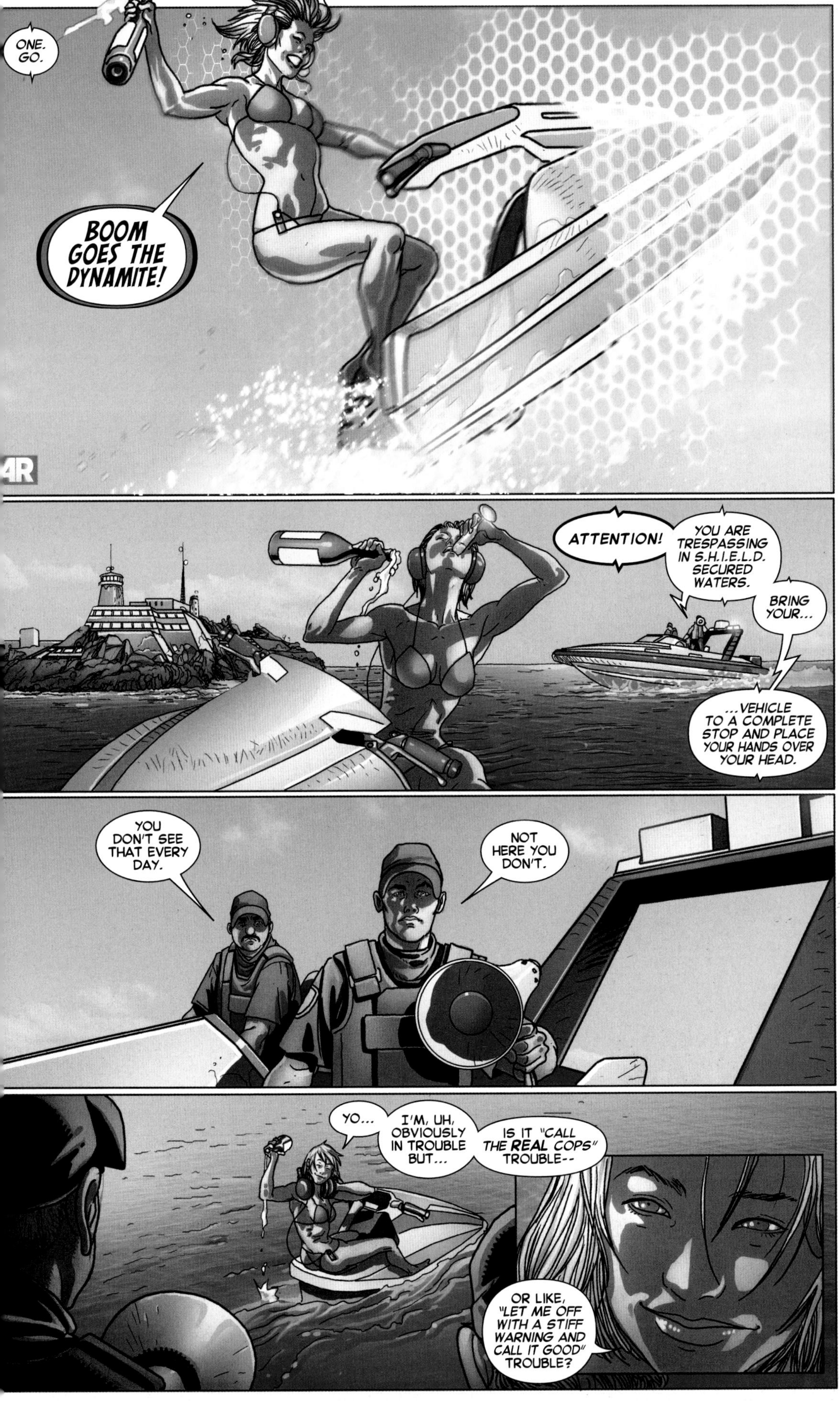
ONE. GO.
BOOM GOES THE DYNAMITE!
4R
ATTENTION!
YOU ARE TRESPASSING IN S.H.I.E.L.D. SECURED WATERS.
BRING YOUR...
...VEHICLE TO A COMPLETE STOP AND PLACE YOUR HANDS OVER YOUR HEAD.
YOU DON'T SEE THAT EVERY DAY.
NOT HERE YOU DON'T.
YO...
I'M, UH, OBVIOUSLY IN TROUBLE BUT...
IS IT "CALL THE REAL COPS" TROUBLE--
OR LIKE, "LET ME OFF WITH A STIFF WARNING AND CALL IT GOOD" TROUBLE?

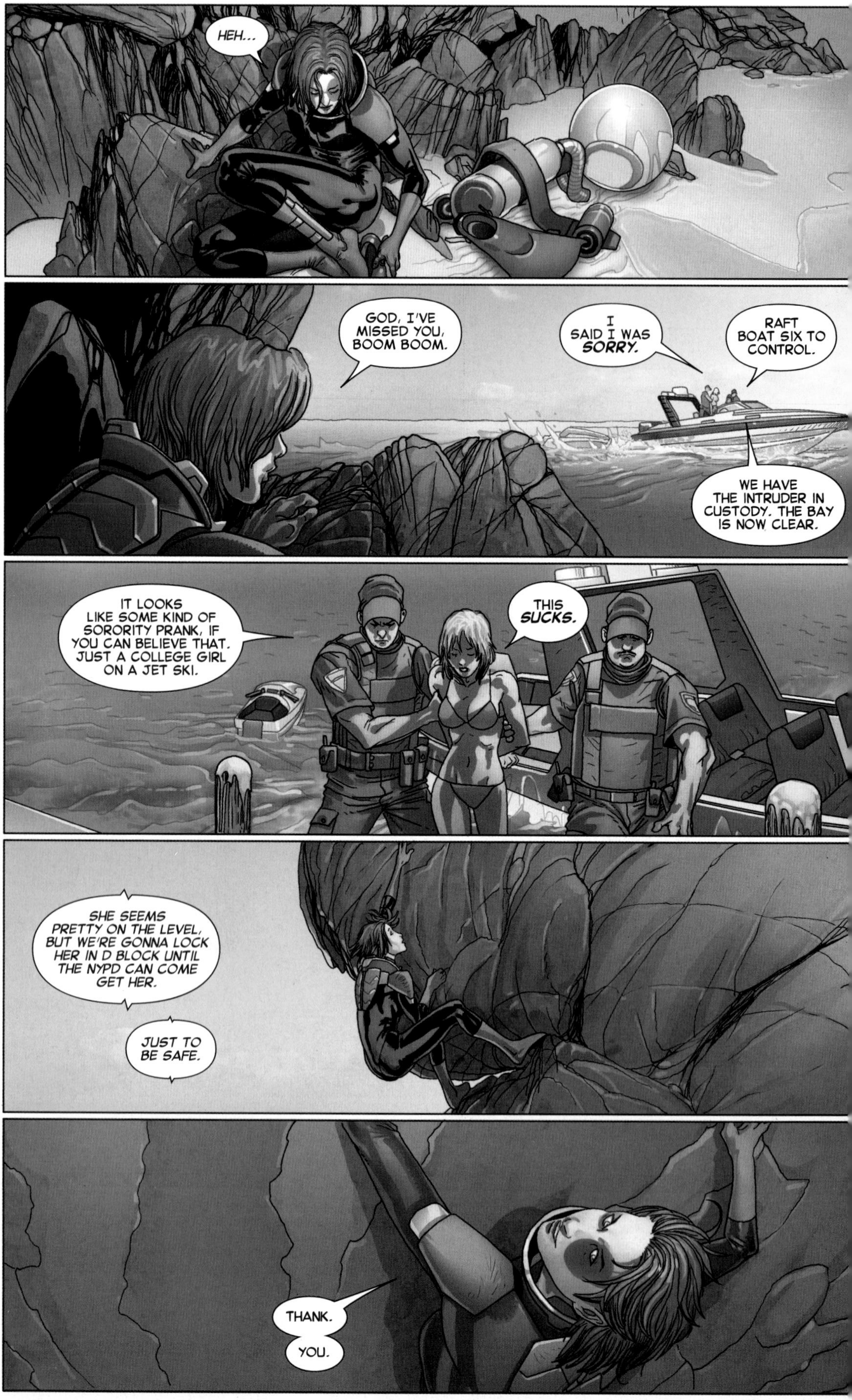
HEH...
GOD, I'VE MISSED YOU, BOOM BOOM.
I SAID I WAS SORRY.
RAFT BOAT SIX TO CONTROL.
WE HAVE THE INTRUDER IN CUSTODY. THE BAY IS NOW CLEAR.
IT LOOKS LIKE SOME KIND OF SORORITY PRANK, IF YOU CAN BELIEVE THAT. JUST A COLLEGE GIRL ON A JET SKI.
THIS SUCKS.
SHE SEEMS PRETTY ON THE LEVEL, BUT WE'RE GONNA LOCK HER IN D BLOCK UNTIL THE NYPD CAN COME GET HER.
JUST TO BE SAFE.
THANK.
YOU.

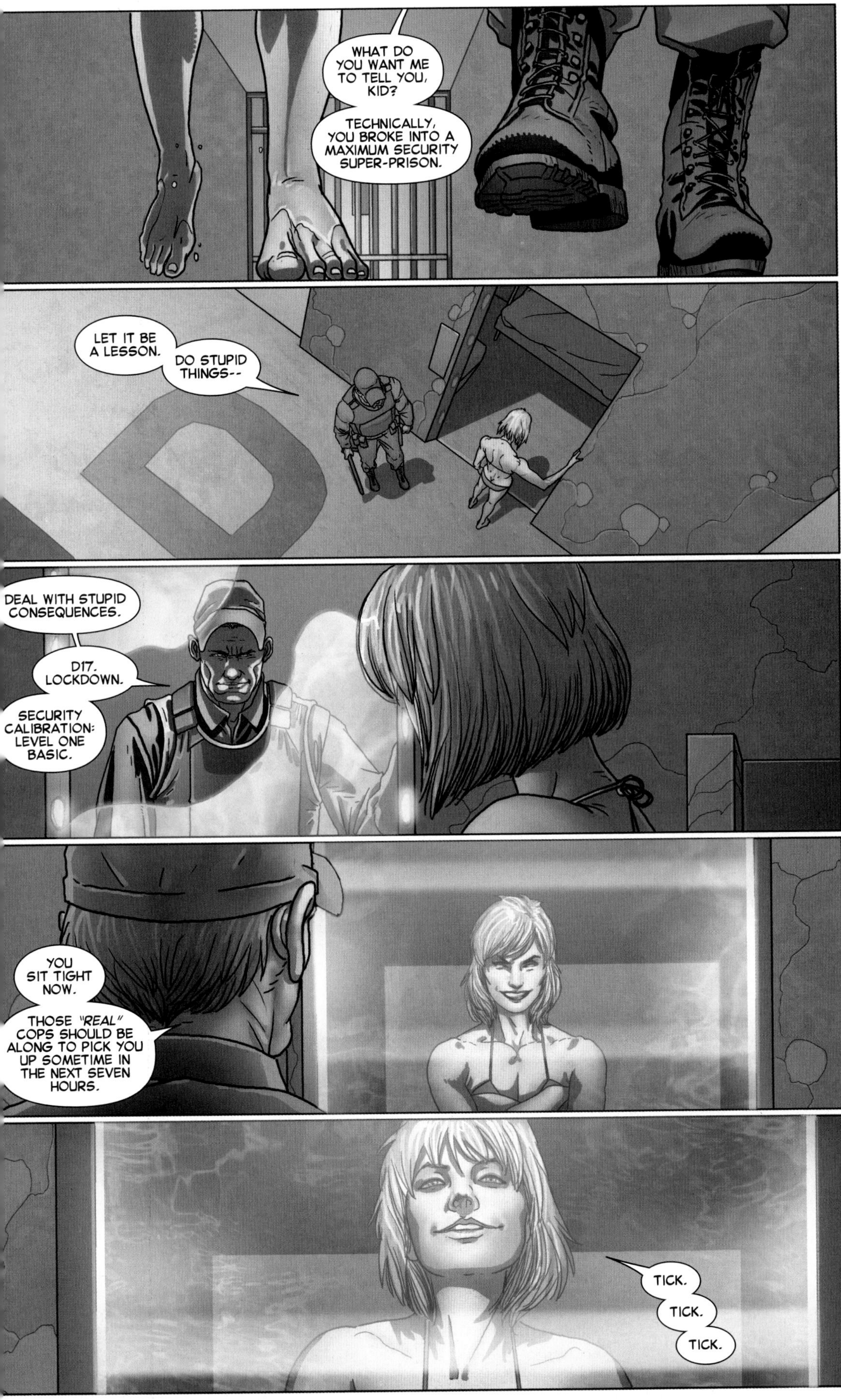
WHAT DO YOU WANT ME TO TELL YOU, KID?
TECHNICALLY, YOU BROKE INTO A MAXIMUM SECURITY SUPER-PRISON.
LET IT BE A LESSON.
DO STUPID THINGS--
DEAL WITH STUPID CONSEQUENCES.
D17. LOCKDOWN.
SECURITY CALIBRATION: LEVEL ONE BASIC.
YOU SIT TIGHT NOW.
THOSE *"REAL"* COPS SHOULD BE ALONG TO PICK YOU UP SOMETIME IN THE NEXT SEVEN HOURS.
TICK.
TICK.
TICK.

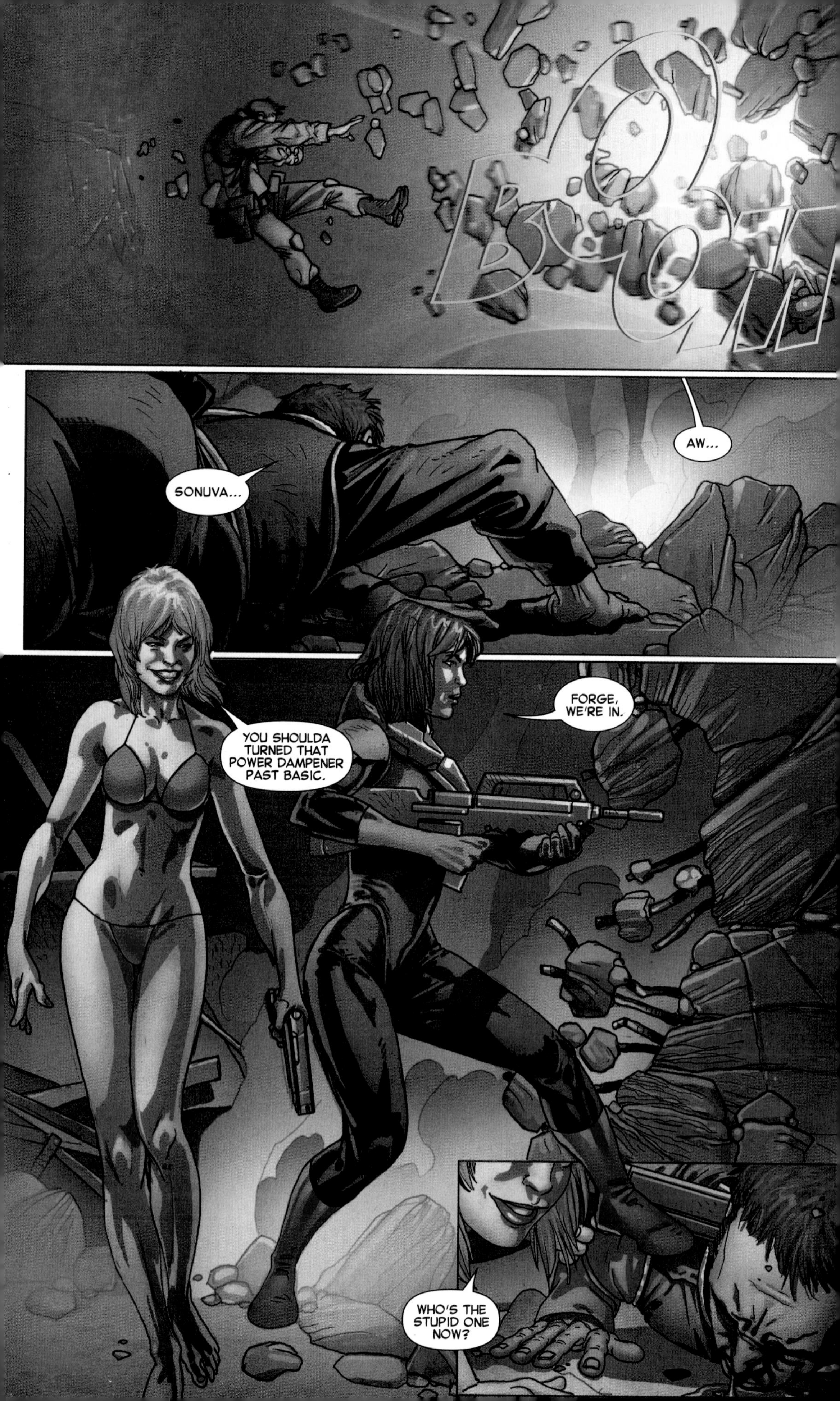
BOOOM
SONUVA...
AW...
YOU SHOULDA TURNED THAT POWER DAMPENER PAST BASIC.
FORGE, WE'RE IN.
WHO'S THE STUPID ONE NOW?

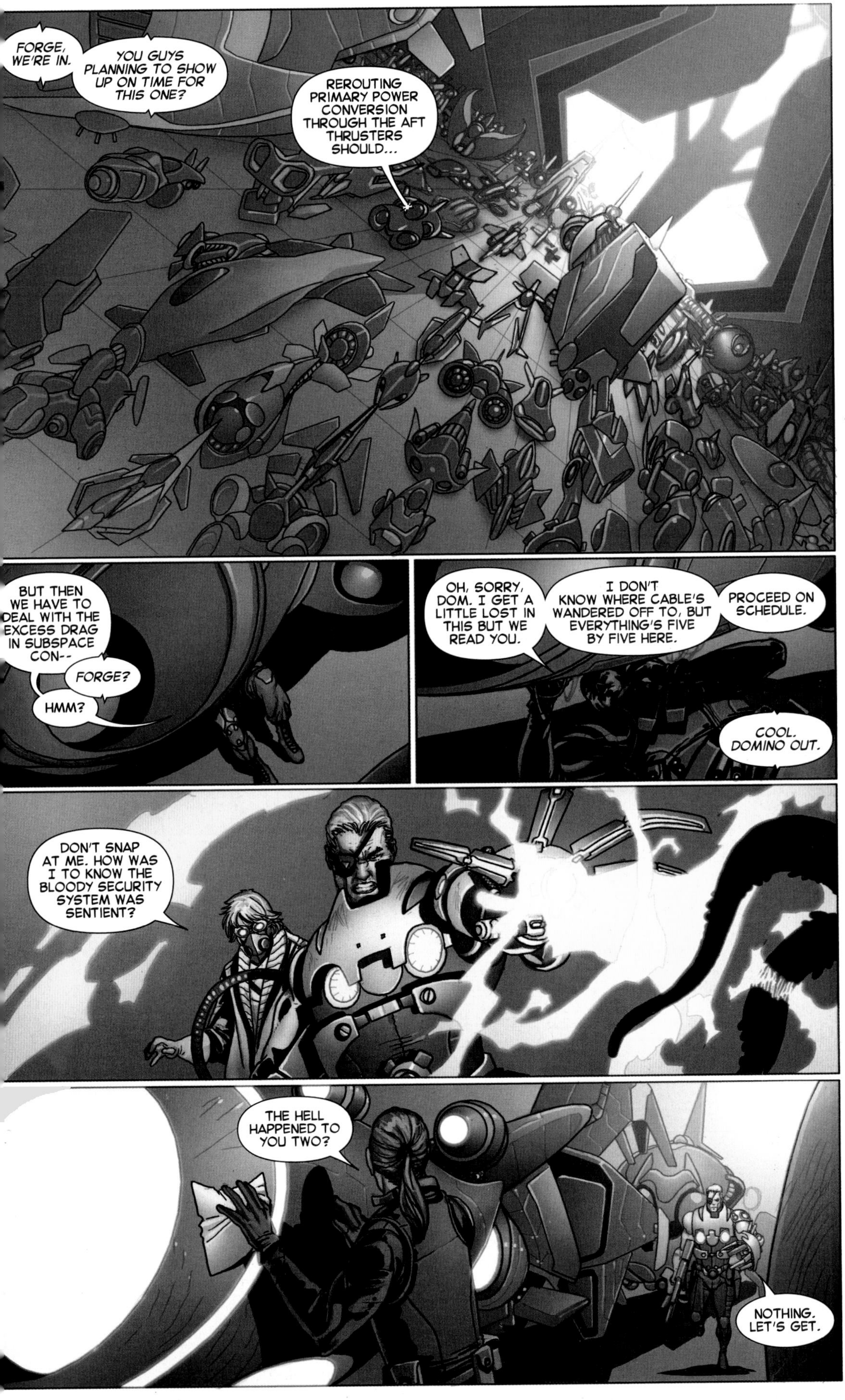
FORGE, WE'RE IN.
YOU GUYS PLANNING TO SHOW UP ON TIME FOR THIS ONE?
REROUTING PRIMARY POWER CONVERSION THROUGH THE AFT THRUSTERS SHOULD...
BUT THEN WE HAVE TO DEAL WITH THE EXCESS DRAG IN SUBSPACE CON--
FORGE?
HMM?
OH, SORRY, DOM. I GET A LITTLE LOST IN THIS BUT WE READ YOU.
I DON'T KNOW WHERE CABLE'S WANDERED OFF TO, BUT EVERYTHING'S FIVE BY FIVE HERE.
PROCEED ON SCHEDULE.
COOL. DOMINO OUT.
DON'T SNAP AT ME. HOW WAS I TO KNOW THE BLOODY SECURITY SYSTEM WAS SENTIENT?
THE HELL HAPPENED TO YOU TWO?
NOTHING. LET'S GET.

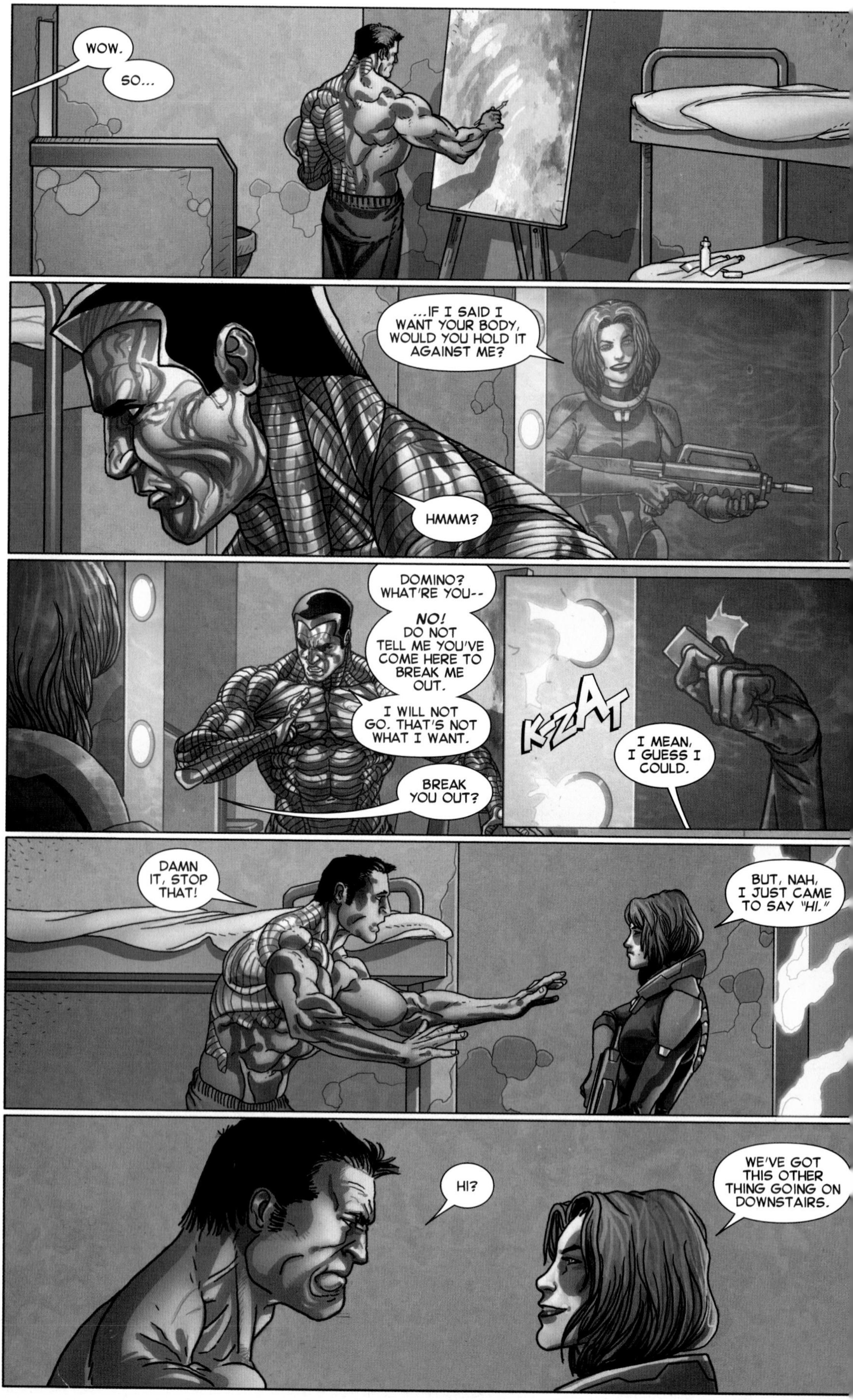

WOW.
SO...
...IF I SAID I WANT YOUR BODY, WOULD YOU HOLD IT AGAINST ME?
HMMM?
DOMINO? WHAT'RE YOU--
NO! DO NOT TELL ME YOU'VE COME HERE TO BREAK ME OUT.
I WILL NOT GO. THAT'S NOT WHAT I WANT.
BREAK YOU OUT?
K-ZAT
I MEAN, I GUESS I COULD.
DAMN IT, STOP THAT!
BUT, NAH, I JUST CAME TO SAY "HI."
HI?
WE'VE GOT THIS OTHER THING GOING ON DOWNSTAIRS.

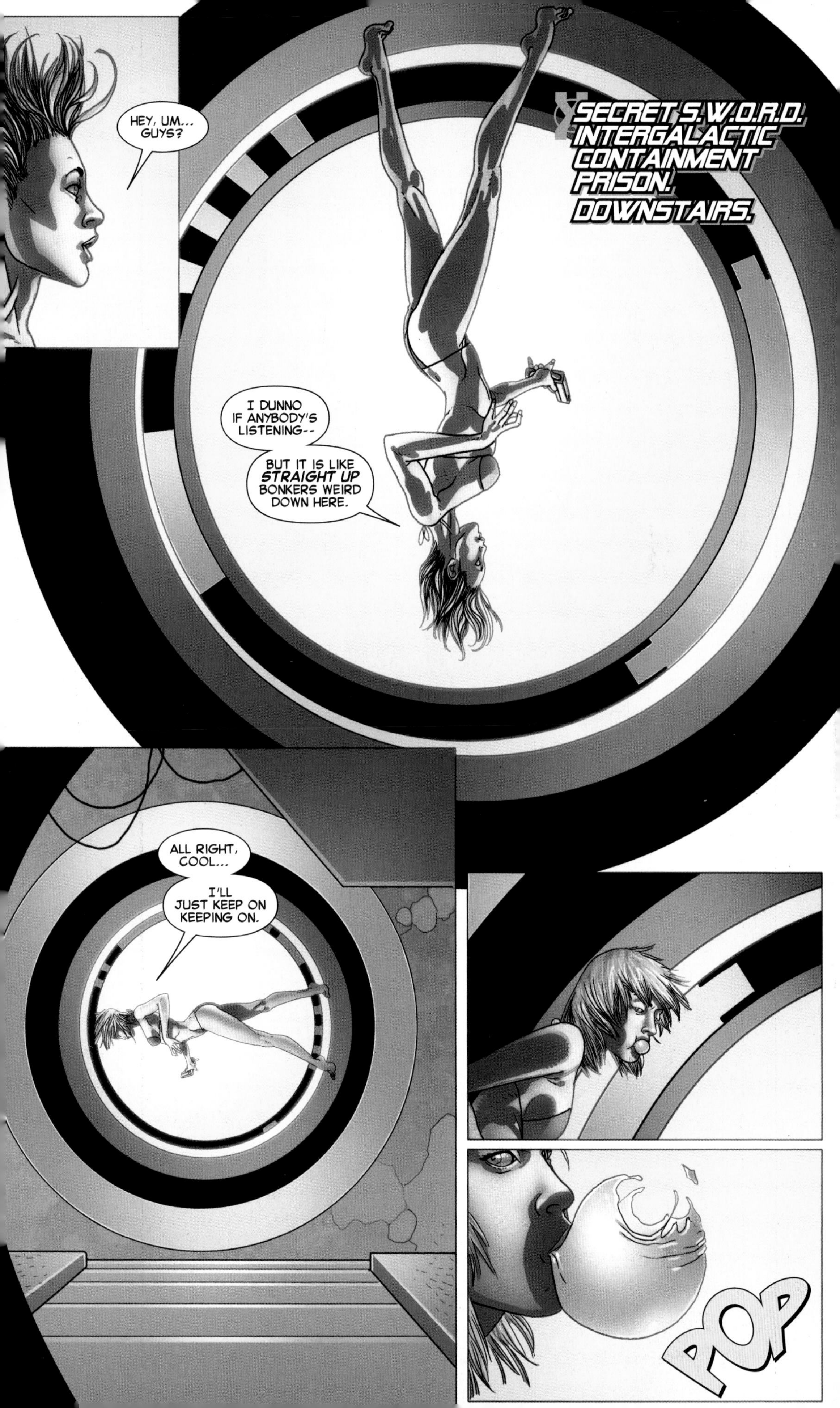
HEY, UM... GUYS?
SECRET S.W.O.R.D. INTERGALACTIC CONTAINMENT PRISON. DOWNSTAIRS.
I DUNNO IF ANYBODY'S LISTENING--
BUT IT IS LIKE STRAIGHT UP BONKERS WEIRD DOWN HERE.
ALL RIGHT, COOL...
I'LL JUST KEEP ON KEEPING ON.
POP

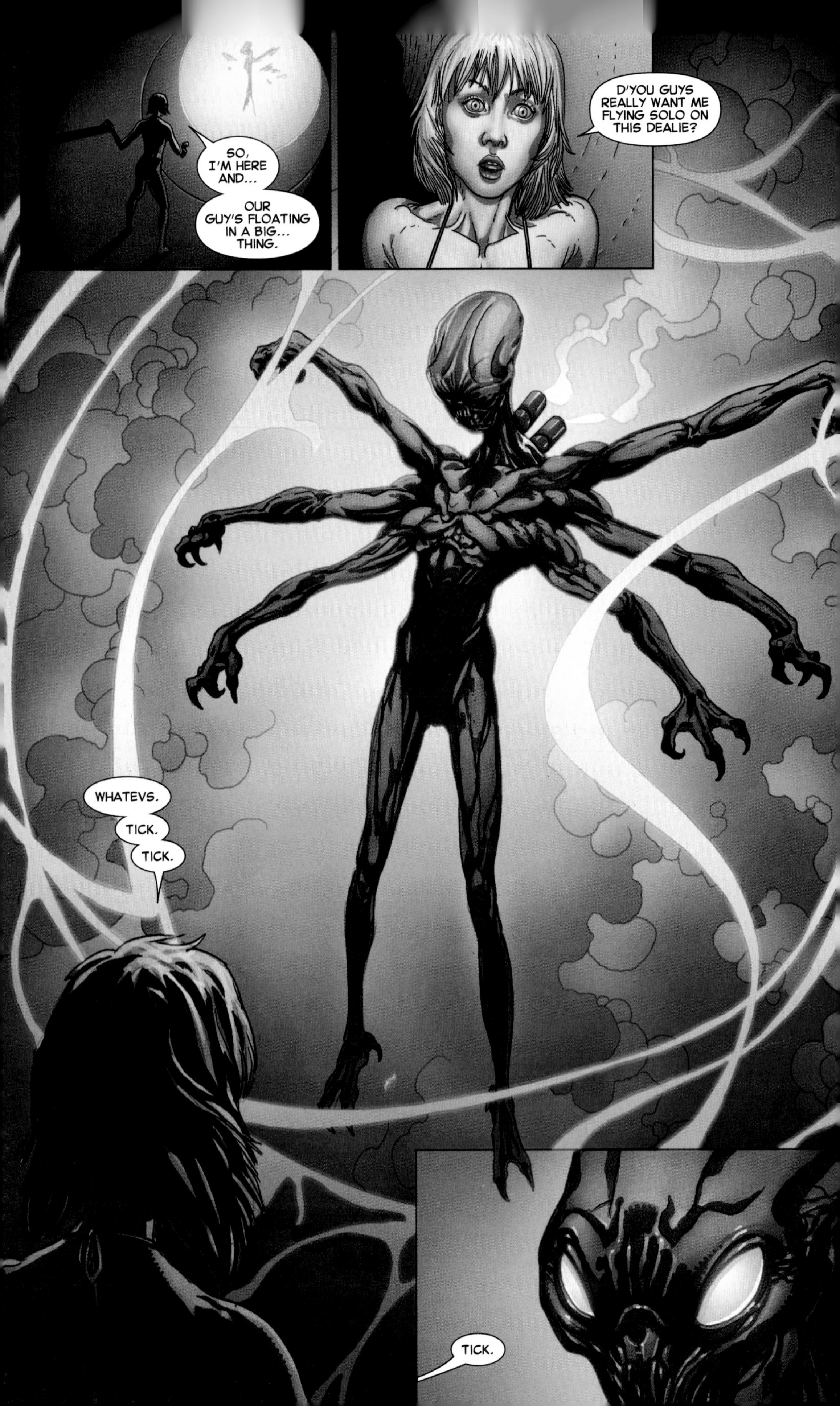
SO, I'M HERE AND...
OUR GUY'S FLOATING IN A BIG... THING.
D'YOU GUYS REALLY WANT ME FLYING SOLO ON THIS DEALIE?
WHATEVS.
TICK.
TICK.
TICK.

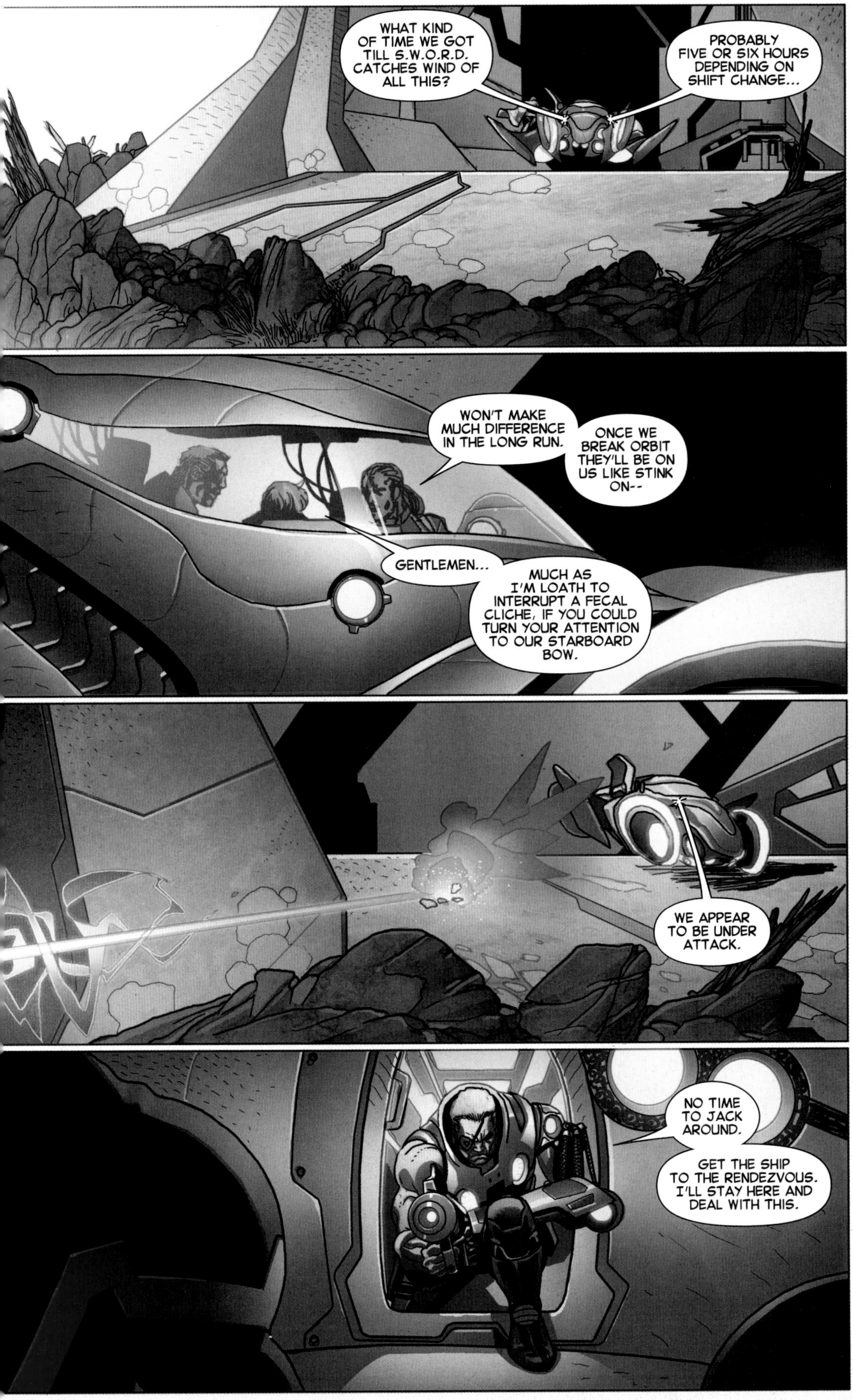

WHAT KIND OF TIME WE GOT TILL S.W.O.R.D. CATCHES WIND OF ALL THIS?
PROBABLY FIVE OR SIX HOURS DEPENDING ON SHIFT CHANGE...
WON'T MAKE MUCH DIFFERENCE IN THE LONG RUN.
ONCE WE BREAK ORBIT THEY'LL BE ON US LIKE STINK ON--
GENTLEMEN...
MUCH AS I'M LOATH TO INTERRUPT A FECAL CLICHE, IF YOU COULD TURN YOUR ATTENTION TO OUR STARBOARD BOW.
WE APPEAR TO BE UNDER ATTACK.
NO TIME TO JACK AROUND.
GET THE SHIP TO THE RENDEZVOUS. I'LL STAY HERE AND DEAL WITH THIS.

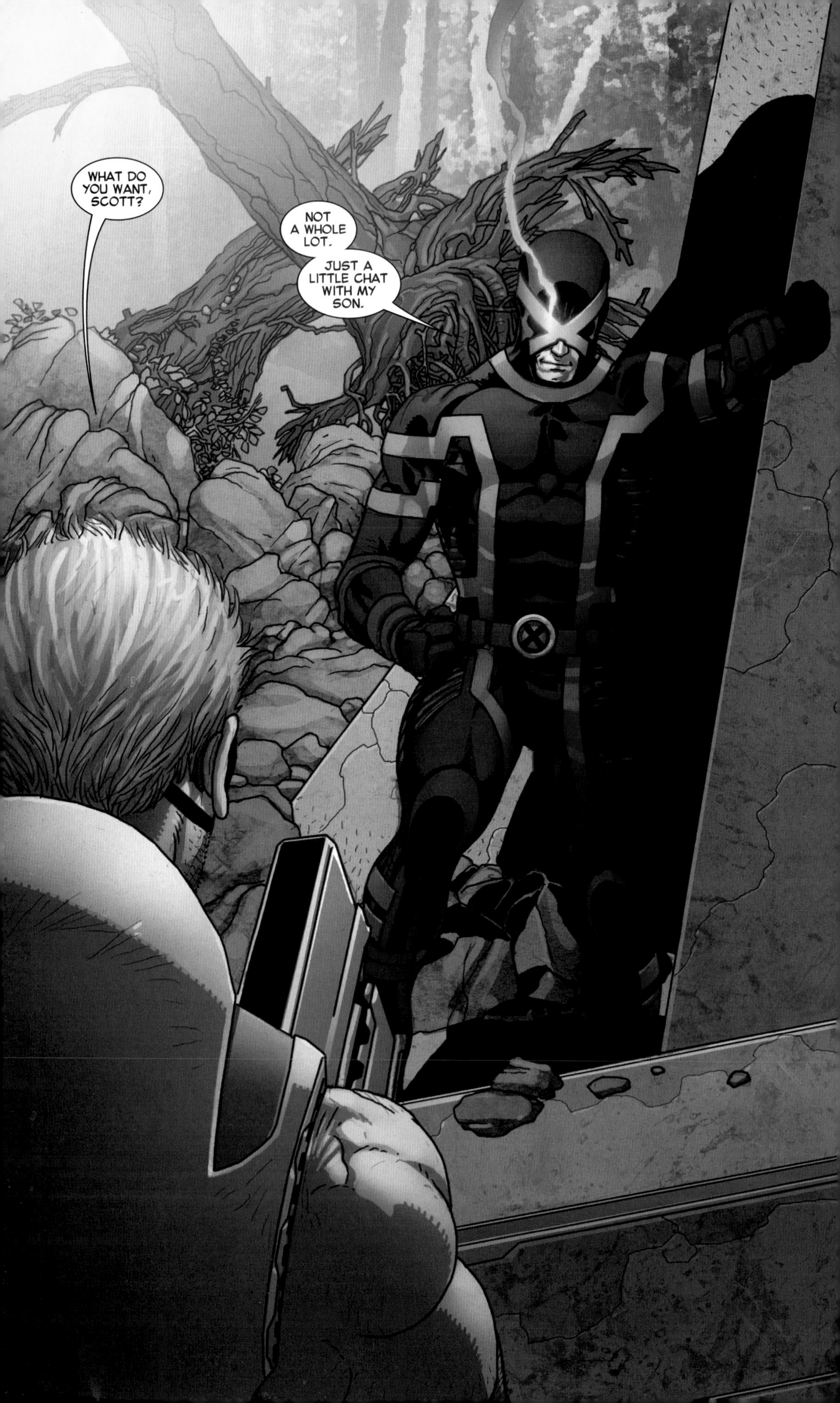
WHAT DO YOU WANT, SCOTT?
NOT A WHOLE LOT.
JUST A LITTLE CHAT WITH MY SON.

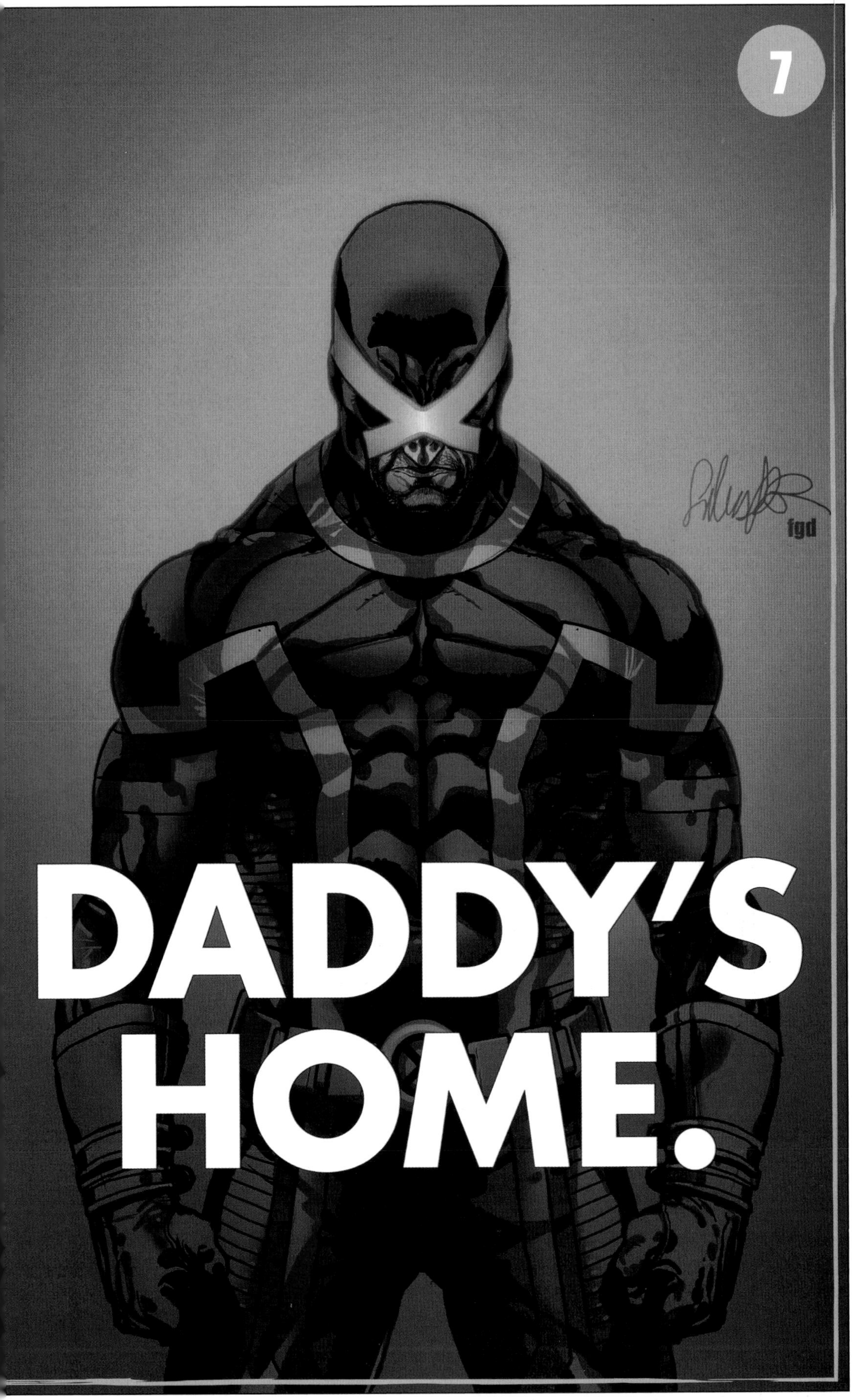
7
fgd
DADDY'S
HOME.

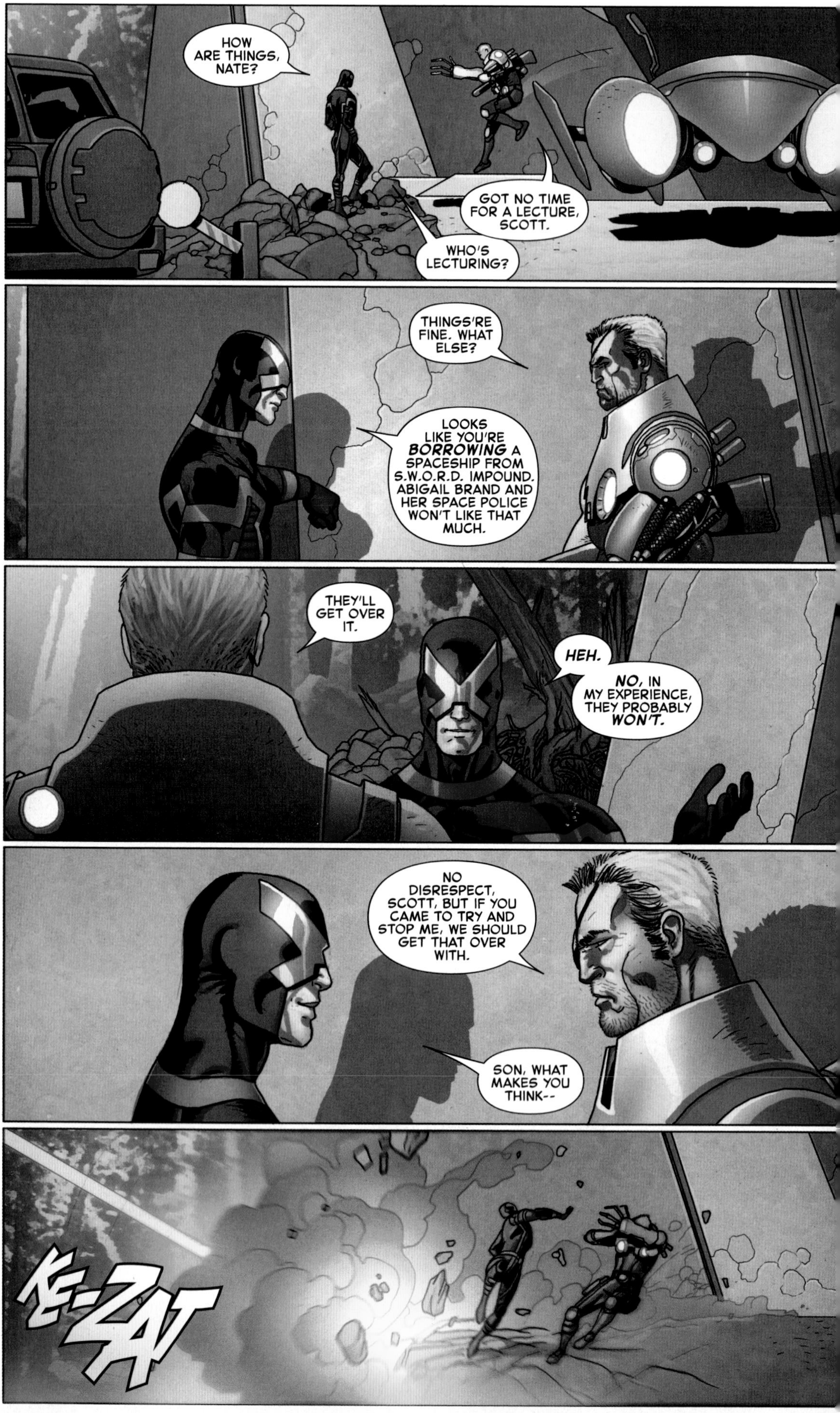
HOW ARE THINGS, NATE?
GOT NO TIME FOR A LECTURE, SCOTT.
WHO'S LECTURING?
THINGS'RE FINE. WHAT ELSE?
LOOKS LIKE YOU'RE BORROWING A SPACESHIP FROM S.W.O.R.D. IMPOUND. ABIGAIL BRAND AND HER SPACE POLICE WON'T LIKE THAT MUCH.
THEY'LL GET OVER IT.
HEH.
NO, IN MY EXPERIENCE, THEY PROBABLY WON'T.
NO DISRESPECT, SCOTT, BUT IF YOU CAME TO TRY AND STOP ME, WE SHOULD GET THAT OVER WITH.
SON, WHAT MAKES YOU THINK--
KE-ZAT

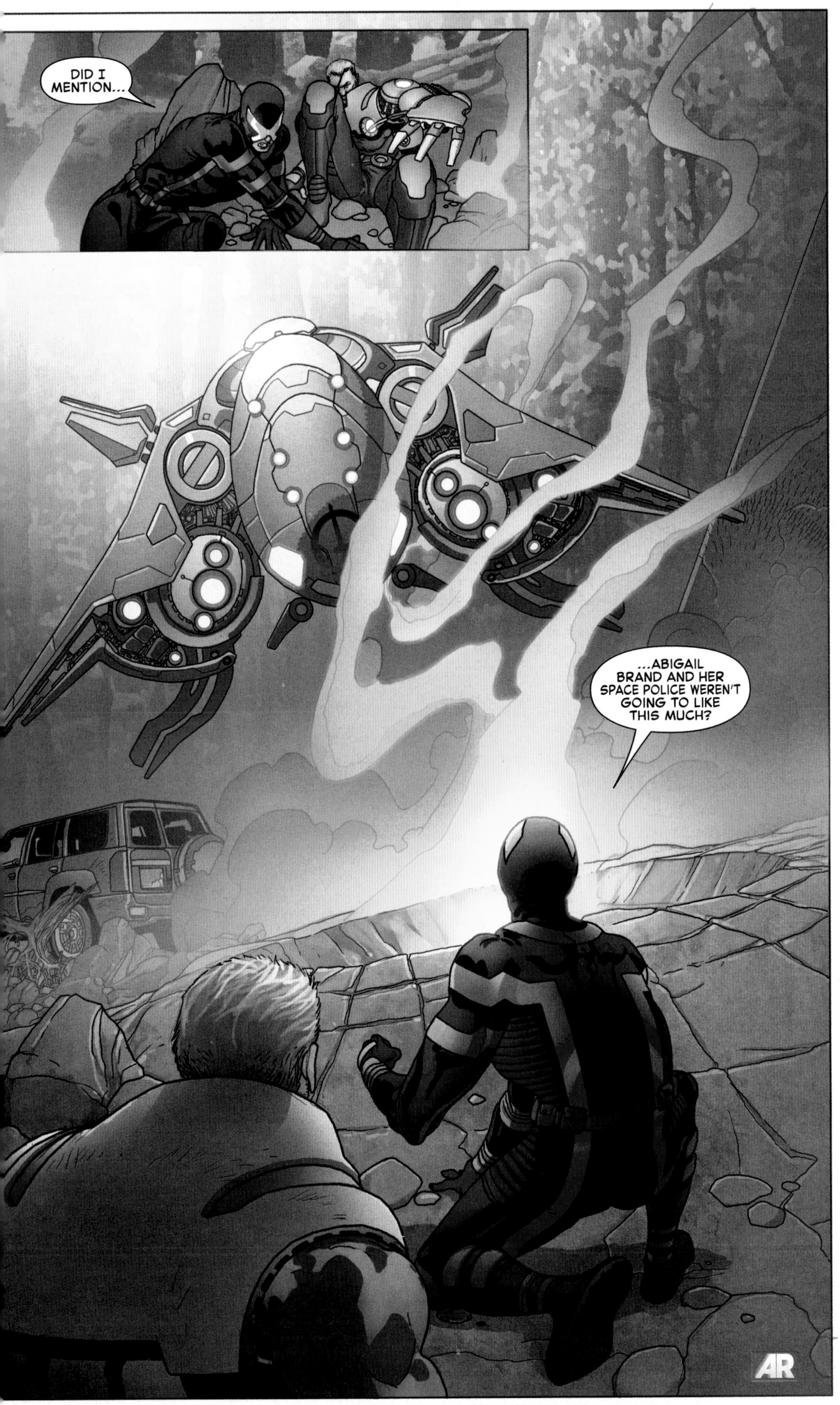
DID I MENTION...
...ABIGAIL BRAND AND HER SPACE POLICE WEREN'T GOING TO LIKE THIS MUCH?

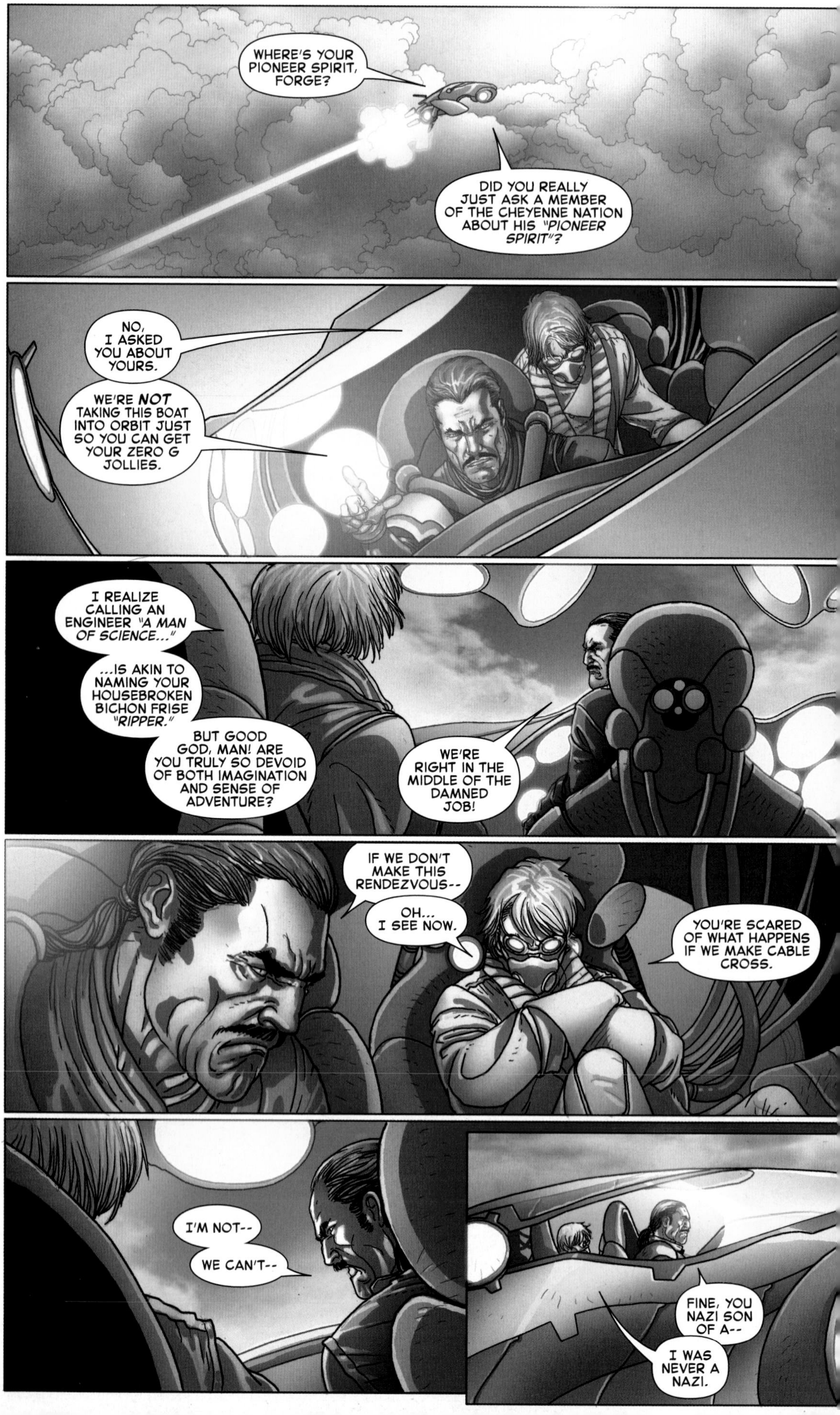

WHERE'S YOUR PIONEER SPIRIT, FORGE?
DID YOU REALLY JUST ASK A MEMBER OF THE CHEYENNE NATION ABOUT HIS "PIONEER SPIRIT"?
NO, I ASKED YOU ABOUT YOURS.
WE'RE NOT TAKING THIS BOAT INTO ORBIT JUST SO YOU CAN GET YOUR ZERO G JOLLIES.
I REALIZE CALLING AN ENGINEER "A MAN OF SCIENCE..."
...IS AKIN TO NAMING YOUR HOUSEBROKEN BICHON FRISE "RIPPER."
BUT GOOD GOD, MAN! ARE YOU TRULY SO DEVOID OF BOTH IMAGINATION AND SENSE OF ADVENTURE?
WE'RE RIGHT IN THE MIDDLE OF THE DAMNED JOB!
IF WE DON'T MAKE THIS RENDEZVOUS--
OH... I SEE NOW.
YOU'RE SCARED OF WHAT HAPPENS IF WE MAKE CABLE CROSS.
I'M NOT--
WE CAN'T--
FINE, YOU NAZI SON OF A--
I WAS NEVER A NAZI.

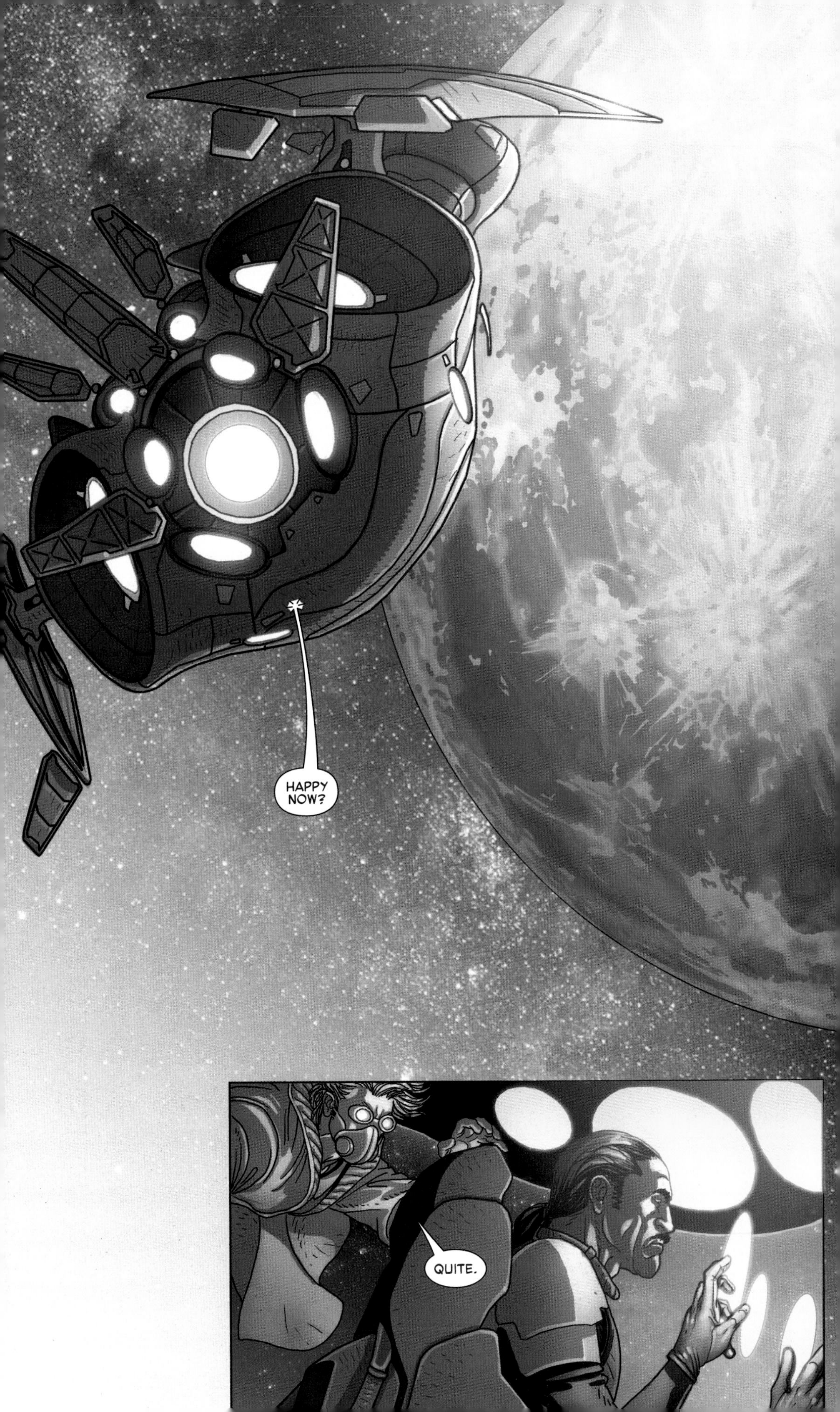
HAPPY NOW?
QUITE.

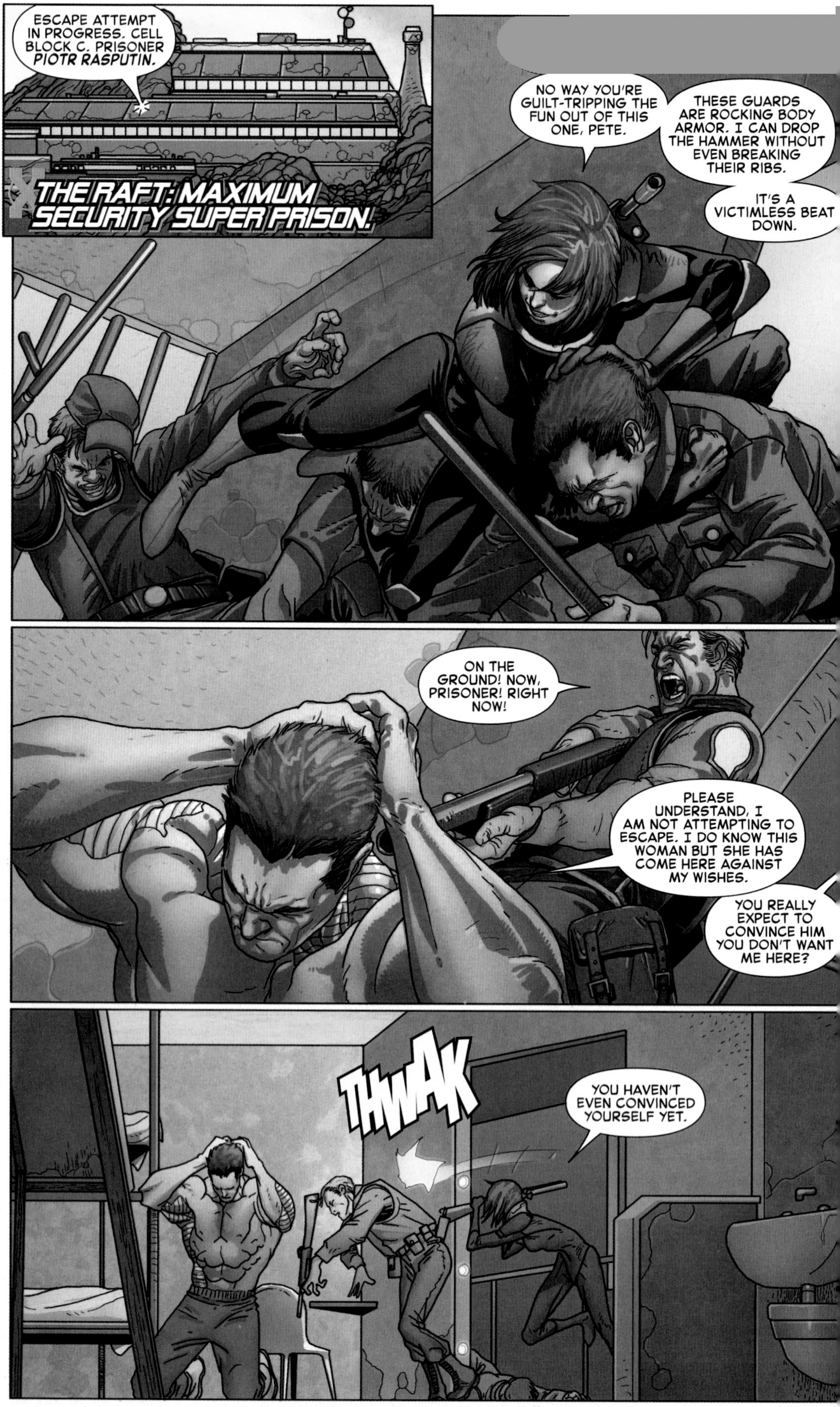
ESCAPE ATTEMPT IN PROGRESS. CELL BLOCK C. PRISONER *PIOTR RASPUTIN.*
THE RAFT: MAXIMUM SECURITY SUPER PRISON.
NO WAY YOU'RE GUILT-TRIPPING THE FUN OUT OF THIS ONE, PETE.
THESE GUARDS ARE ROCKING BODY ARMOR. I CAN DROP THE HAMMER WITHOUT EVEN BREAKING THEIR RIBS.
IT'S A VICTIMLESS BEAT DOWN.
ON THE GROUND! NOW, PRISONER! RIGHT NOW!
PLEASE UNDERSTAND, I AM NOT ATTEMPTING TO ESCAPE. I DO KNOW THIS WOMAN BUT SHE HAS COME HERE AGAINST MY WISHES.
YOU REALLY EXPECT TO CONVINCE HIM YOU DON'T WANT ME HERE?
THWAK
YOU HAVEN'T EVEN CONVINCED YOURSELF YET.

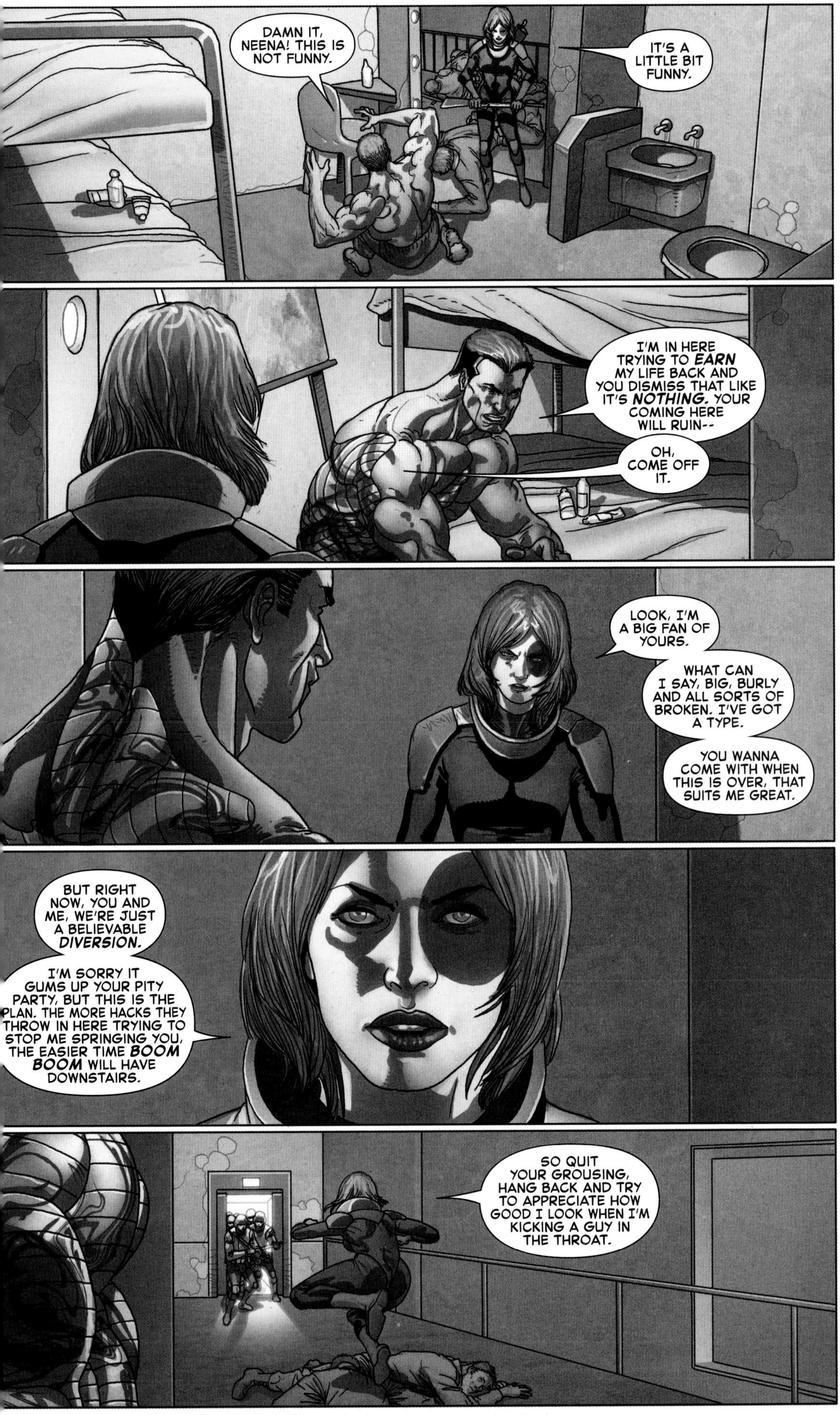
DAMN IT, NEENA! THIS IS NOT FUNNY.
IT'S A LITTLE BIT FUNNY.
I'M IN HERE TRYING TO EARN MY LIFE BACK AND YOU DISMISS THAT LIKE IT'S NOTHING. YOUR COMING HERE WILL RUIN--
OH, COME OFF IT.
LOOK, I'M A BIG FAN OF YOURS.
WHAT CAN I SAY, BIG, BURLY AND ALL SORTS OF BROKEN. I'VE GOT A TYPE.
YOU WANNA COME WITH WHEN THIS IS OVER, THAT SUITS ME GREAT.
BUT RIGHT NOW, YOU AND ME, WE'RE JUST A BELIEVABLE DIVERSION.
I'M SORRY IT GUMS UP YOUR PITY PARTY, BUT THIS IS THE PLAN. THE MORE HACKS THEY THROW IN HERE TRYING TO STOP ME SPRINGING YOU, THE EASIER TIME BOOM BOOM WILL HAVE DOWNSTAIRS.
SO QUIT YOUR GROUSING, HANG BACK AND TRY TO APPRECIATE HOW GOOD I LOOK WHEN I'M KICKING A GUY IN THE THROAT.

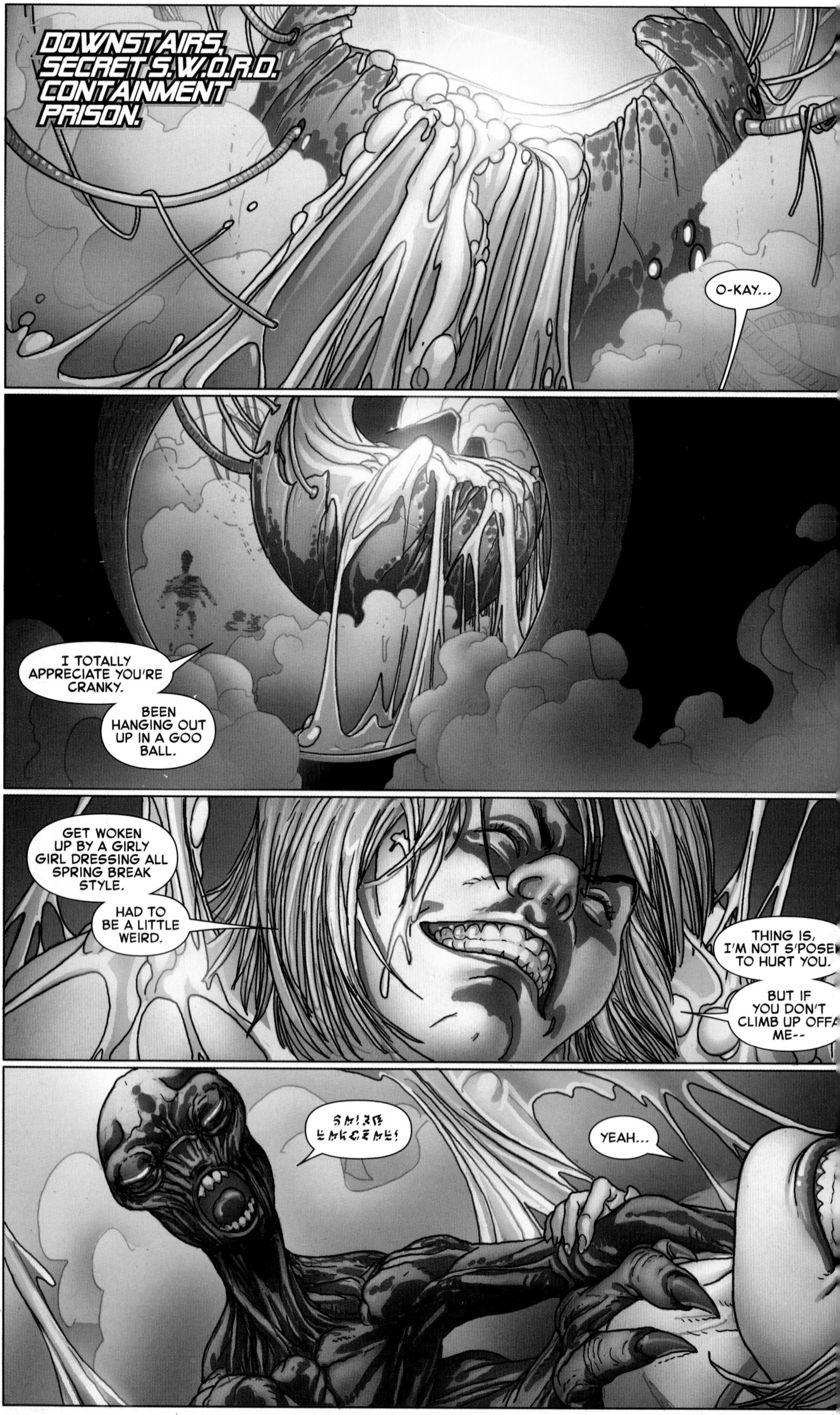
DOWNSTAIRS, SECRET S.W.O.R.D. CONTAINMENT PRISON.
O-KAY...
I TOTALLY APPRECIATE YOU'RE CRANKY.
BEEN HANGING OUT UP IN A GOO BALL.
GET WOKEN UP BY A GIRLY GIRL DRESSING ALL SPRING BREAK STYLE.
HAD TO BE A LITTLE WEIRD.
THING IS, I'M NOT S'POSE TO HURT YOU.
BUT IF YOU DON'T CLIMB UP OFFA ME--
YEAH...

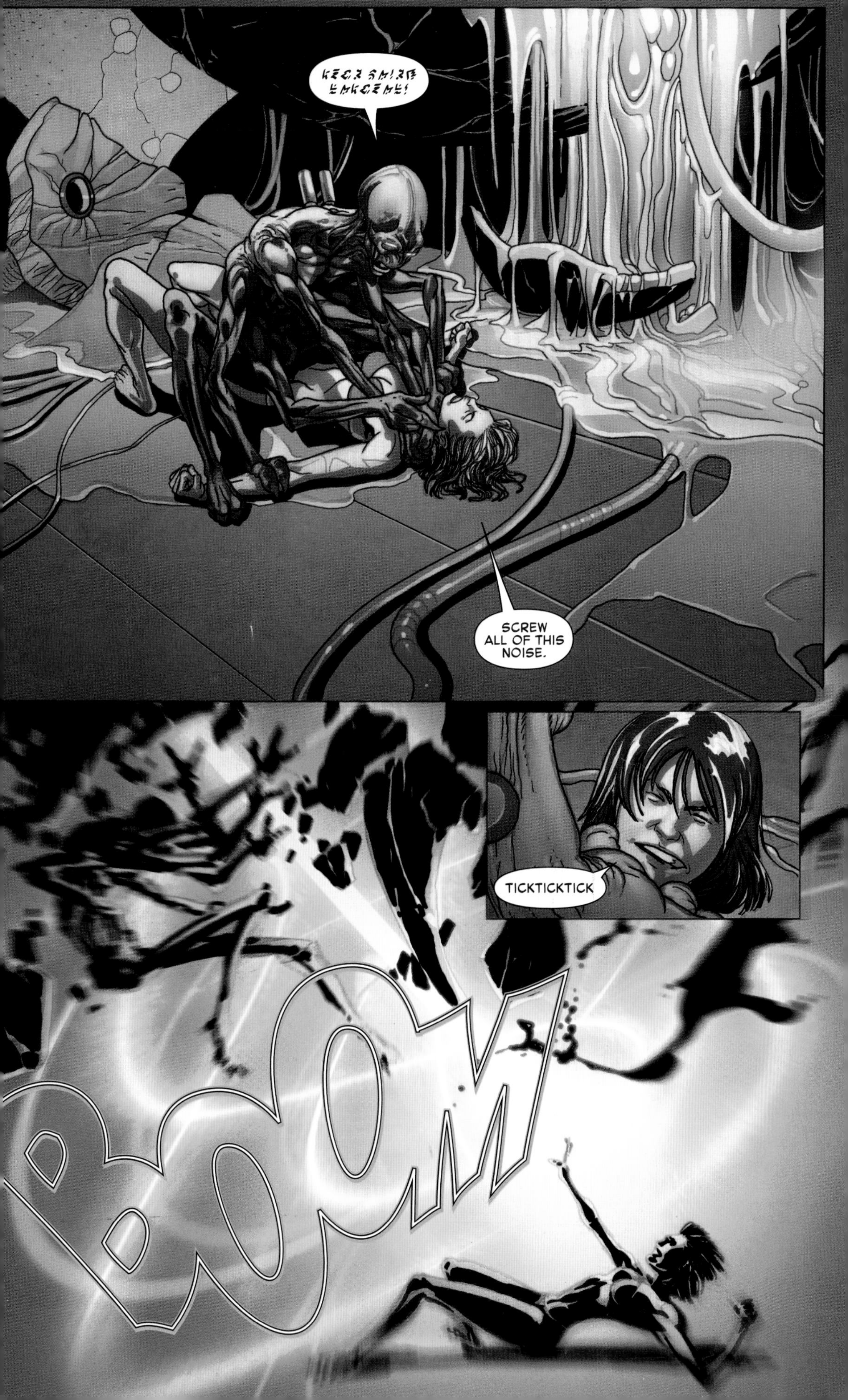
SCREW ALL OF THIS NOISE.
TICKTICKTICK
BOOM

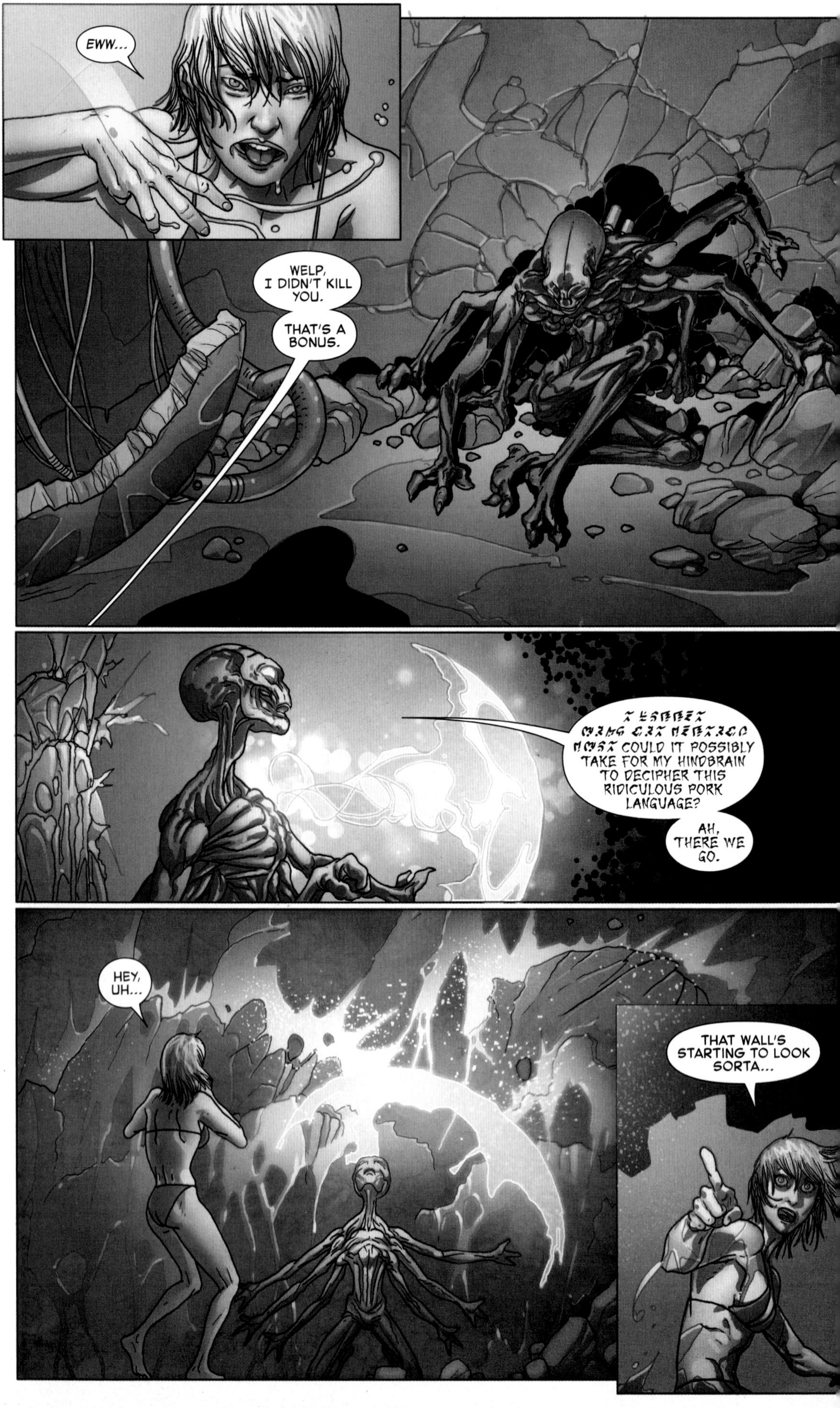
EWW...
WELP, I DIDN'T KILL YOU.
THAT'S A BONUS.
COULD IT POSSIBLY TAKE FOR MY HINDBRAIN TO DECIPHER THIS RIDICULOUS PORK LANGUAGE?
AH, THERE WE GO.
HEY, UH...
THAT WALL'S STARTING TO LOOK SORTA...

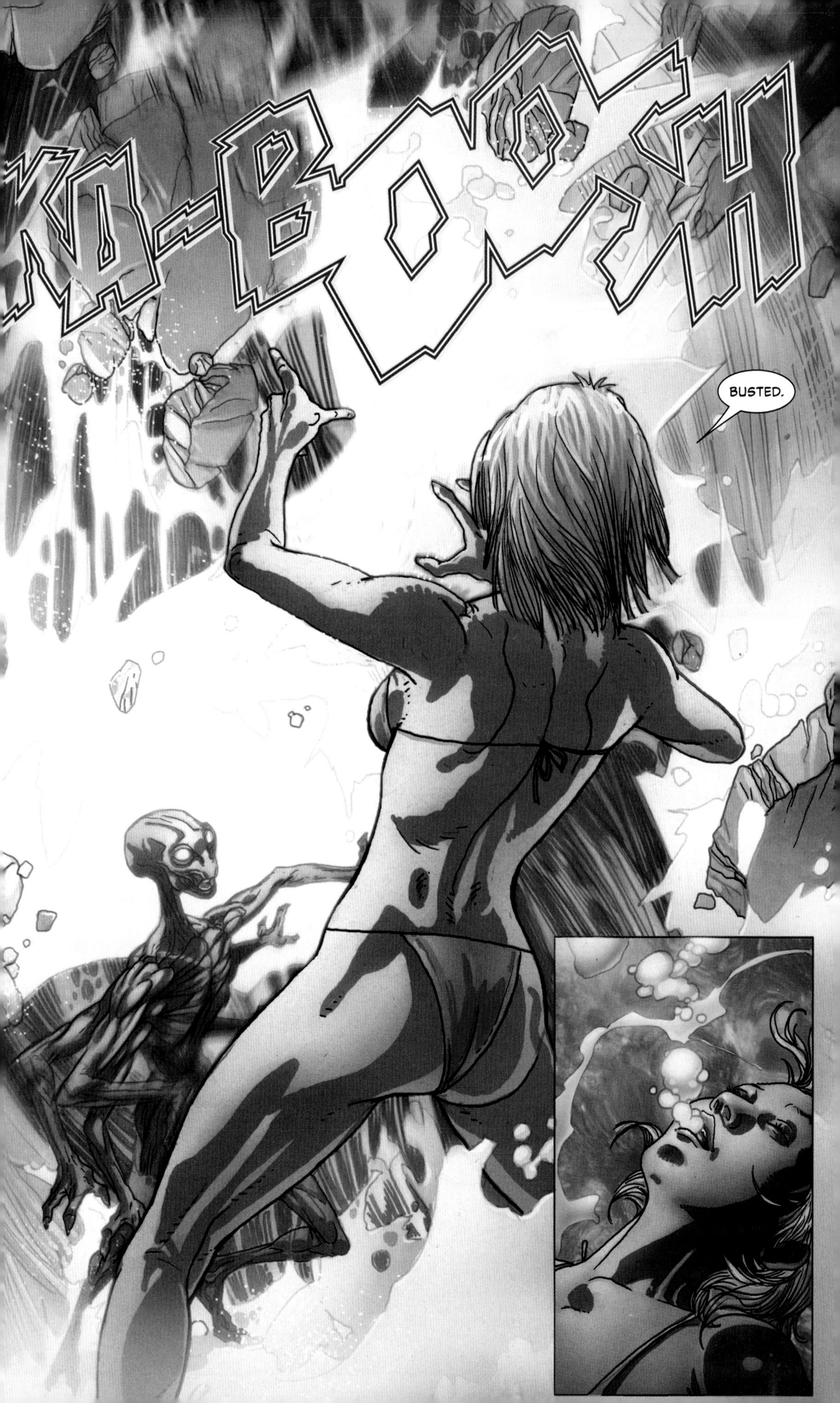
KA-BOOM
BUSTED.

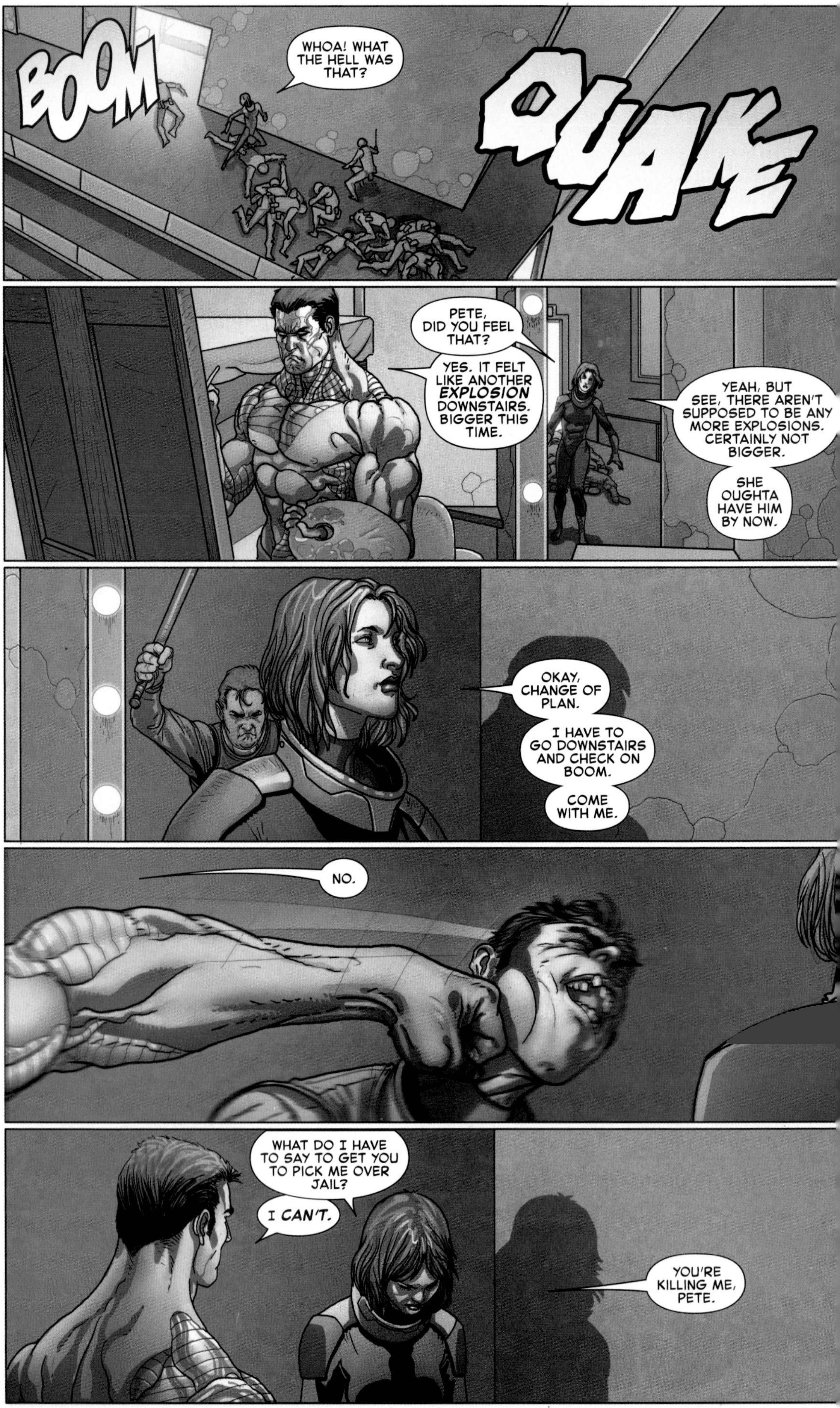
BOOM
WHOA! WHAT THE HELL WAS THAT?
QUAKE
PETE, DID YOU FEEL THAT?
YES. IT FELT LIKE ANOTHER EXPLOSION DOWNSTAIRS. BIGGER THIS TIME.
YEAH, BUT SEE, THERE AREN'T SUPPOSED TO BE ANY MORE EXPLOSIONS. CERTAINLY NOT BIGGER.
SHE OUGHTA HAVE HIM BY NOW.
OKAY, CHANGE OF PLAN.
I HAVE TO GO DOWNSTAIRS AND CHECK ON BOOM.
COME WITH ME.
NO.
WHAT DO I HAVE TO SAY TO GET YOU TO PICK ME OVER JAIL?
I CAN'T.
YOU'RE KILLING ME, PETE.

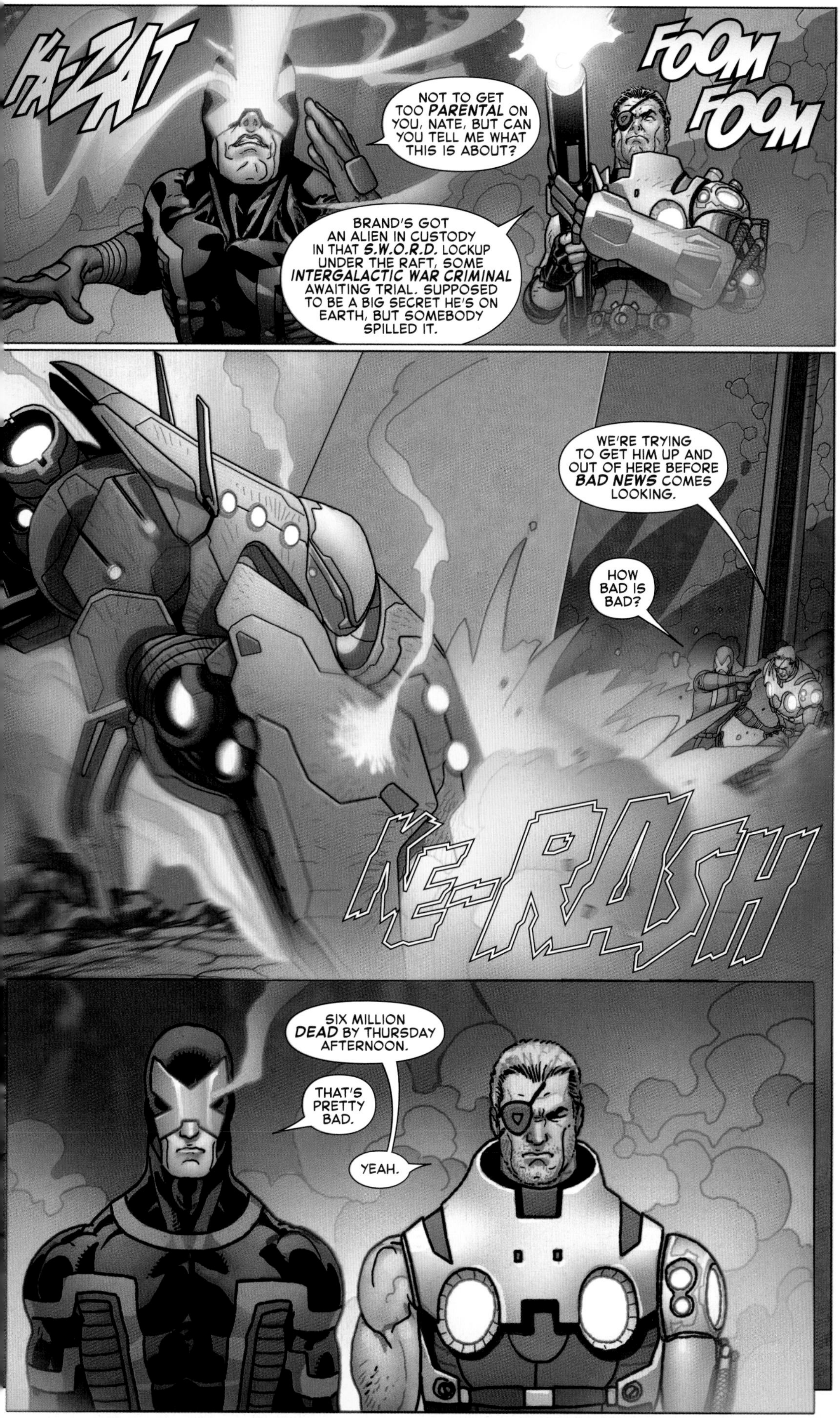
KA-ZAT
NOT TO GET TOO PARENTAL ON YOU, NATE, BUT CAN YOU TELL ME WHAT THIS IS ABOUT?
FOOM FOOM
BRAND'S GOT AN ALIEN IN CUSTODY IN THAT S.W.O.R.D. LOCKUP UNDER THE RAFT, SOME INTERGALACTIC WAR CRIMINAL AWAITING TRIAL. SUPPOSED TO BE A BIG SECRET HE'S ON EARTH, BUT SOMEBODY SPILLED IT.
WE'RE TRYING TO GET HIM UP AND OUT OF HERE BEFORE BAD NEWS COMES LOOKING.
HOW BAD IS BAD?
KE-RASH
SIX MILLION DEAD BY THURSDAY AFTERNOON.
THAT'S PRETTY BAD.
YEAH.

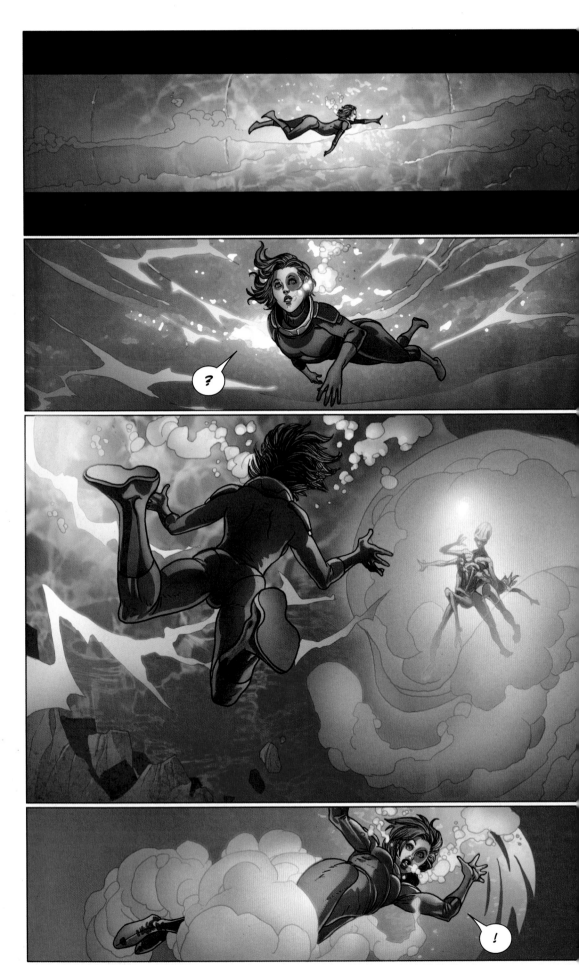

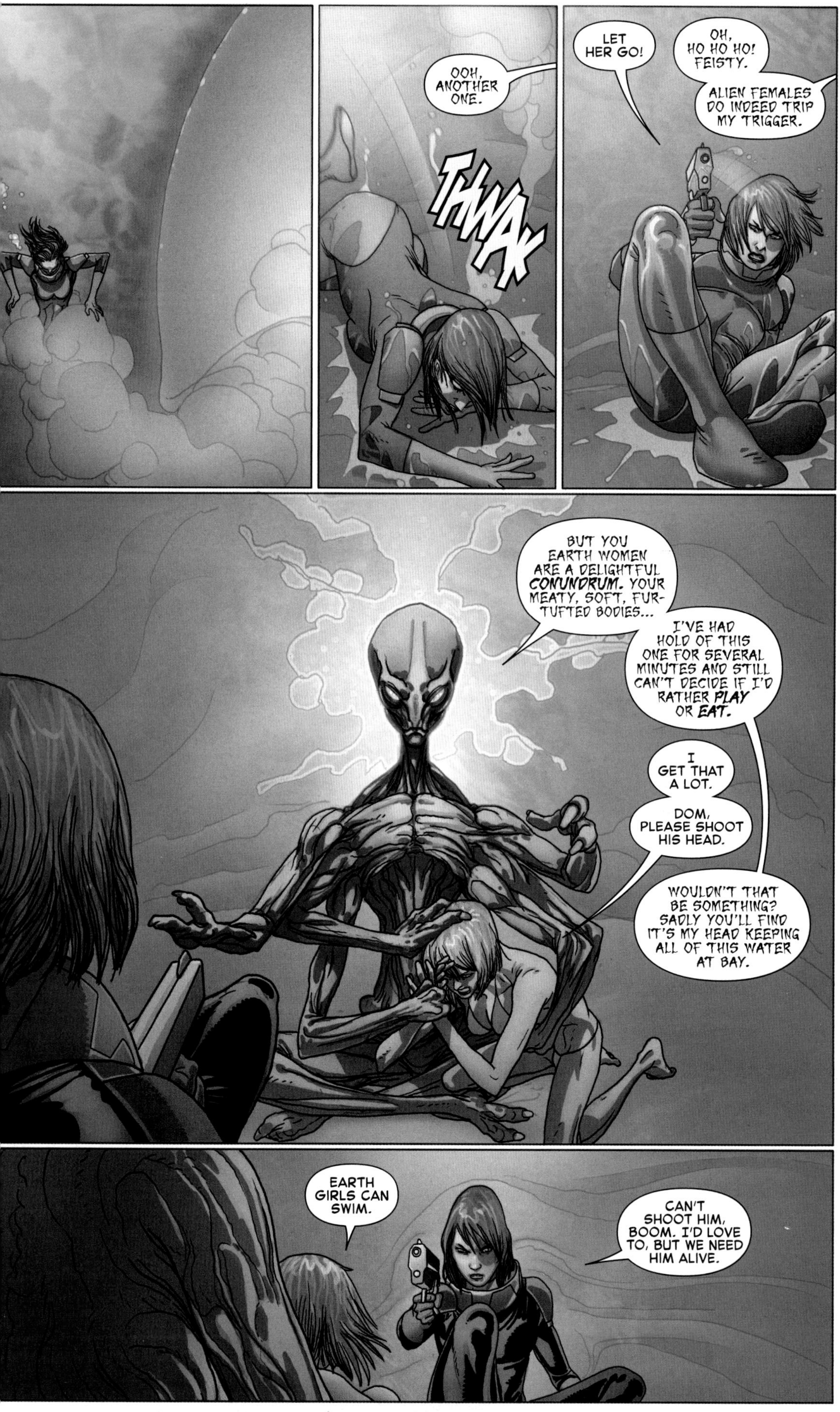
OOH, ANOTHER ONE.
THWAK
LET HER GO!
OH, HO HO HO! FEISTY.
ALIEN FEMALES DO INDEED TRIP MY TRIGGER.
BUT YOU EARTH WOMEN ARE A DELIGHTFUL CONUNDRUM. YOUR MEATY, SOFT, FUR-TUFTED BODIES...
I'VE HAD HOLD OF THIS ONE FOR SEVERAL MINUTES AND STILL CAN'T DECIDE IF I'D RATHER PLAY OR EAT.
I GET THAT A LOT.
DOM, PLEASE SHOOT HIS HEAD.
WOULDN'T THAT BE SOMETHING? SADLY YOU'LL FIND IT'S MY HEAD KEEPING ALL OF THIS WATER AT BAY.
EARTH GIRLS CAN SWIM.
CAN'T SHOOT HIM, BOOM. I'D LOVE TO, BUT WE NEED HIM ALIVE.

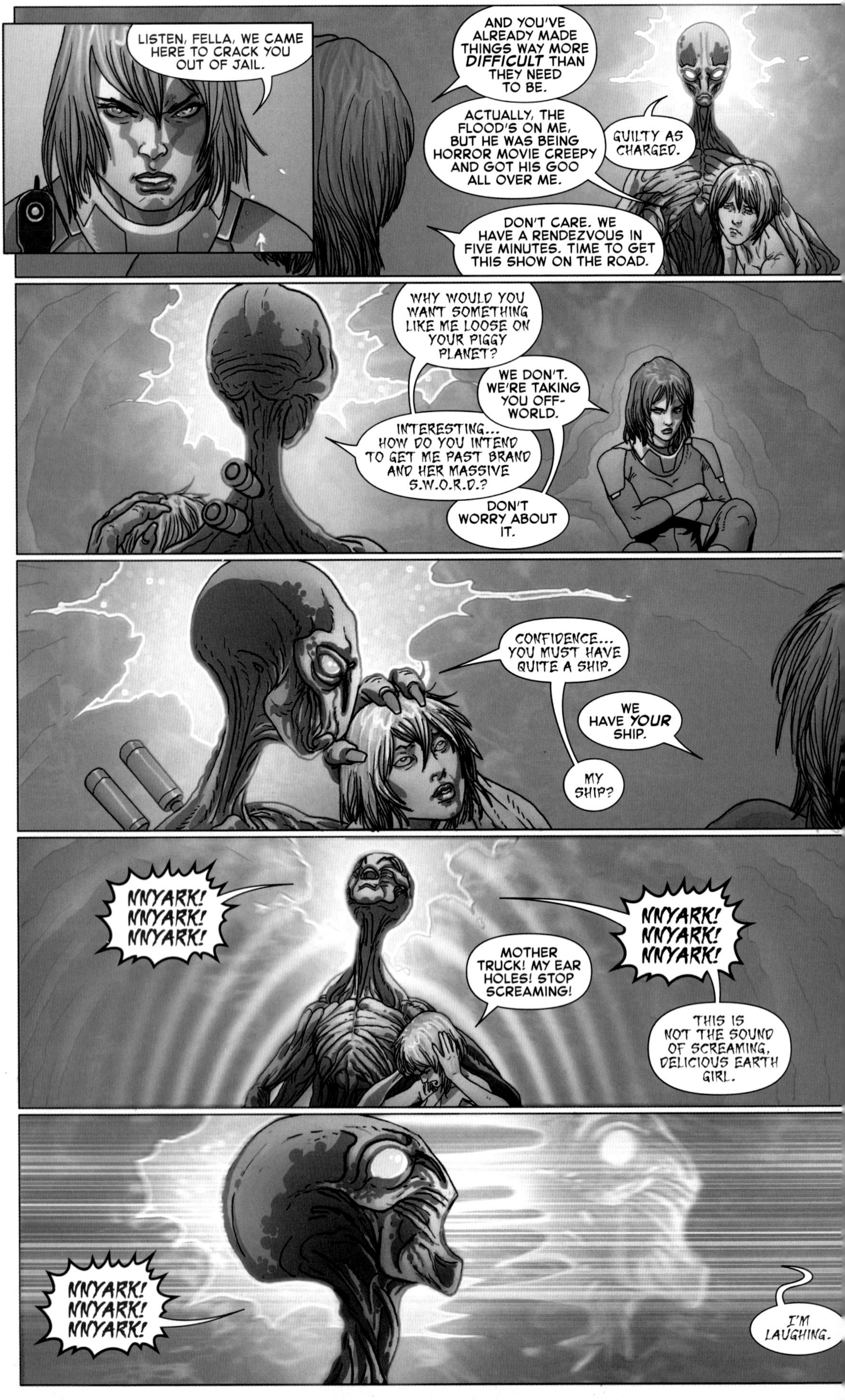
LISTEN, FELLA, WE CAME HERE TO CRACK YOU OUT OF JAIL.
AND YOU'VE ALREADY MADE THINGS WAY MORE DIFFICULT THAN THEY NEED TO BE.
ACTUALLY, THE FLOOD'S ON ME, BUT HE WAS BEING HORROR MOVIE CREEPY AND GOT HIS GOO ALL OVER ME.
GUILTY AS CHARGED.
DON'T CARE. WE HAVE A RENDEZVOUS IN FIVE MINUTES. TIME TO GET THIS SHOW ON THE ROAD.
WHY WOULD YOU WANT SOMETHING LIKE ME LOOSE ON YOUR PIGGY PLANET?
WE DON'T. WE'RE TAKING YOU OFF-WORLD.
INTERESTING... HOW DO YOU INTEND TO GET ME PAST BRAND AND HER MASSIVE S.W.O.R.D.?
DON'T WORRY ABOUT IT.
CONFIDENCE... YOU MUST HAVE QUITE A SHIP.
WE HAVE YOUR SHIP.
MY SHIP?
NNYARK! NNYARK! NNYARK!
NNYARK! NNYARK! NNYARK!
MOTHER TRUCK! MY EAR HOLES! STOP SCREAMING!
THIS IS NOT THE SOUND OF SCREAMING, DELICIOUS EARTH GIRL.
NNYARK! NNYARK! NNYARK!
I'M LAUGHING.

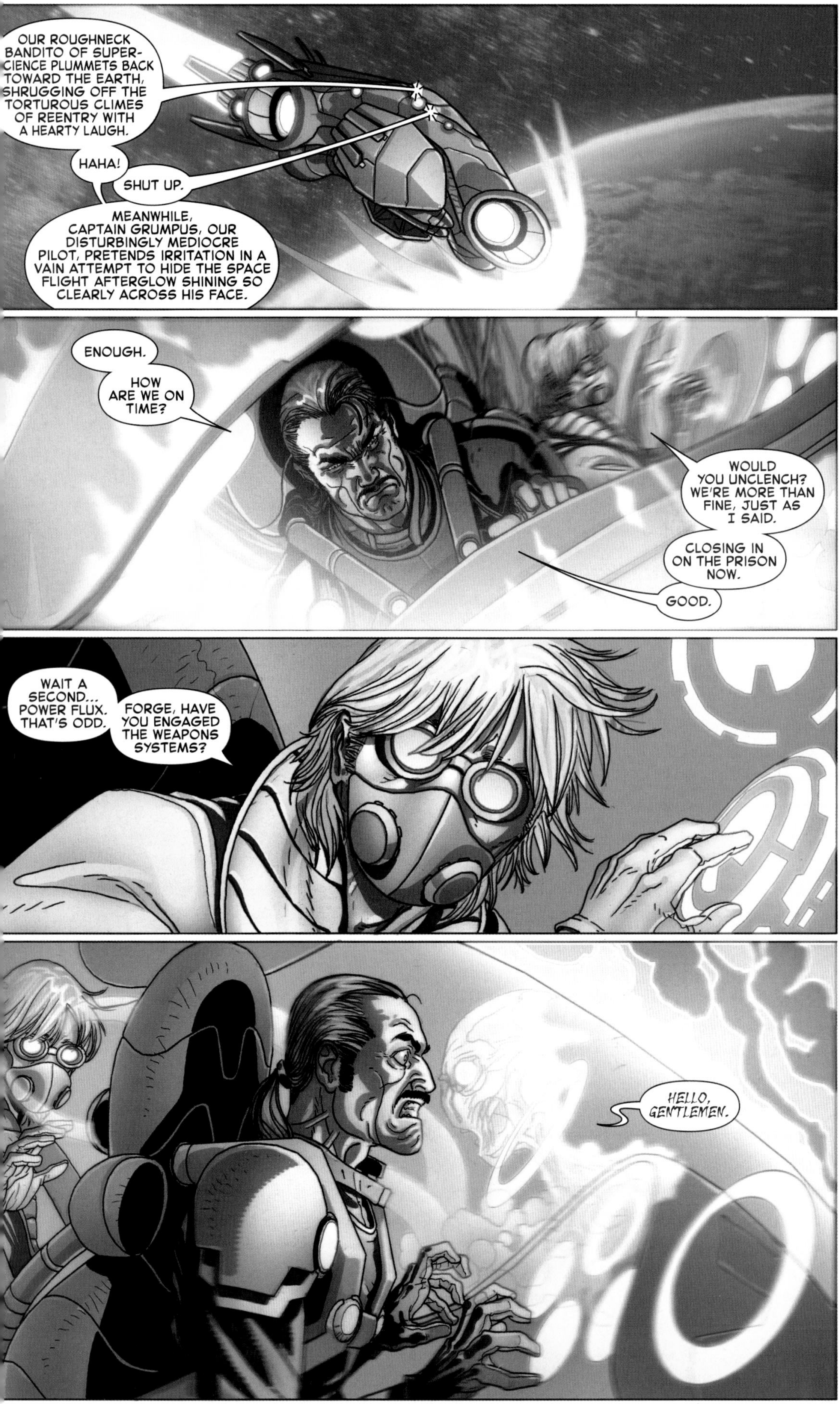

OUR ROUGHNECK BANDITO OF SUPER-CIENCE PLUMMETS BACK TOWARD THE EARTH, SHRUGGING OFF THE TORTUROUS CLIMES OF REENTRY WITH A HEARTY LAUGH.
HAHA!
SHUT UP.
MEANWHILE, CAPTAIN GRUMPUS, OUR DISTURBINGLY MEDIOCRE PILOT, PRETENDS IRRITATION IN A VAIN ATTEMPT TO HIDE THE SPACE FLIGHT AFTERGLOW SHINING SO CLEARLY ACROSS HIS FACE.
ENOUGH.
HOW ARE WE ON TIME?
WOULD YOU UNCLENCH? WE'RE MORE THAN FINE, JUST AS I SAID.
CLOSING IN ON THE PRISON NOW.
GOOD.
WAIT A SECOND... POWER FLUX. THAT'S ODD.
FORGE, HAVE YOU ENGAGED THE WEAPONS SYSTEMS?
HELLO, GENTLEMEN.

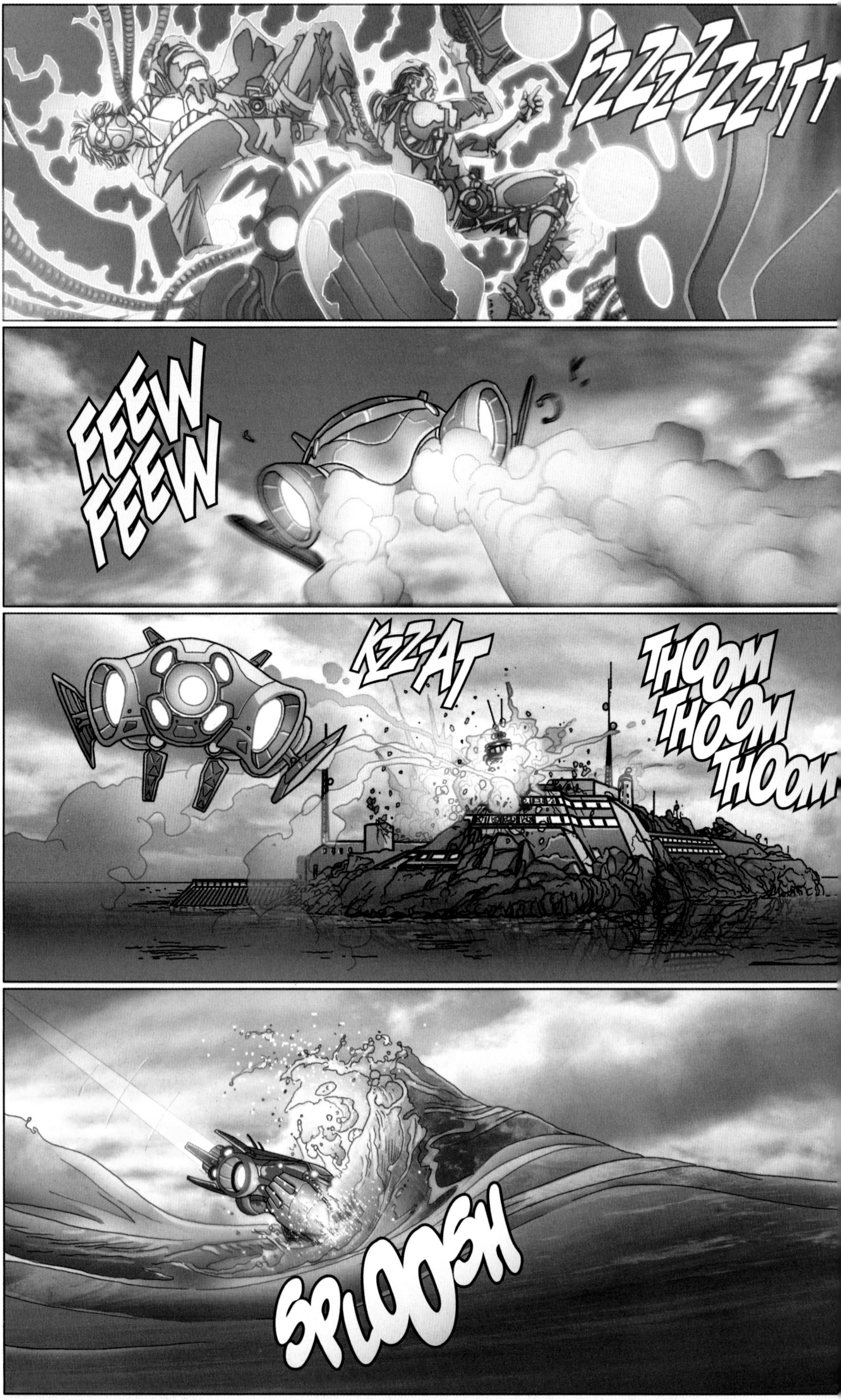
FZZZZZZTTT
FEEW FEEW
KZZ-AT
THOOM THOOM THOOM
SPLOOSH

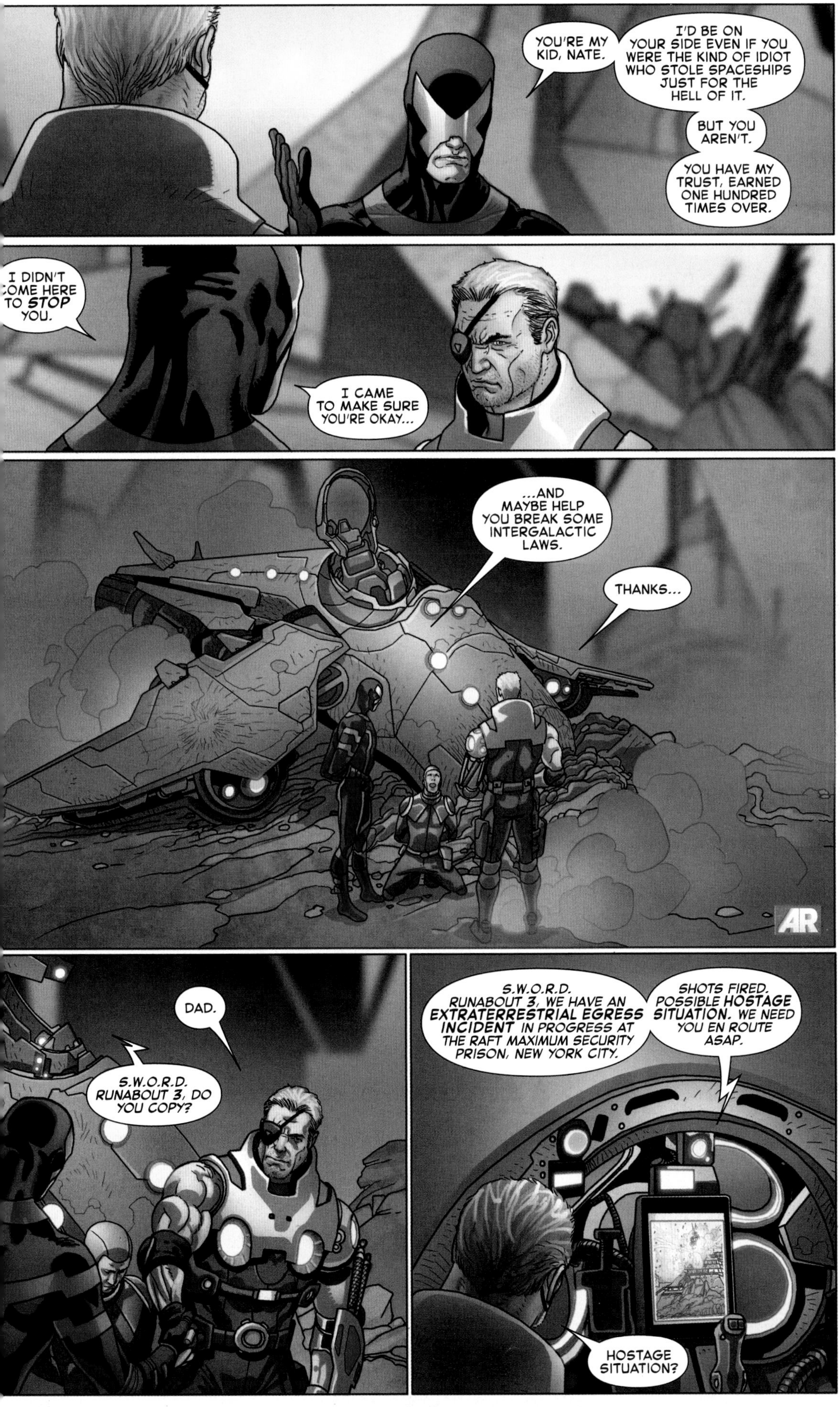
YOU'RE MY KID, NATE.
I'D BE ON YOUR SIDE EVEN IF YOU WERE THE KIND OF IDIOT WHO STOLE SPACESHIPS JUST FOR THE HELL OF IT.
BUT YOU AREN'T.
YOU HAVE MY TRUST, EARNED ONE HUNDRED TIMES OVER.
I DIDN'T COME HERE TO STOP YOU.
I CAME TO MAKE SURE YOU'RE OKAY...
...AND MAYBE HELP YOU BREAK SOME INTERGALACTIC LAWS.
THANKS...
DAD.
S.W.O.R.D. RUNABOUT 3, DO YOU COPY?
S.W.O.R.D. RUNABOUT 3, WE HAVE AN EXTRATERRESTRIAL EGRESS INCIDENT IN PROGRESS AT THE RAFT MAXIMUM SECURITY PRISON, NEW YORK CITY.
SHOTS FIRED. POSSIBLE HOSTAGE SITUATION. WE NEED YOU EN ROUTE ASAP.
HOSTAGE SITUATION?

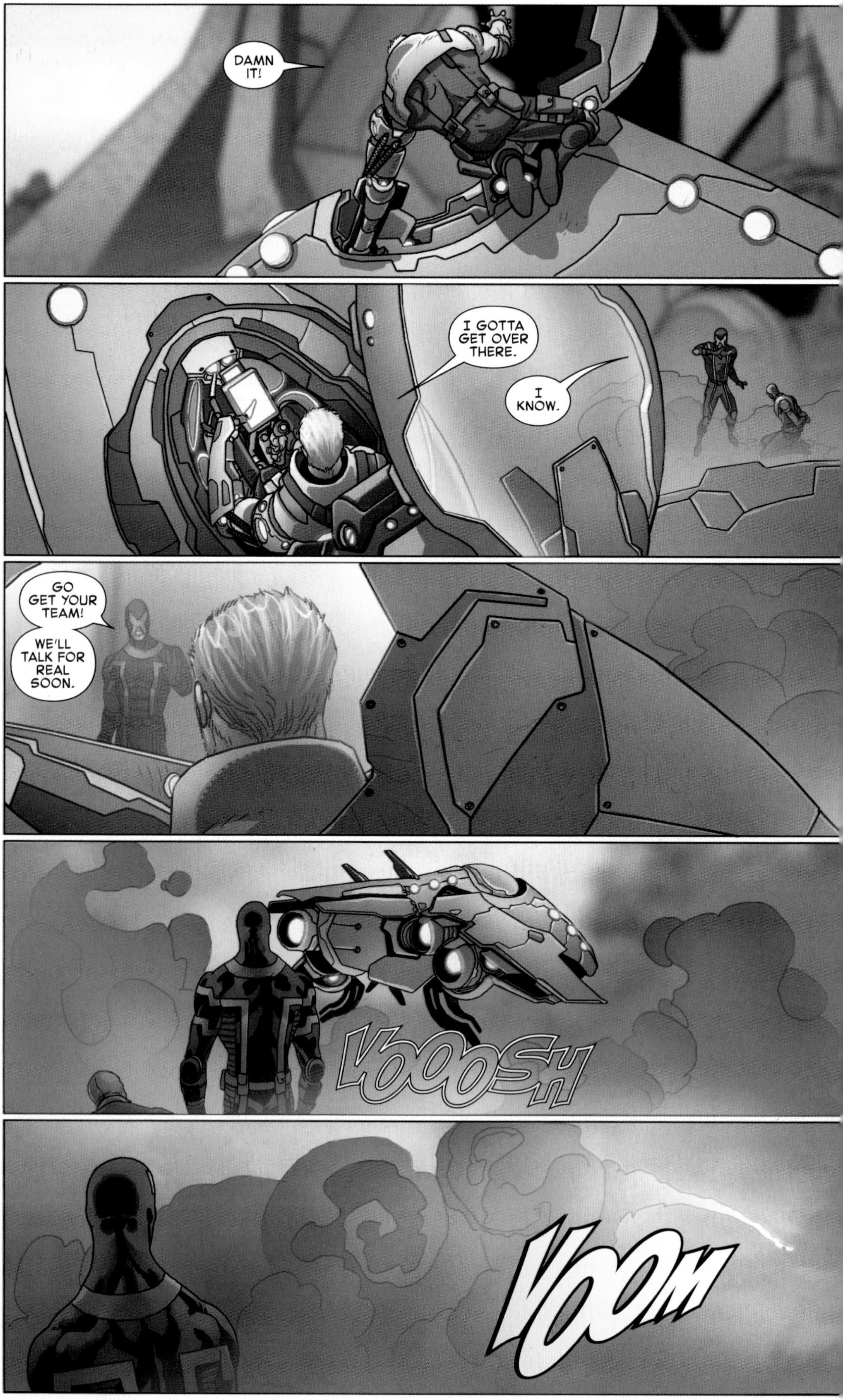
DAMN IT!
I GOTTA GET OVER THERE.
I KNOW.
GO GET YOUR TEAM!
WE'LL TALK FOR REAL SOON.
VOOOSH
VOOM

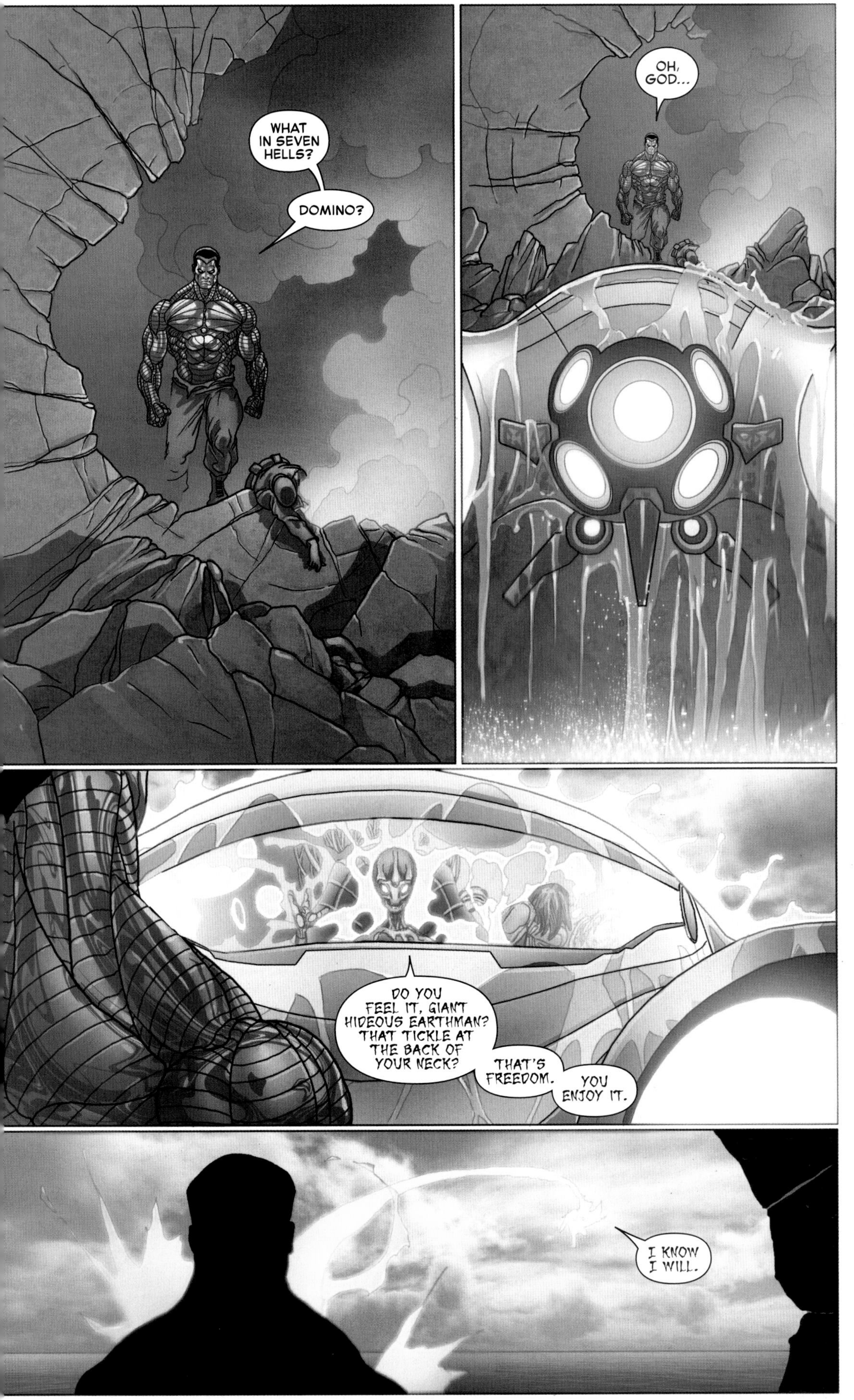
WHAT IN SEVEN HELLS?
DOMINO?
OH, GOD...
DO YOU FEEL IT, GIANT HIDEOUS EARTHMAN? THAT TICKLE AT THE BACK OF YOUR NECK?
THAT'S FREEDOM.
YOU ENJOY IT.
I KNOW I WILL.

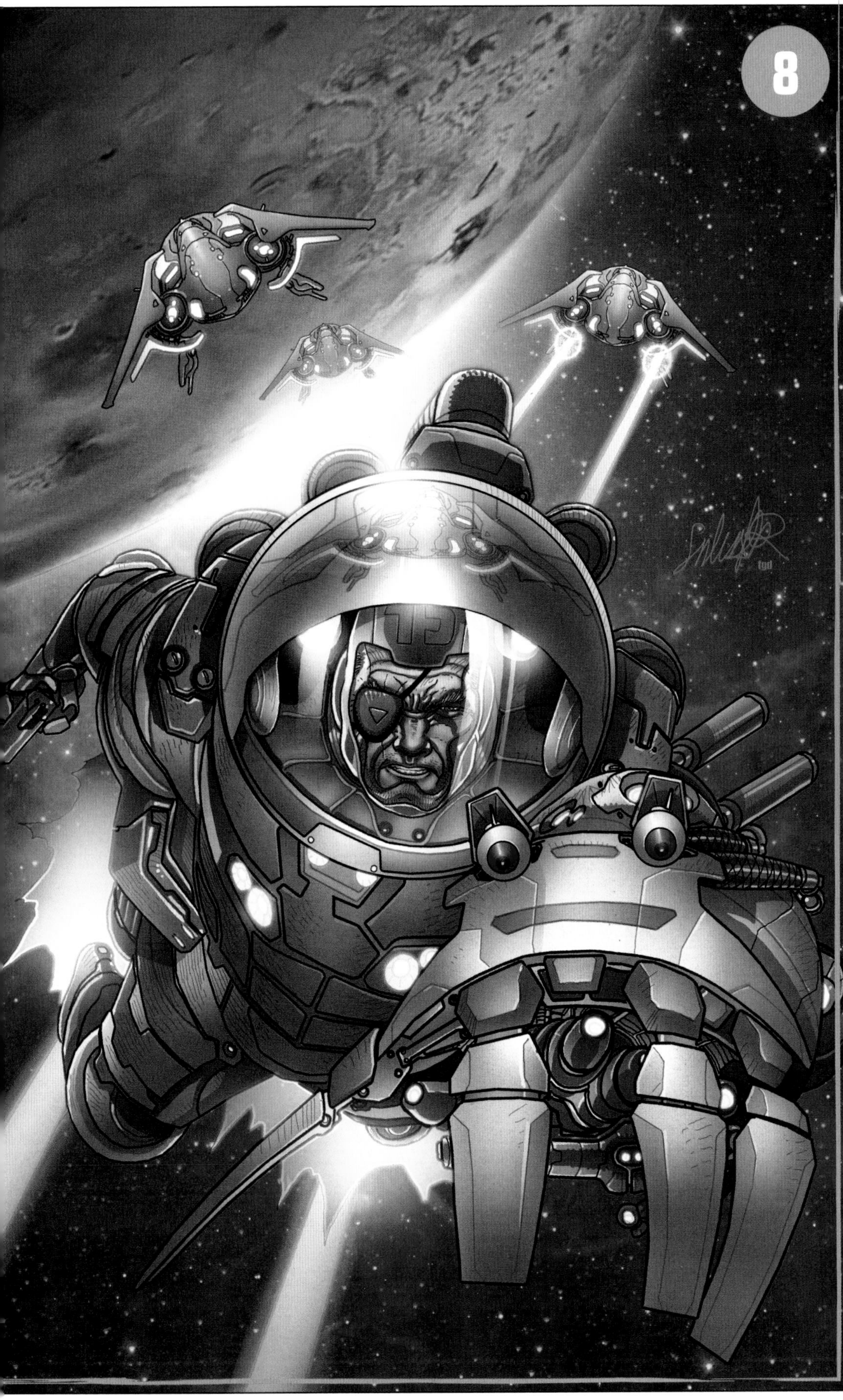
8

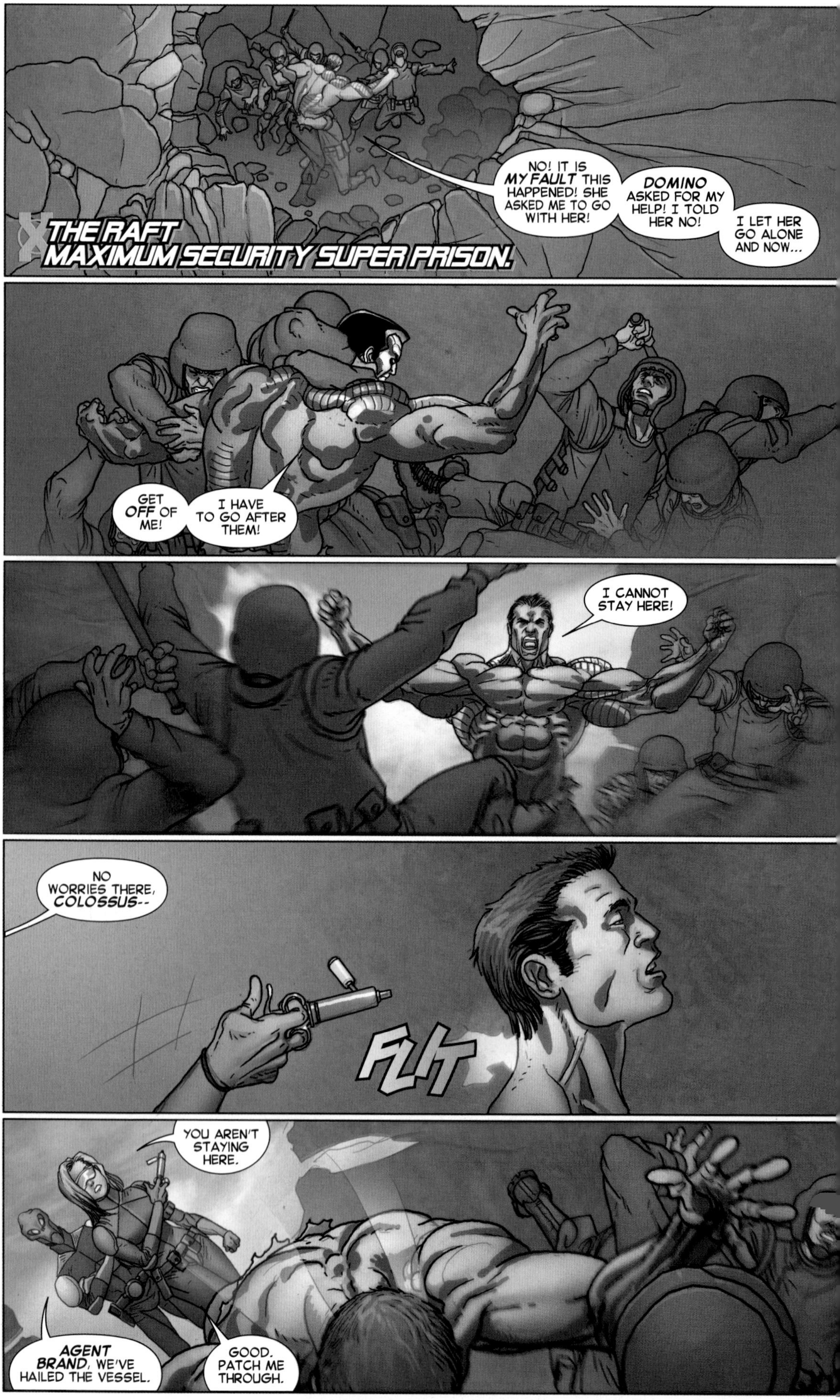
THE RAFT
MAXIMUM SECURITY SUPER PRISON.
NO! IT IS MY FAULT THIS HAPPENED! SHE ASKED ME TO GO WITH HER!
DOMINO ASKED FOR MY HELP! I TOLD HER NO!
I LET HER GO ALONE AND NOW...
GET OFF OF ME!
I HAVE TO GO AFTER THEM!
I CANNOT STAY HERE!
NO WORRIES THERE, COLOSSUS--
FLIT
YOU AREN'T STAYING HERE.
AGENT BRAND, WE'VE HAILED THE VESSEL.
GOOD. PATCH ME THROUGH.

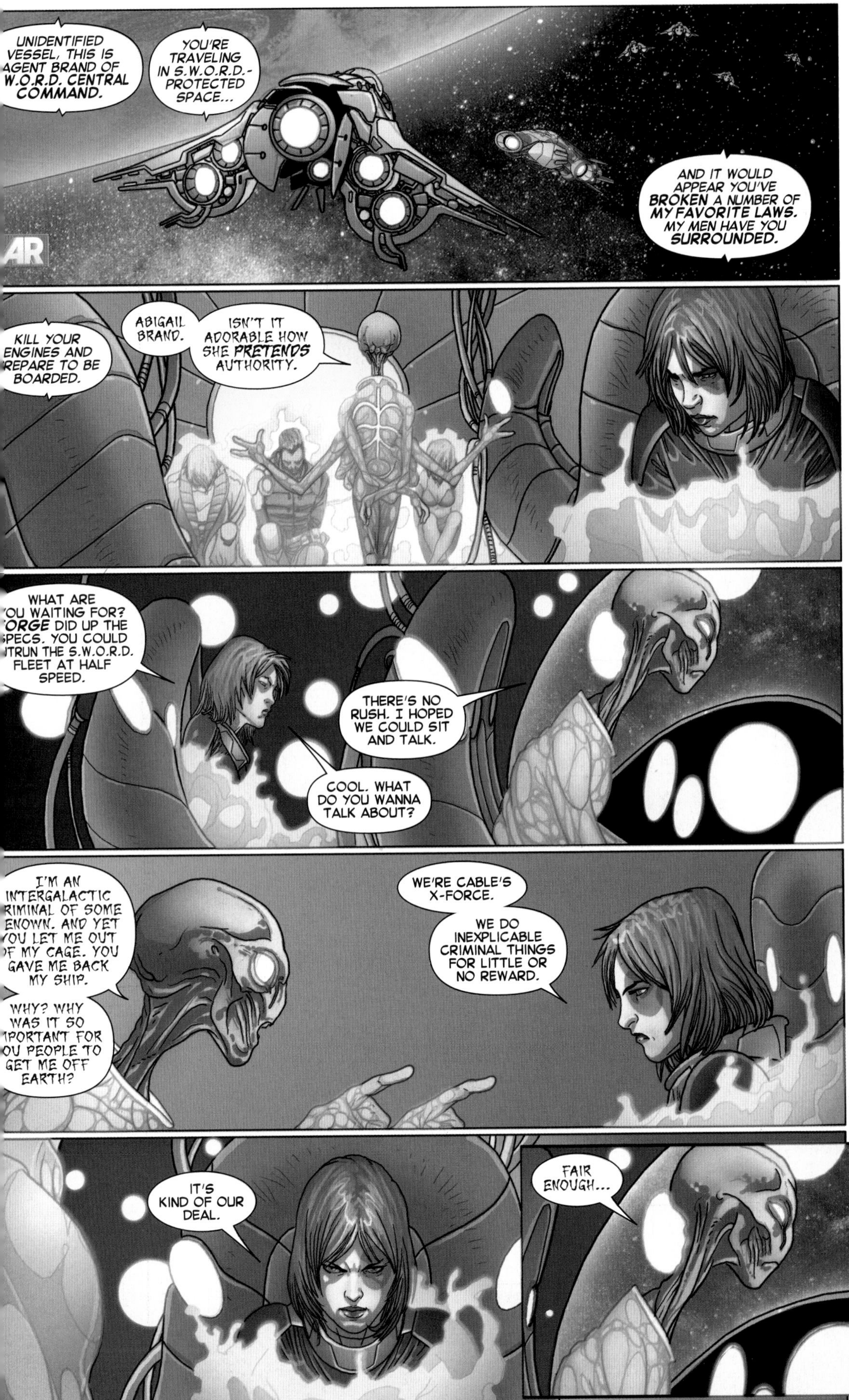

UNIDENTIFIED VESSEL, THIS IS AGENT BRAND OF W.O.R.D. CENTRAL COMMAND.
YOU'RE TRAVELING IN S.W.O.R.D.-PROTECTED SPACE...
AND IT WOULD APPEAR YOU'VE BROKEN A NUMBER OF MY FAVORITE LAWS. MY MEN HAVE YOU SURROUNDED.
KILL YOUR ENGINES AND REPARE TO BE BOARDED.
ABIGAIL BRAND.
ISN'T IT ADORABLE HOW SHE PRETENDS AUTHORITY.
WHAT ARE OU WAITING FOR? ORGE DID UP THE PECS. YOU COULD UTRUN THE S.W.O.R.D. FLEET AT HALF SPEED.
THERE'S NO RUSH. I HOPED WE COULD SIT AND TALK.
COOL. WHAT DO YOU WANNA TALK ABOUT?
I'M AN INTERGALACTIC RIMINAL OF SOME ENOWN. AND YET OU LET ME OUT F MY CAGE. YOU GAVE ME BACK MY SHIP.
WHY? WHY WAS IT SO PORTANT FOR OU PEOPLE TO GET ME OFF EARTH?
WE'RE CABLE'S X-FORCE.
WE DO INEXPLICABLE CRIMINAL THINGS FOR LITTLE OR NO REWARD.
IT'S KIND OF OUR DEAL.
FAIR ENOUGH...

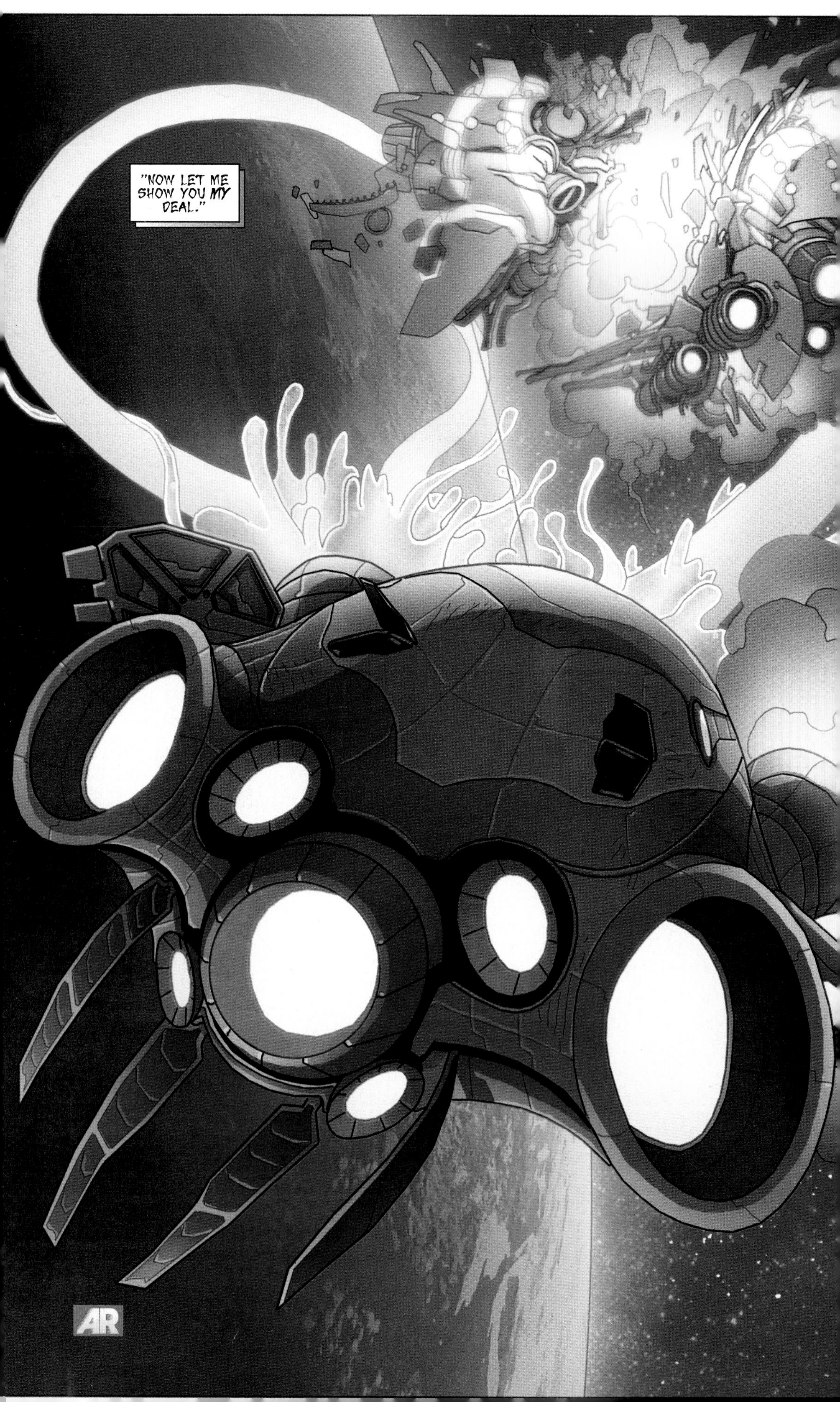
"NOW LET ME SHOW YOU MY DEAL."

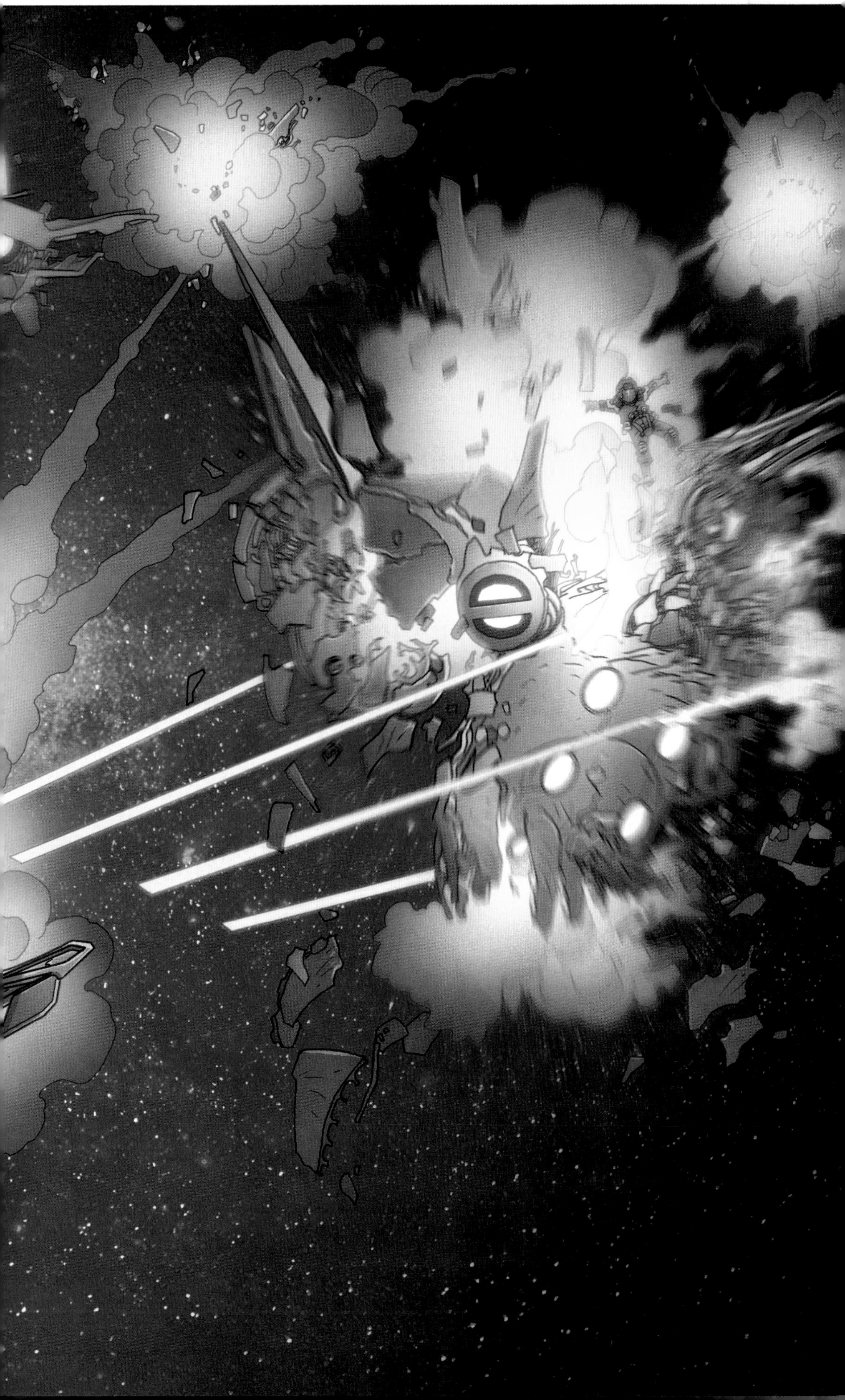

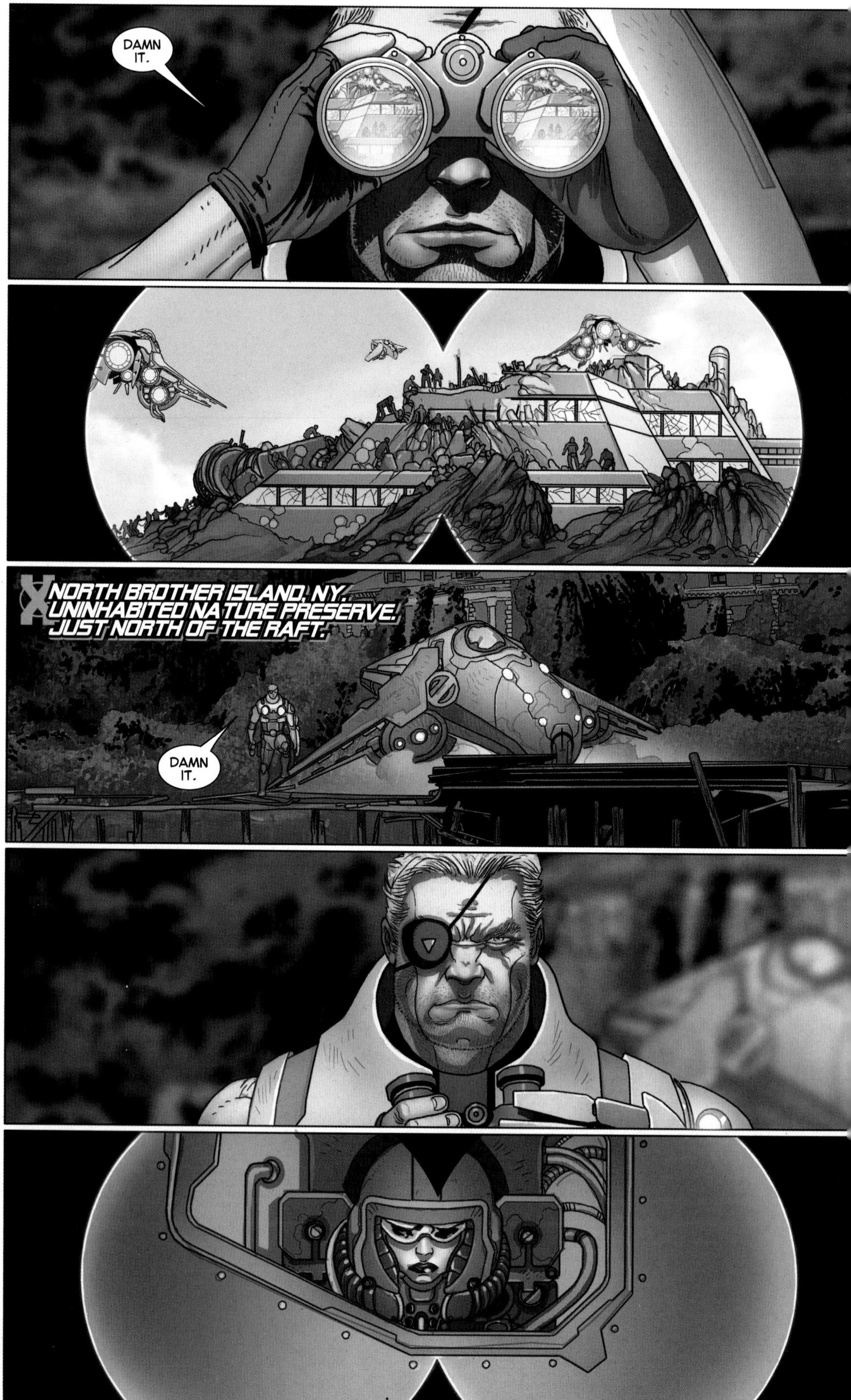
DAMN IT.
NORTH BROTHER ISLAND, NY. UNINHABITED NATURE PRESERVE. JUST NORTH OF THE RAFT.
DAMN IT.

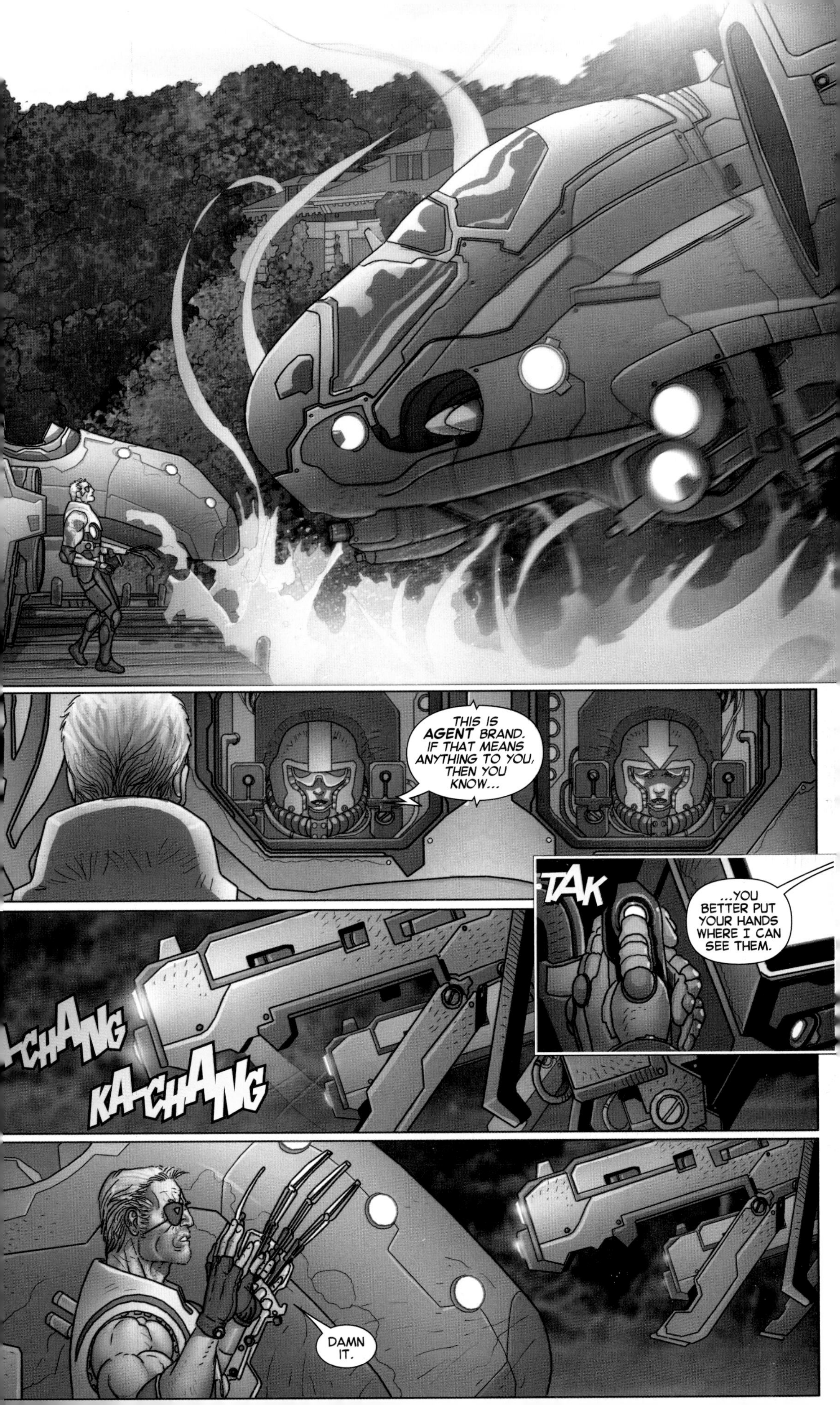

THIS IS AGENT BRAND. IF THAT MEANS ANYTHING TO YOU, THEN YOU KNOW...
TAK
...YOU BETTER PUT YOUR HANDS WHERE I CAN SEE THEM.
-CHANG
KA-CHANG
DAMN IT.

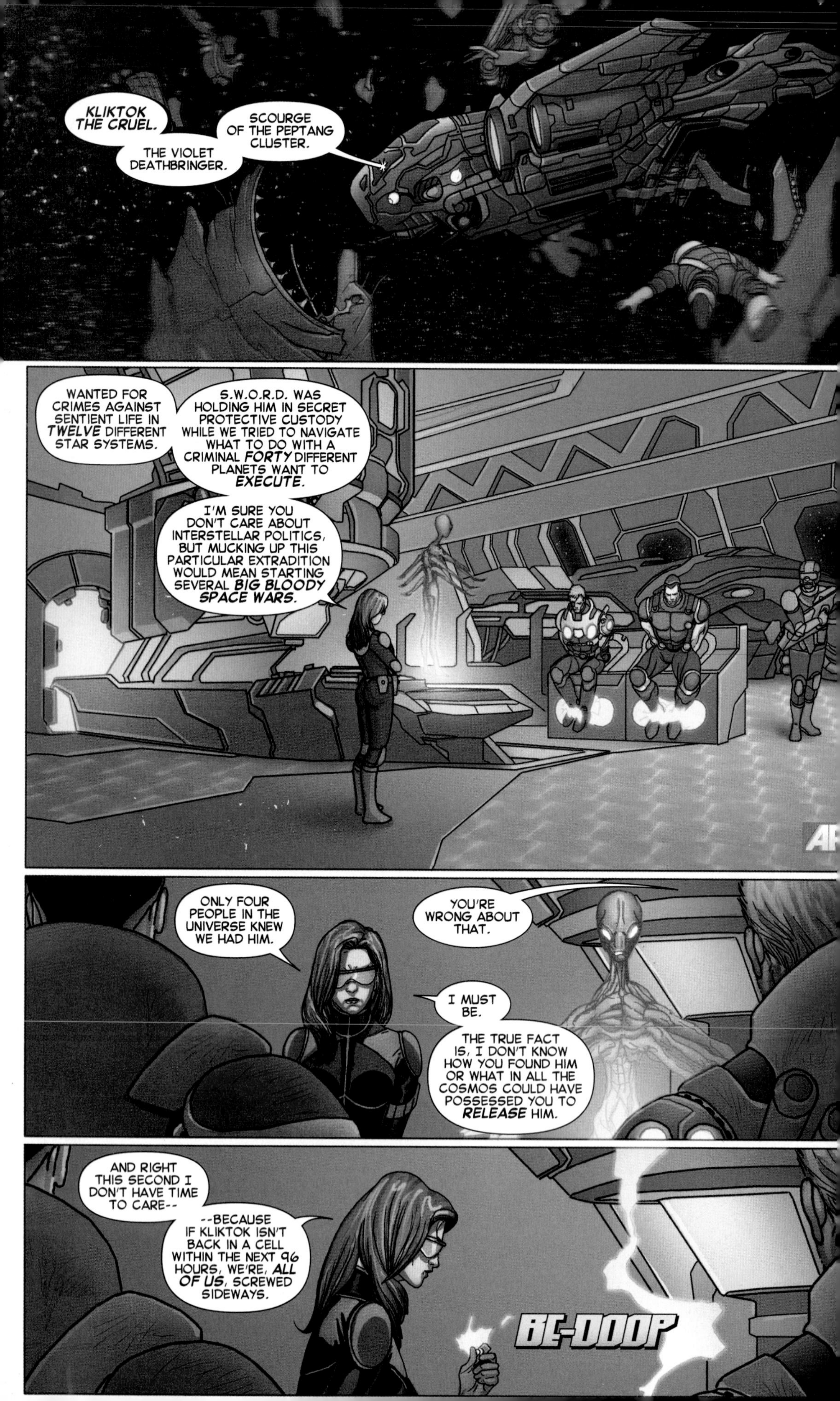
KLIKTOK THE CRUEL.
THE VIOLET DEATHBRINGER.
SCOURGE OF THE PEPTANG CLUSTER.
WANTED FOR CRIMES AGAINST SENTIENT LIFE IN TWELVE DIFFERENT STAR SYSTEMS.
S.W.O.R.D. WAS HOLDING HIM IN SECRET PROTECTIVE CUSTODY WHILE WE TRIED TO NAVIGATE WHAT TO DO WITH A CRIMINAL FORTY DIFFERENT PLANETS WANT TO EXECUTE.
I'M SURE YOU DON'T CARE ABOUT INTERSTELLAR POLITICS, BUT MUCKING UP THIS PARTICULAR EXTRADITION WOULD MEAN STARTING SEVERAL BIG BLOODY SPACE WARS.
ONLY FOUR PEOPLE IN THE UNIVERSE KNEW WE HAD HIM.
YOU'RE WRONG ABOUT THAT.
I MUST BE.
THE TRUE FACT IS, I DON'T KNOW HOW YOU FOUND HIM OR WHAT IN ALL THE COSMOS COULD HAVE POSSESSED YOU TO RELEASE HIM.
AND RIGHT THIS SECOND I DON'T HAVE TIME TO CARE--
--BECAUSE IF KLIKTOK ISN'T BACK IN A CELL WITHIN THE NEXT 96 HOURS, WE'RE, ALL OF US, SCREWED SIDEWAYS.
BE-DOOP

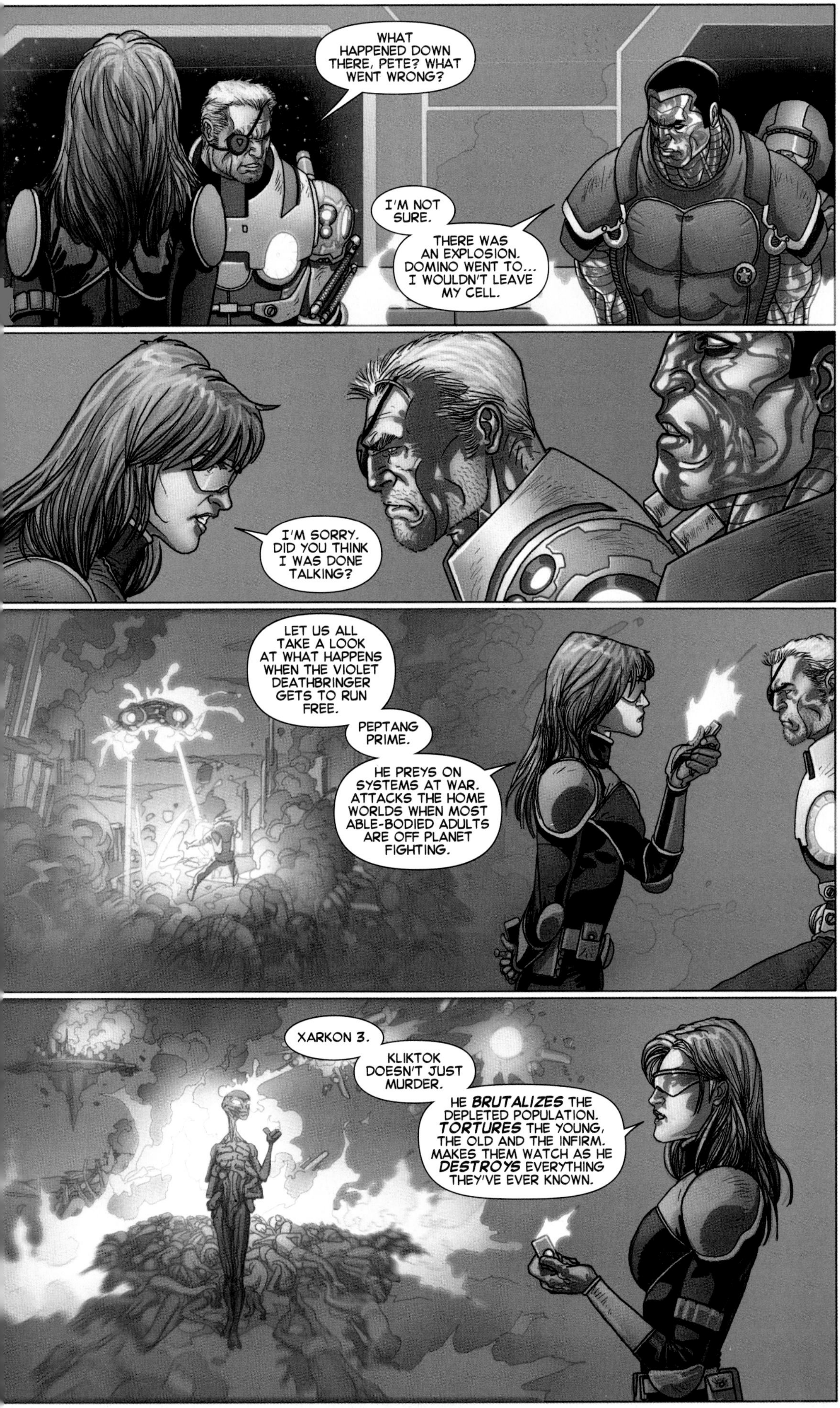
WHAT HAPPENED DOWN THERE, PETE? WHAT WENT WRONG?
I'M NOT SURE.
THERE WAS AN EXPLOSION. DOMINO WENT TO... I WOULDN'T LEAVE MY CELL.
I'M SORRY. DID YOU THINK I WAS DONE TALKING?
LET US ALL TAKE A LOOK AT WHAT HAPPENS WHEN THE VIOLET DEATHBRINGER GETS TO RUN FREE.
PEPTANG PRIME.
HE PREYS ON SYSTEMS AT WAR. ATTACKS THE HOME WORLDS WHEN MOST ABLE-BODIED ADULTS ARE OFF PLANET FIGHTING.
XARKON 3.
KLIKTOK DOESN'T JUST MURDER.
HE BRUTALIZES THE DEPLETED POPULATION. TORTURES THE YOUNG, THE OLD AND THE INFIRM. MAKES THEM WATCH AS HE DESTROYS EVERYTHING THEY'VE EVER KNOWN.

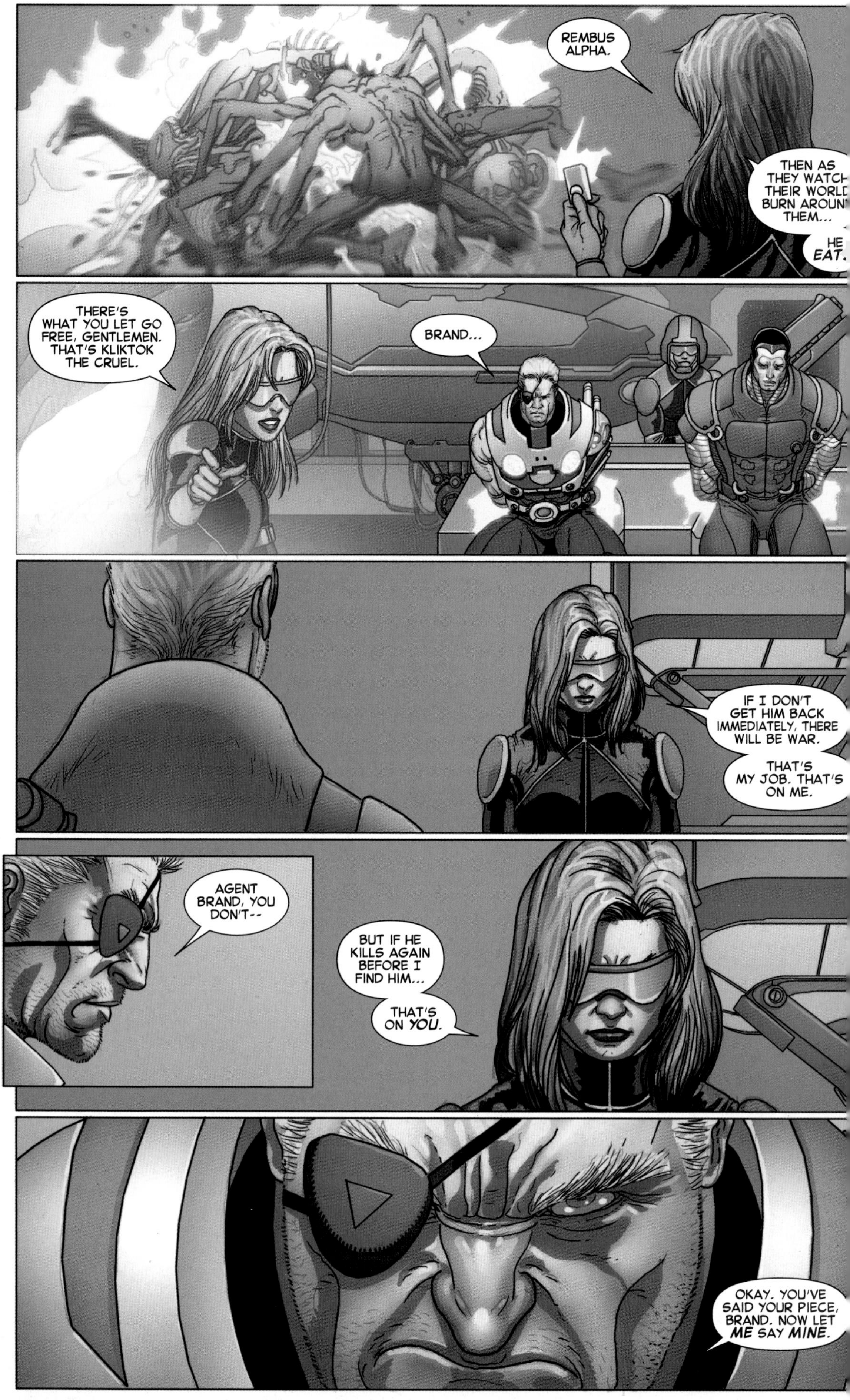

REMBUS ALPHA.
THEN AS THEY WATCH THEIR WORLD BURN AROUN THEM...
HE EAT.
THERE'S WHAT YOU LET GO FREE, GENTLEMEN. THAT'S KLIKTOK THE CRUEL.
BRAND...
IF I DON'T GET HIM BACK IMMEDIATELY, THERE WILL BE WAR.
THAT'S MY JOB. THAT'S ON ME.
AGENT BRAND, YOU DON'T--
BUT IF HE KILLS AGAIN BEFORE I FIND HIM...
THAT'S ON YOU.
OKAY. YOU'VE SAID YOUR PIECE, BRAND. NOW LET ME SAY MINE.

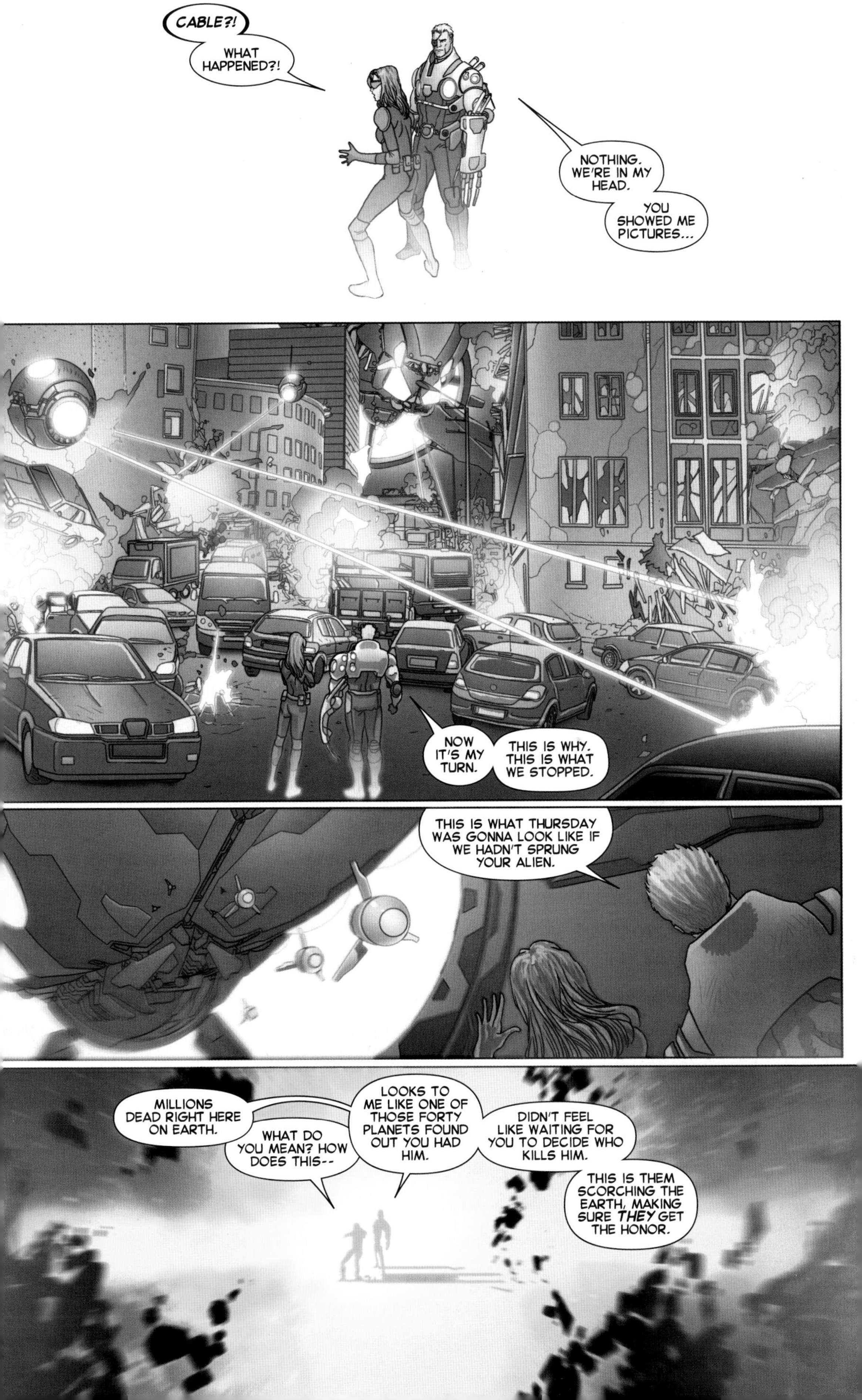
CABLE?!
WHAT HAPPENED?!
NOTHING. WE'RE IN MY HEAD.
YOU SHOWED ME PICTURES...
NOW IT'S MY TURN.
THIS IS WHY. THIS IS WHAT WE STOPPED.
THIS IS WHAT THURSDAY WAS GONNA LOOK LIKE IF WE HADN'T SPRUNG YOUR ALIEN.
MILLIONS DEAD RIGHT HERE ON EARTH.
WHAT DO YOU MEAN? HOW DOES THIS--
LOOKS TO ME LIKE ONE OF THOSE FORTY PLANETS FOUND OUT YOU HAD HIM.
DIDN'T FEEL LIKE WAITING FOR YOU TO DECIDE WHO KILLS HIM.
THIS IS THEM SCORCHING THE EARTH, MAKING SURE THEY GET THE HONOR.

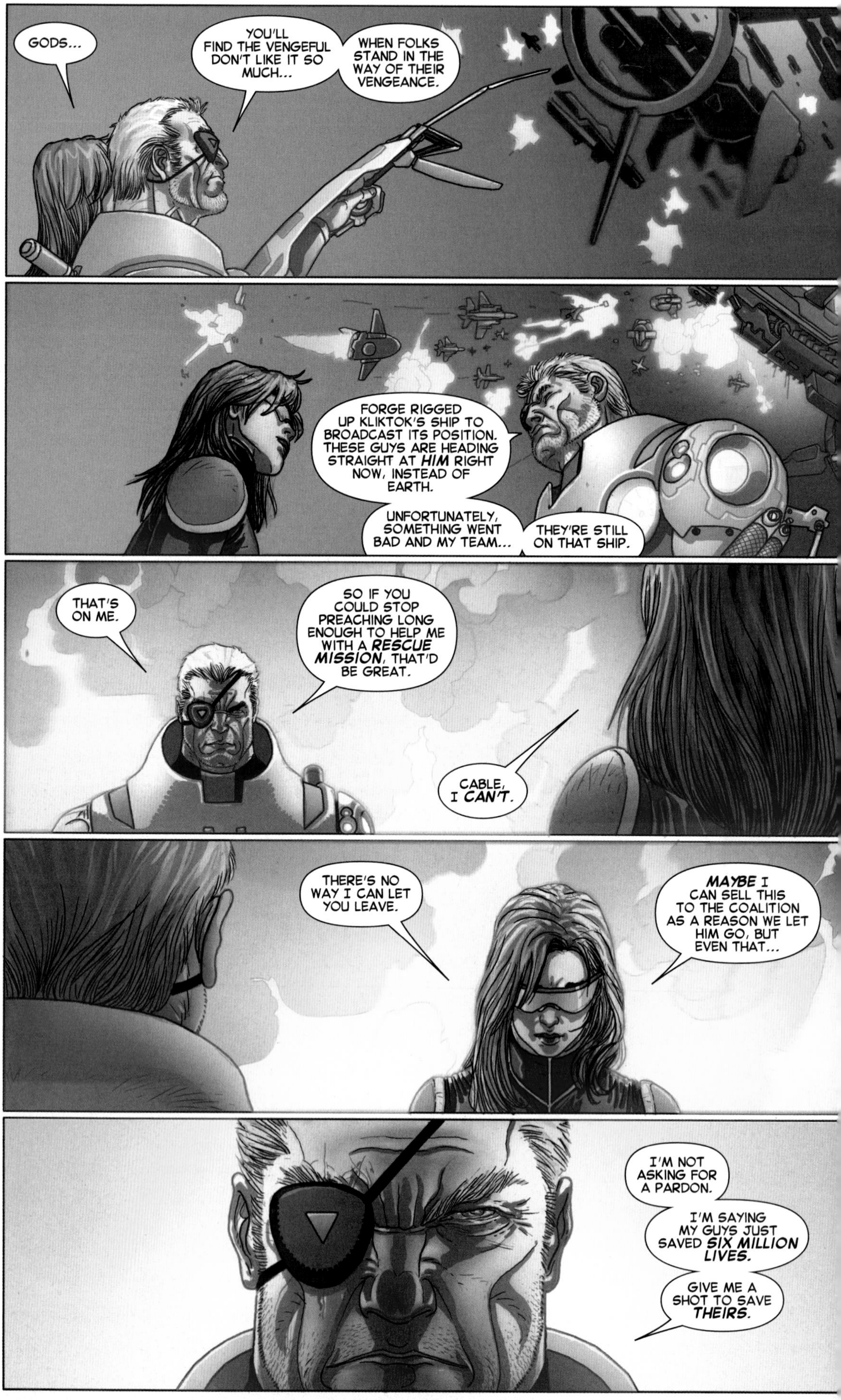
GODS...
YOU'LL FIND THE VENGEFUL DON'T LIKE IT SO MUCH...
WHEN FOLKS STAND IN THE WAY OF THEIR VENGEANCE.
FORGE RIGGED UP KLIKTOK'S SHIP TO BROADCAST ITS POSITION. THESE GUYS ARE HEADING STRAIGHT AT HIM RIGHT NOW, INSTEAD OF EARTH.
UNFORTUNATELY, SOMETHING WENT BAD AND MY TEAM...
THEY'RE STILL ON THAT SHIP.
THAT'S ON ME.
SO IF YOU COULD STOP PREACHING LONG ENOUGH TO HELP ME WITH A RESCUE MISSION, THAT'D BE GREAT.
CABLE, I CAN'T.
THERE'S NO WAY I CAN LET YOU LEAVE.
MAYBE I CAN SELL THIS TO THE COALITION AS A REASON WE LET HIM GO, BUT EVEN THAT...
I'M NOT ASKING FOR A PARDON.
I'M SAYING MY GUYS JUST SAVED SIX MILLION LIVES.
GIVE ME A SHOT TO SAVE THEIRS.

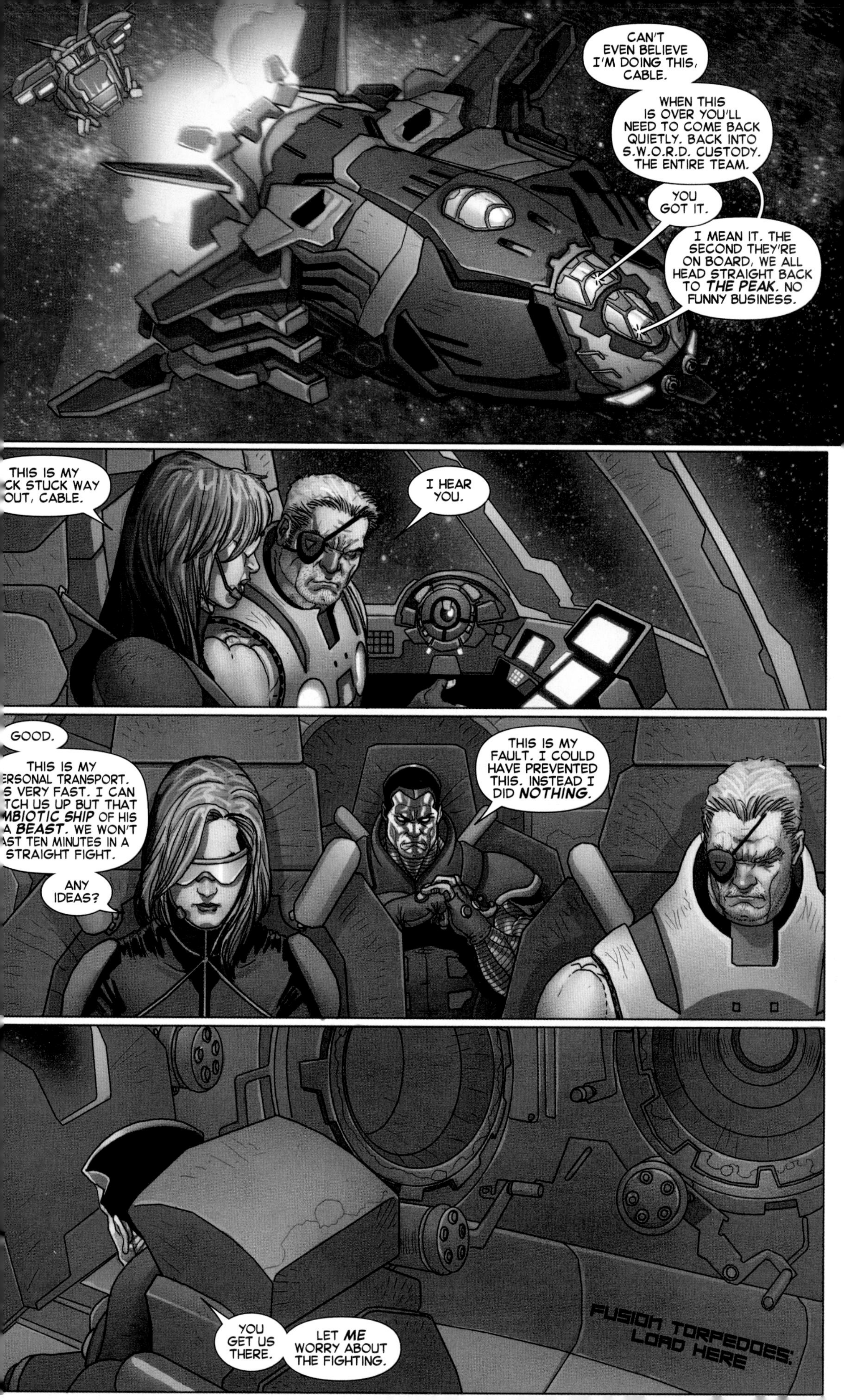

CAN'T EVEN BELIEVE I'M DOING THIS, CABLE.
WHEN THIS IS OVER YOU'LL NEED TO COME BACK QUIETLY. BACK INTO S.W.O.R.D. CUSTODY. THE ENTIRE TEAM.
YOU GOT IT.
I MEAN IT. THE SECOND THEY'RE ON BOARD, WE ALL HEAD STRAIGHT BACK TO THE PEAK. NO FUNNY BUSINESS.
THIS IS MY CK STUCK WAY OUT, CABLE.
I HEAR YOU.
GOOD.
THIS IS MY RSONAL TRANSPORT. S VERY FAST. I CAN TCH US UP BUT THAT MBIOTIC SHIP OF HIS A BEAST. WE WON'T AST TEN MINUTES IN A STRAIGHT FIGHT.
ANY IDEAS?
THIS IS MY FAULT. I COULD HAVE PREVENTED THIS. INSTEAD I DID NOTHING.
YOU GET US THERE.
LET ME WORRY ABOUT THE FIGHTING.
FUSION TORPEDOES: LOAD HERE

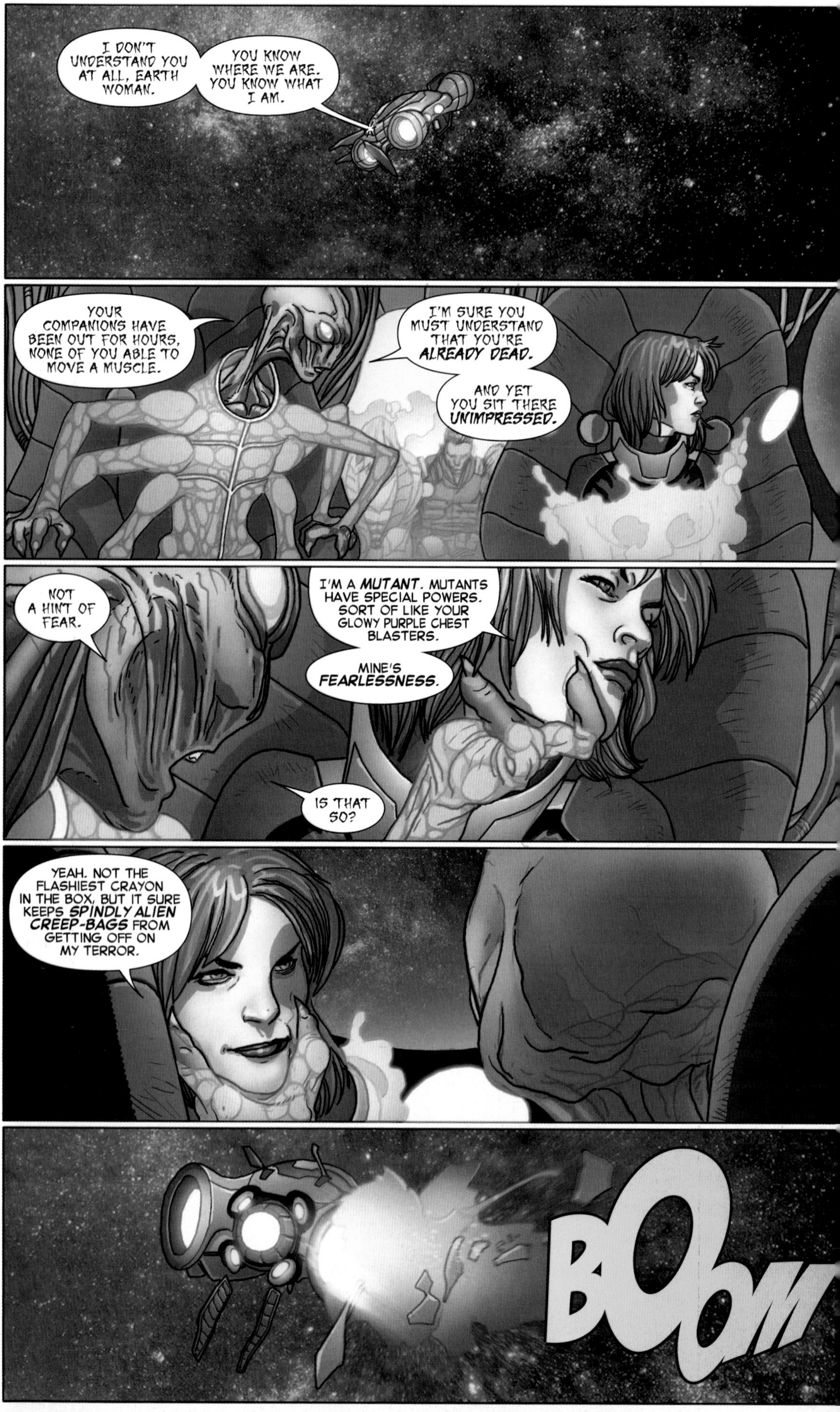

I DON'T UNDERSTAND YOU AT ALL, EARTH WOMAN.
YOU KNOW WHERE WE ARE. YOU KNOW WHAT I AM.
YOUR COMPANIONS HAVE BEEN OUT FOR HOURS, NONE OF YOU ABLE TO MOVE A MUSCLE.
I'M SURE YOU MUST UNDERSTAND THAT YOU'RE ALREADY DEAD.
AND YET YOU SIT THERE UNIMPRESSED.
NOT A HINT OF FEAR.
I'M A MUTANT. MUTANTS HAVE SPECIAL POWERS. SORT OF LIKE YOUR GLOWY PURPLE CHEST BLASTERS.
MINE'S FEARLESSNESS.
IS THAT SO?
YEAH. NOT THE FLASHIEST CRAYON IN THE BOX, BUT IT SURE KEEPS SPINDLY ALIEN CREEP-BAGS FROM GETTING OFF ON MY TERROR.
BOOM

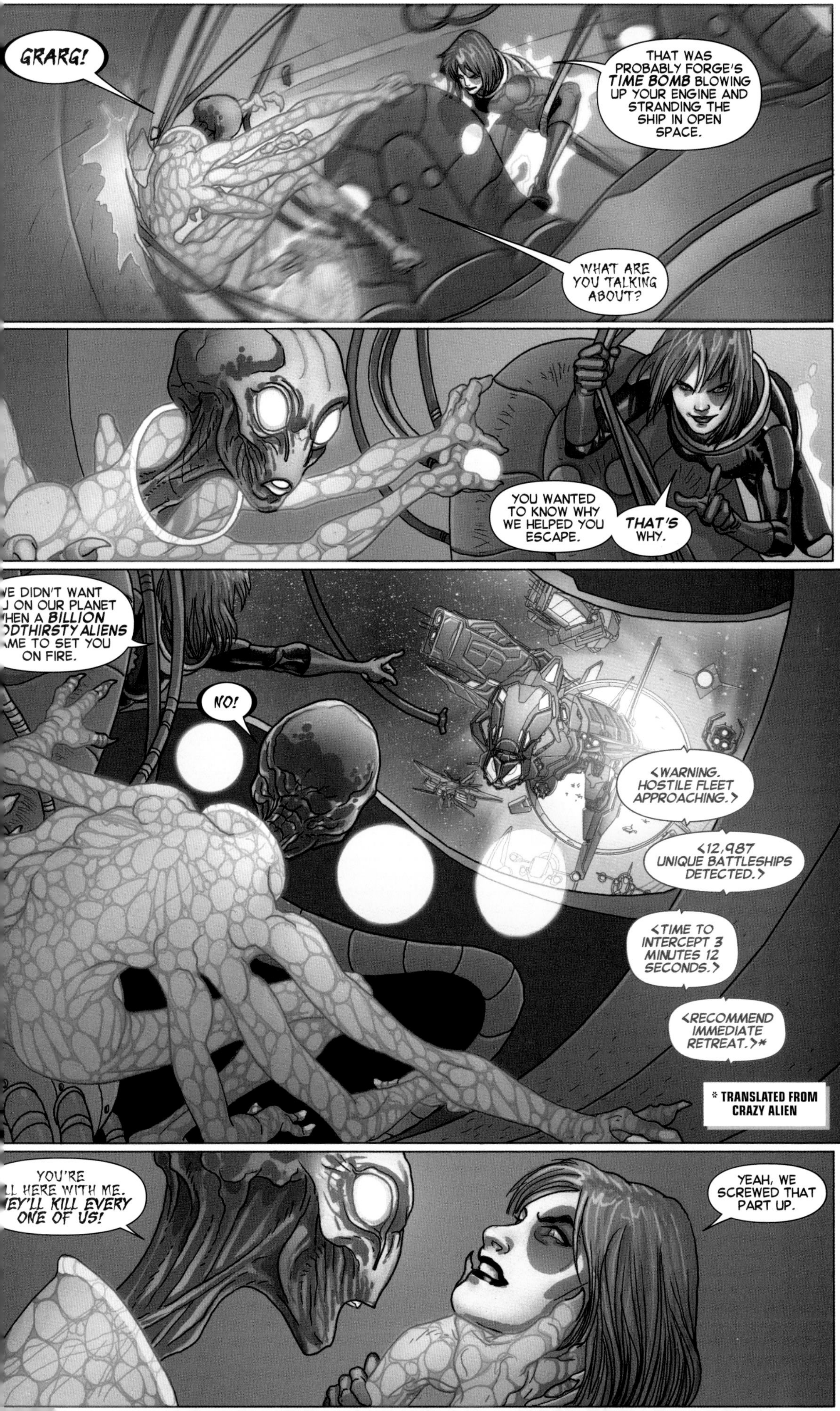

GRARG!
THAT WAS PROBABLY FORGE'S TIME BOMB BLOWING UP YOUR ENGINE AND STRANDING THE SHIP IN OPEN SPACE.
WHAT ARE YOU TALKING ABOUT?
YOU WANTED TO KNOW WHY WE HELPED YOU ESCAPE.
THAT'S WHY.
NO!
<WARNING. HOSTILE FLEET APPROACHING.>
<12,987 UNIQUE BATTLESHIPS DETECTED.>
<TIME TO INTERCEPT 3 MINUTES 12 SECONDS.>
<RECOMMEND IMMEDIATE RETREAT.>*
* TRANSLATED FROM CRAZY ALIEN
YEAH, WE SCREWED THAT PART UP.

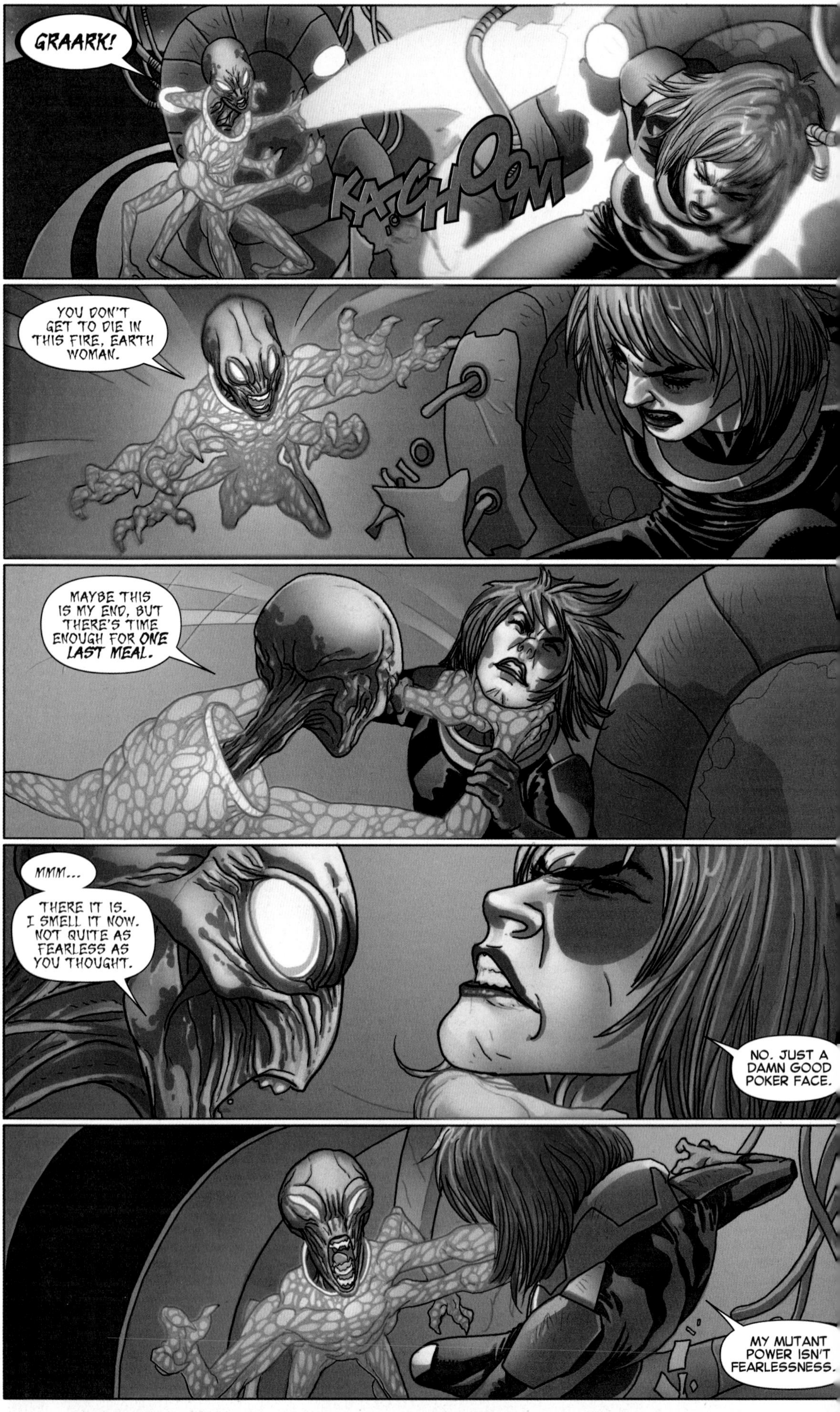
GRAARK!
KA-CHOOOM
YOU DON'T GET TO DIE IN THIS FIRE, EARTH WOMAN.
MAYBE THIS IS MY END, BUT THERE'S TIME ENOUGH FOR ONE LAST MEAL.
MMM...
THERE IT IS. I SMELL IT NOW. NOT QUITE AS FEARLESS AS YOU THOUGHT.
NO. JUST A DAMN GOOD POKER FACE.
MY MUTANT POWER ISN'T FEARLESSNESS.

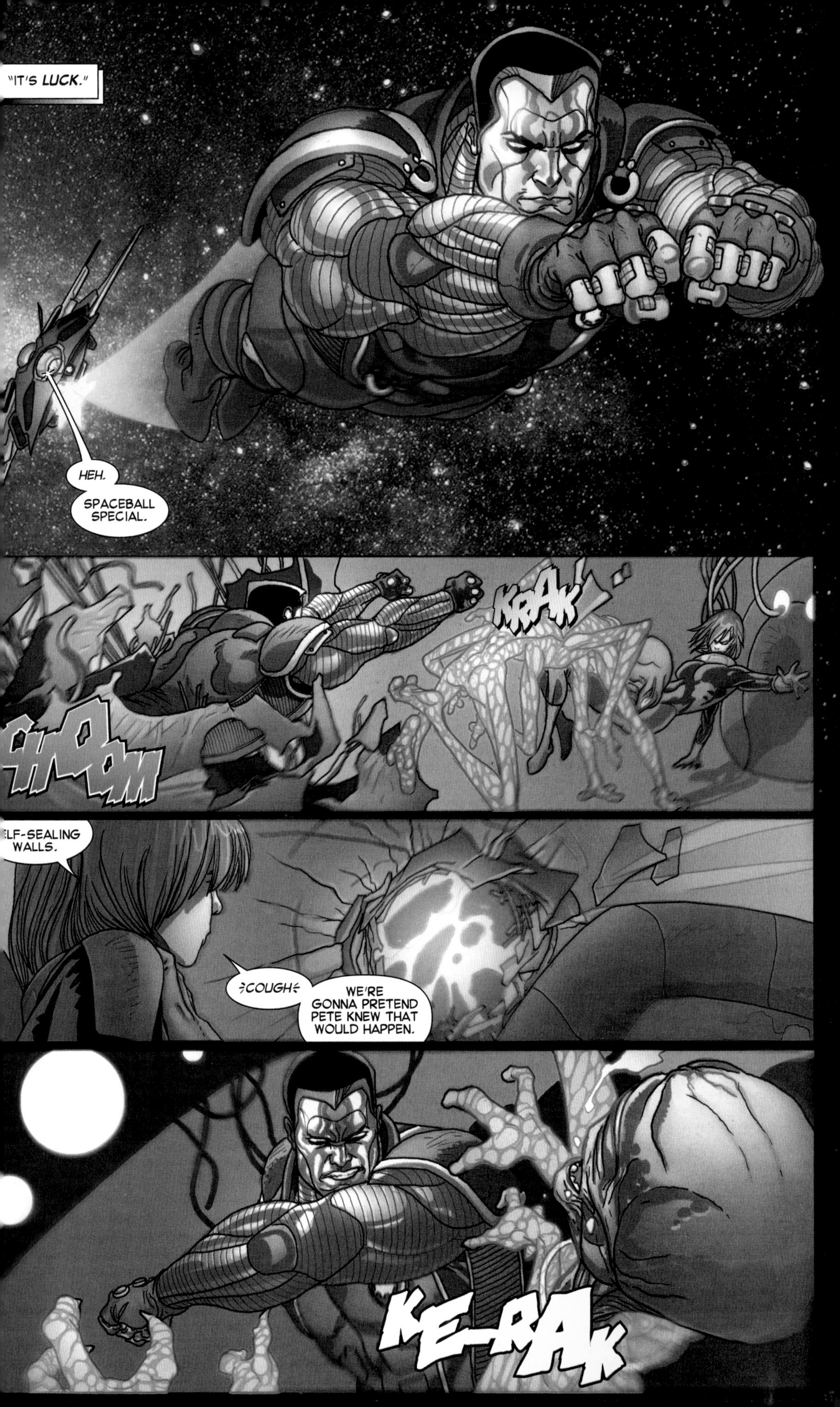

"IT'S LUCK."
HEH.
SPACEBALL SPECIAL.
KRAK
CHOOM
ELF-SEALING WALLS.
COUGH
WE'RE GONNA PRETEND PETE KNEW THAT WOULD HAPPEN.
KE-RAK

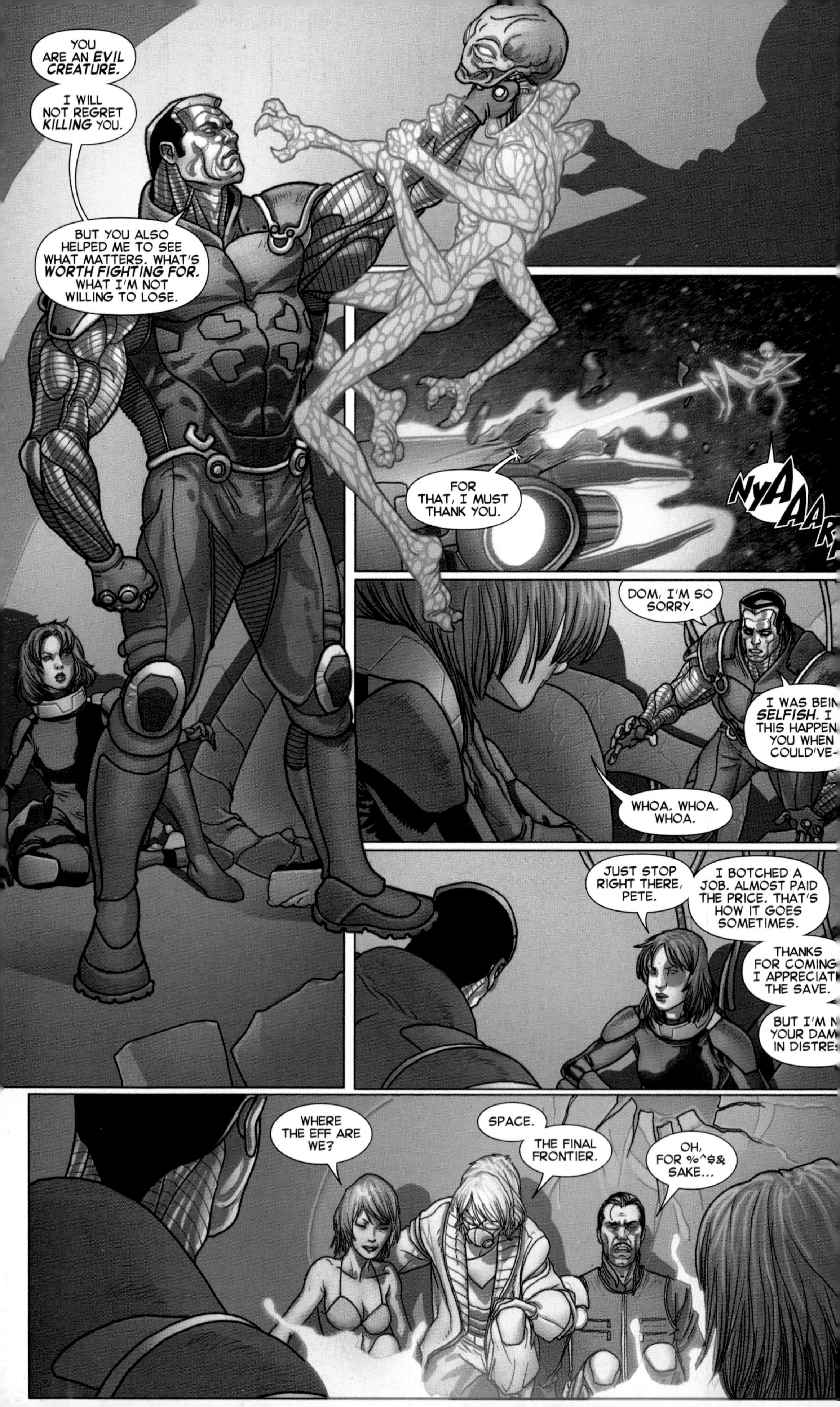
YOU ARE AN EVIL CREATURE.
I WILL NOT REGRET KILLING YOU.
BUT YOU ALSO HELPED ME TO SEE WHAT MATTERS. WHAT'S WORTH FIGHTING FOR. WHAT I'M NOT WILLING TO LOSE.
FOR THAT, I MUST THANK YOU.
NYAAAR
DOM, I'M SO SORRY.
I WAS BEIN SELFISH. I THIS HAPPEN YOU WHEN COULD'VE-
WHOA. WHOA. WHOA.
JUST STOP RIGHT THERE, PETE.
I BOTCHED A JOB. ALMOST PAID THE PRICE. THAT'S HOW IT GOES SOMETIMES.
THANKS FOR COMING I APPRECIAT THE SAVE.
BUT I'M N YOUR DAM IN DISTRE
WHERE THE EFF ARE WE?
SPACE.
THE FINAL FRONTIER.
OH, FOR %^$& SAKE...

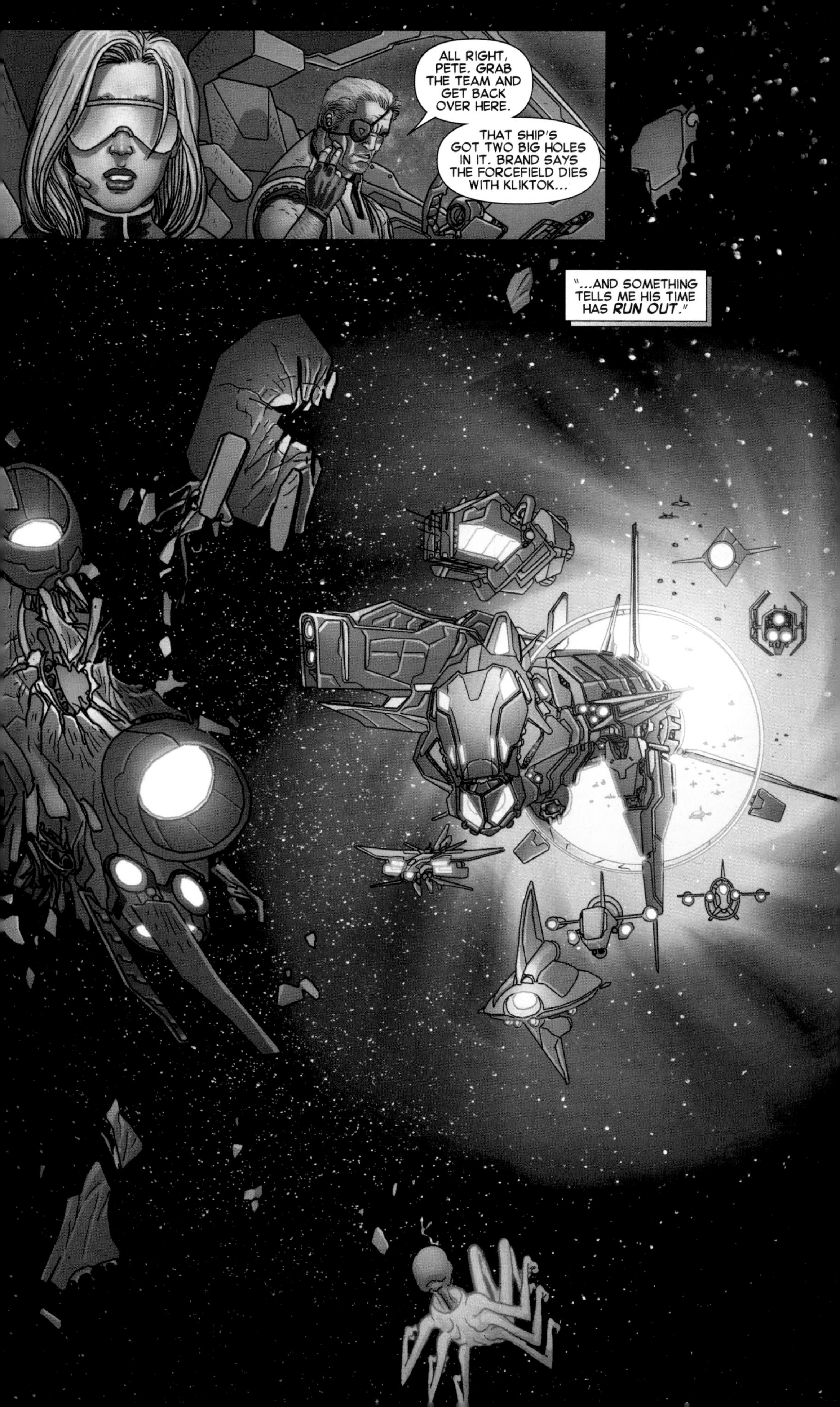
ALL RIGHT, PETE. GRAB THE TEAM AND GET BACK OVER HERE.
THAT SHIP'S GOT TWO BIG HOLES IN IT. BRAND SAYS THE FORCEFIELD DIES WITH KLIKTOK...
"...AND SOMETHING TELLS ME HIS TIME HAS *RUN OUT*."

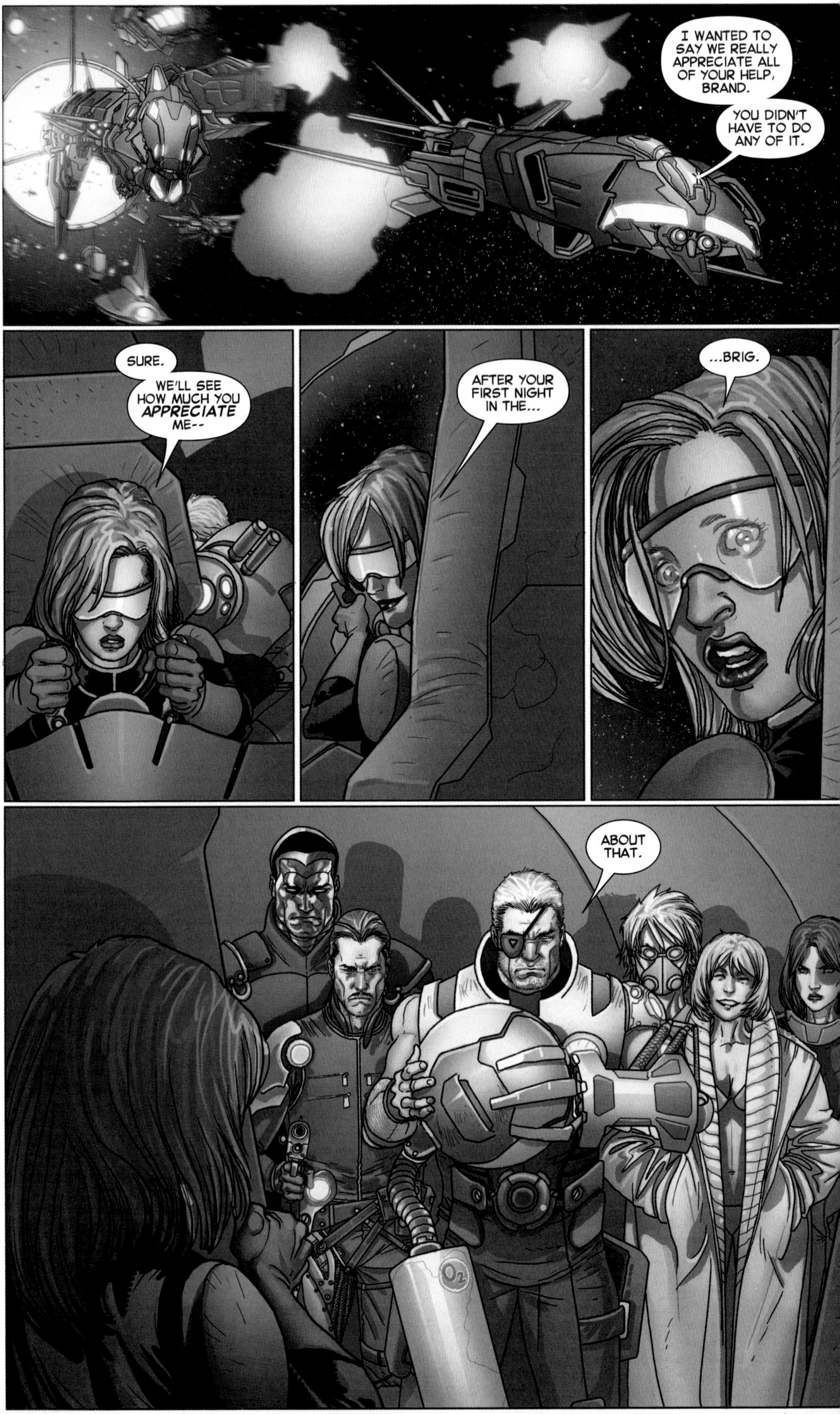
I WANTED TO SAY WE REALLY APPRECIATE ALL OF YOUR HELP, BRAND.
YOU DIDN'T HAVE TO DO ANY OF IT.
SURE.
WE'LL SEE HOW MUCH YOU *APPRECIATE* ME--
AFTER YOUR FIRST NIGHT IN THE...
...BRIG.
ABOUT THAT.
O2

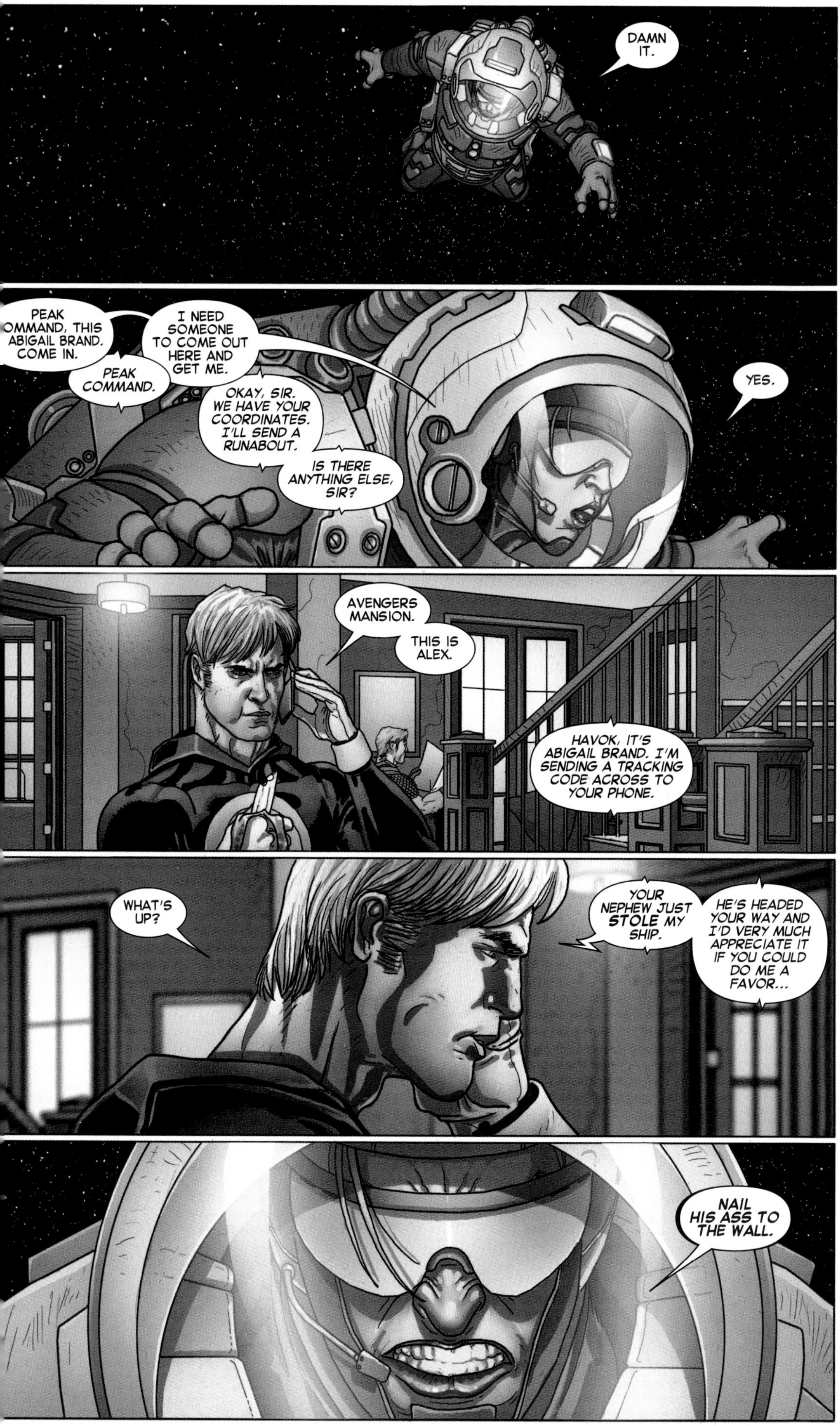
DAMN IT.
PEAK COMMAND, THIS ABIGAIL BRAND. COME IN.
PEAK COMMAND.
I NEED SOMEONE TO COME OUT HERE AND GET ME.
OKAY, SIR. WE HAVE YOUR COORDINATES. I'LL SEND A RUNABOUT.
IS THERE ANYTHING ELSE, SIR?
YES.
AVENGERS MANSION.
THIS IS ALEX.
HAVOK, IT'S ABIGAIL BRAND. I'M SENDING A TRACKING CODE ACROSS TO YOUR PHONE.
WHAT'S UP?
YOUR NEPHEW JUST STOLE MY SHIP.
HE'S HEADED YOUR WAY AND I'D VERY MUCH APPRECIATE IT IF YOU COULD DO ME A FAVOR...
NAIL HIS ASS TO THE WALL.

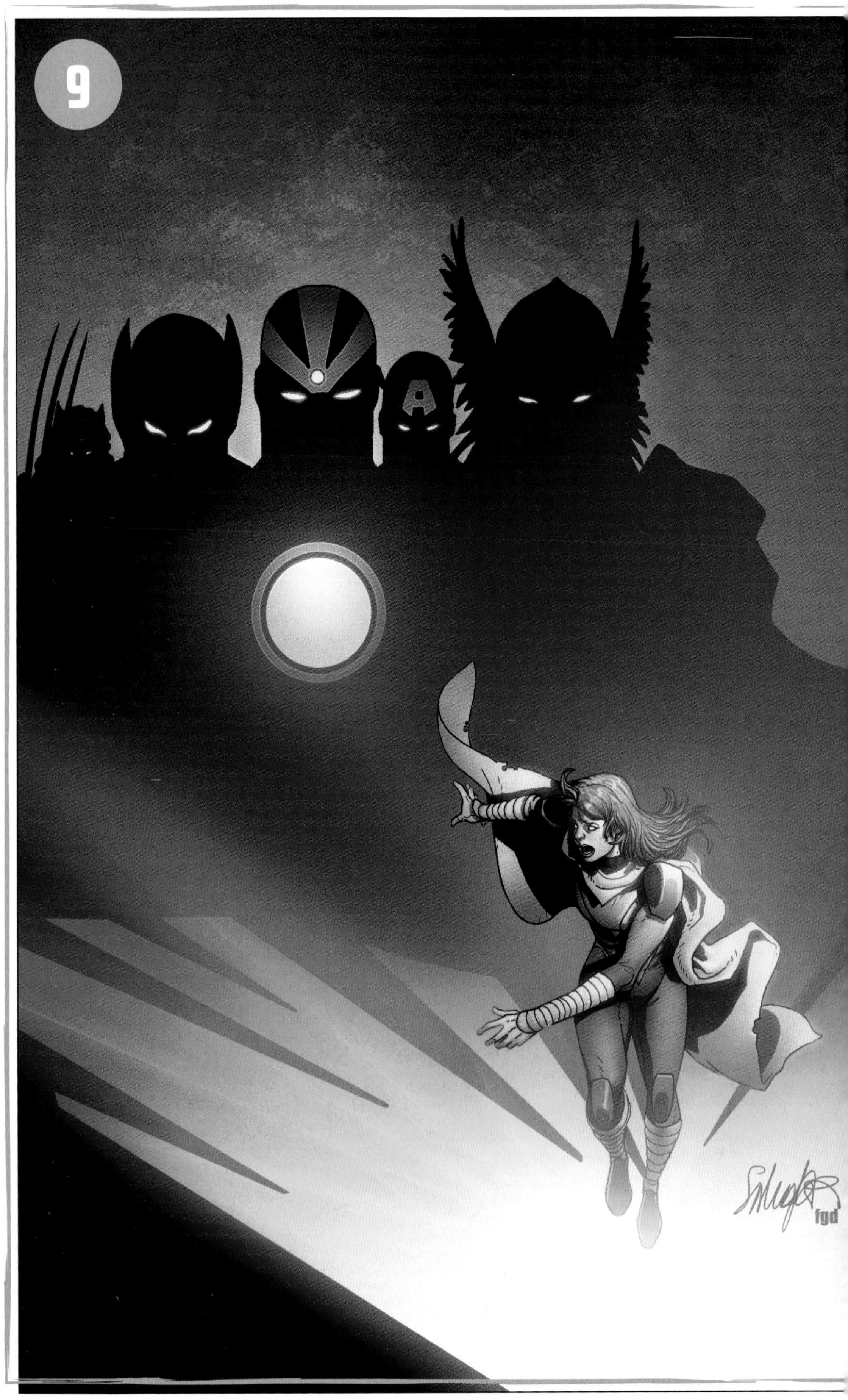
9
fgd

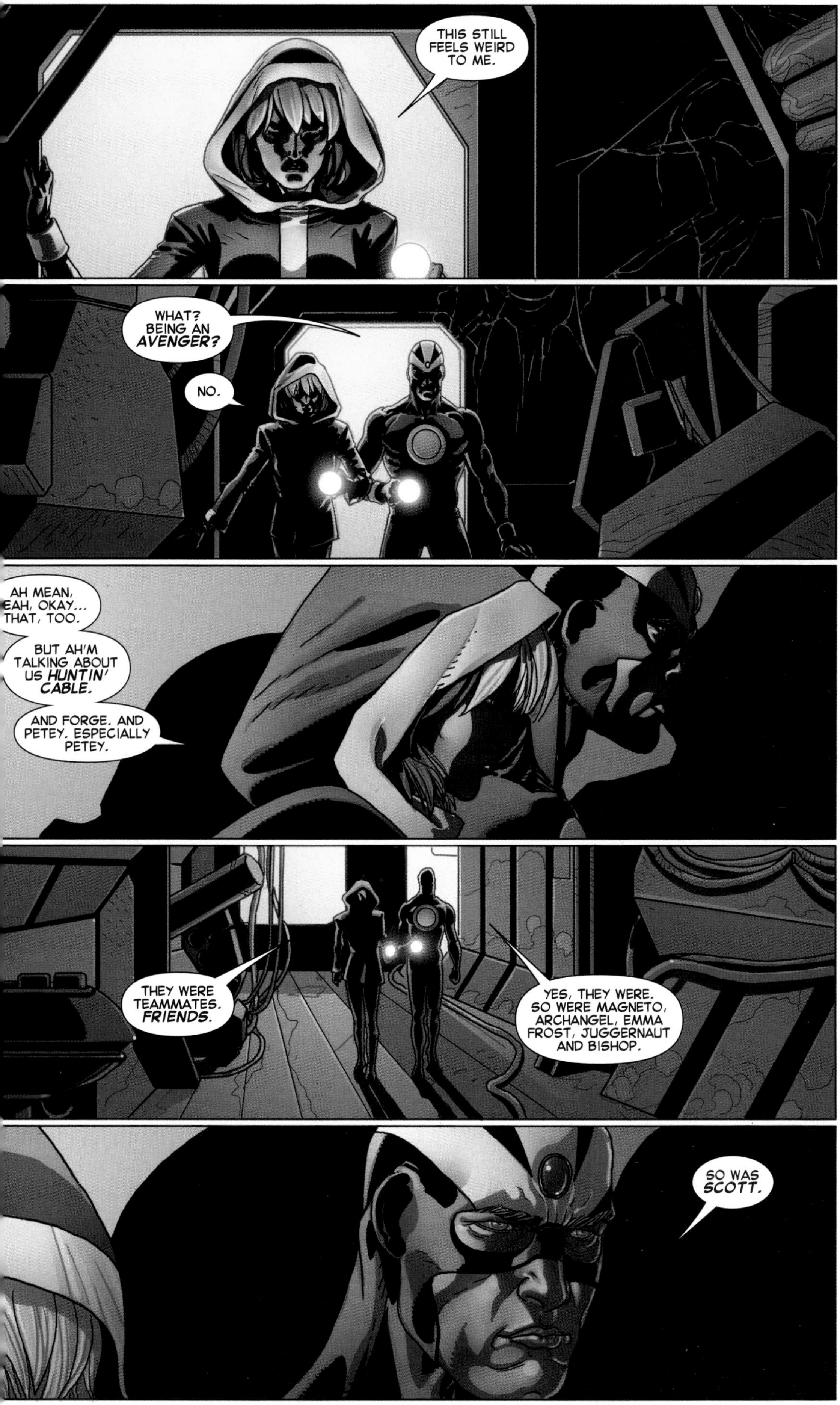
THIS STILL FEELS WEIRD TO ME.
WHAT? BEING AN *AVENGER?*
NO.
AH MEAN, EAH, OKAY... THAT, TOO.
BUT AH'M TALKING ABOUT US *HUNTIN' CABLE.*
AND FORGE. AND PETEY. ESPECIALLY PETEY.
THEY WERE TEAMMATES. *FRIENDS.*
YES, THEY WERE. SO WERE MAGNETO, ARCHANGEL, EMMA FROST, JUGGERNAUT AND BISHOP.
SO WAS *SCOTT.*

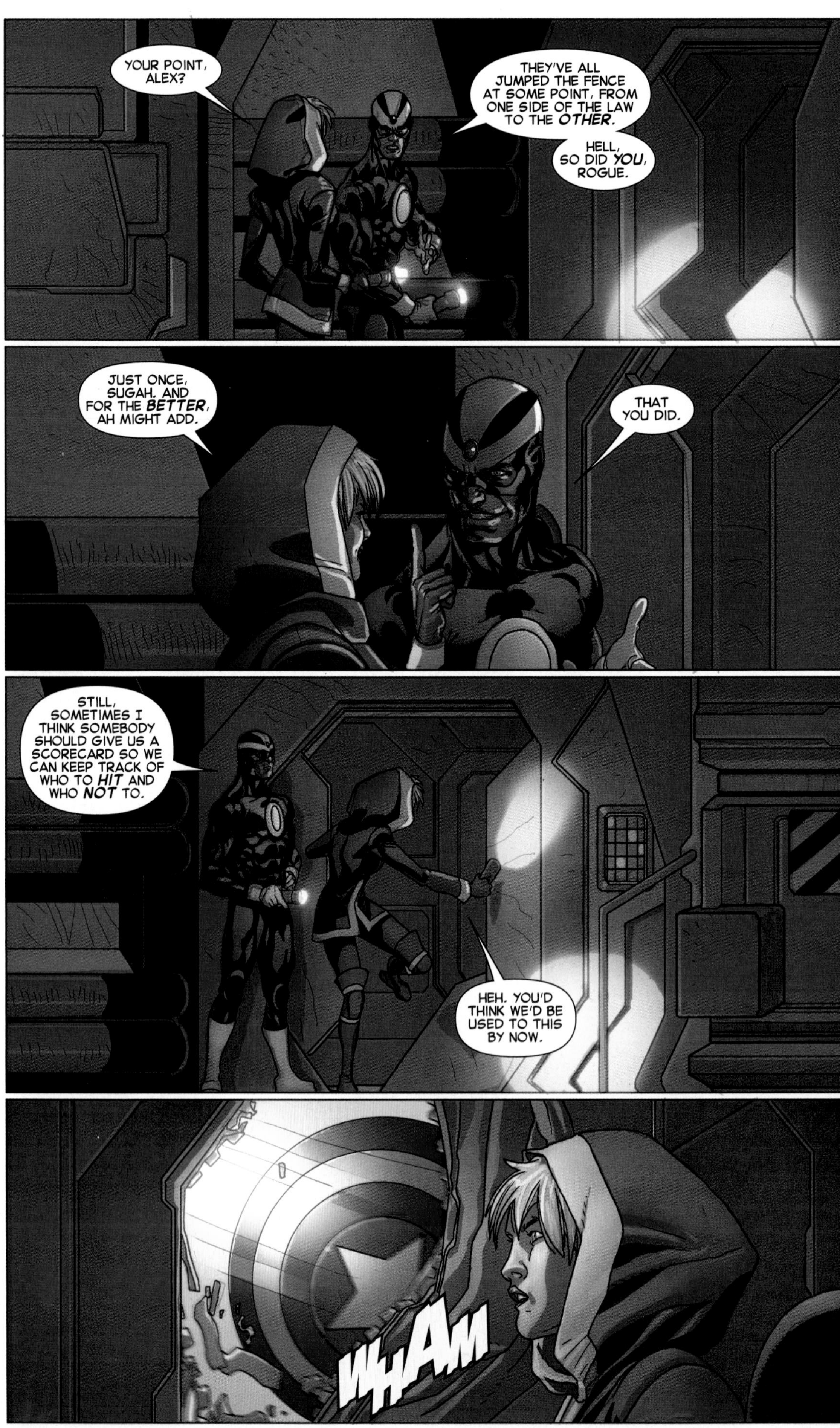
YOUR POINT, ALEX?
THEY'VE ALL JUMPED THE FENCE AT SOME POINT, FROM ONE SIDE OF THE LAW TO THE *OTHER*.
HELL, SO DID *YOU*, ROGUE.
JUST ONCE, SUGAH. AND FOR THE *BETTER*, AH MIGHT ADD.
THAT YOU DID.
STILL, SOMETIMES I THINK SOMEBODY SHOULD GIVE US A SCORECARD SO WE CAN KEEP TRACK OF WHO TO *HIT* AND WHO *NOT* TO.
HEH. YOU'D THINK WE'D BE USED TO THIS BY NOW.
WHAM

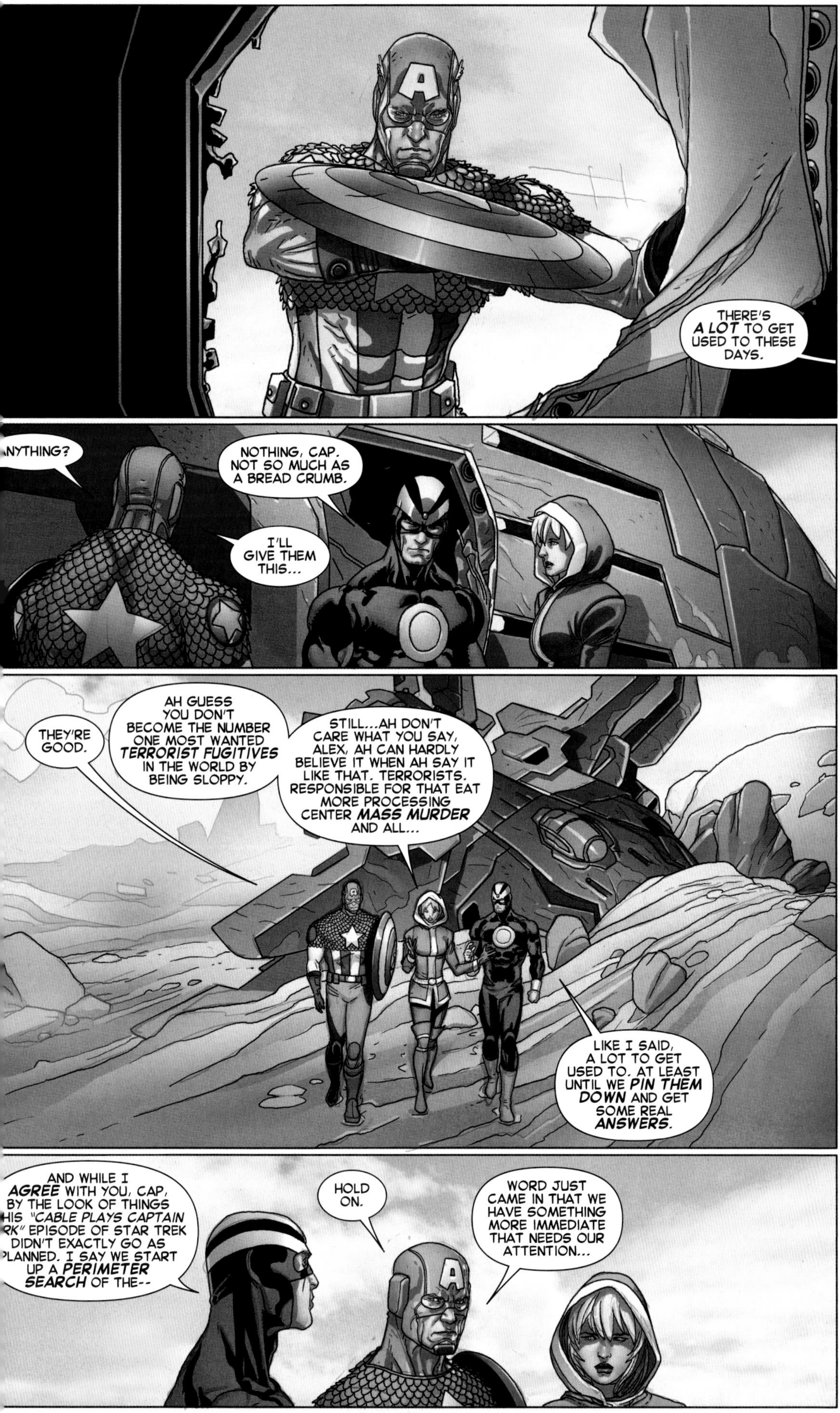

THERE'S A LOT TO GET USED TO THESE DAYS.
NYTHING?
NOTHING, CAP. NOT SO MUCH AS A BREAD CRUMB.
I'LL GIVE THEM THIS...
THEY'RE GOOD.
AH GUESS YOU DON'T BECOME THE NUMBER ONE MOST WANTED TERRORIST FUGITIVES IN THE WORLD BY BEING SLOPPY.
STILL...AH DON'T CARE WHAT YOU SAY, ALEX, AH CAN HARDLY BELIEVE IT WHEN AH SAY IT LIKE THAT. TERRORISTS. RESPONSIBLE FOR THAT EAT MORE PROCESSING CENTER MASS MURDER AND ALL...
LIKE I SAID, A LOT TO GET USED TO. AT LEAST UNTIL WE PIN THEM DOWN AND GET SOME REAL ANSWERS.
AND WHILE I AGREE WITH YOU, CAP, BY THE LOOK OF THINGS HIS "CABLE PLAYS CAPTAIN RK" EPISODE OF STAR TREK DIDN'T EXACTLY GO AS LANNED. I SAY WE START UP A PERIMETER SEARCH OF THE--
HOLD ON.
WORD JUST CAME IN THAT WE HAVE SOMETHING MORE IMMEDIATE THAT NEEDS OUR ATTENTION...

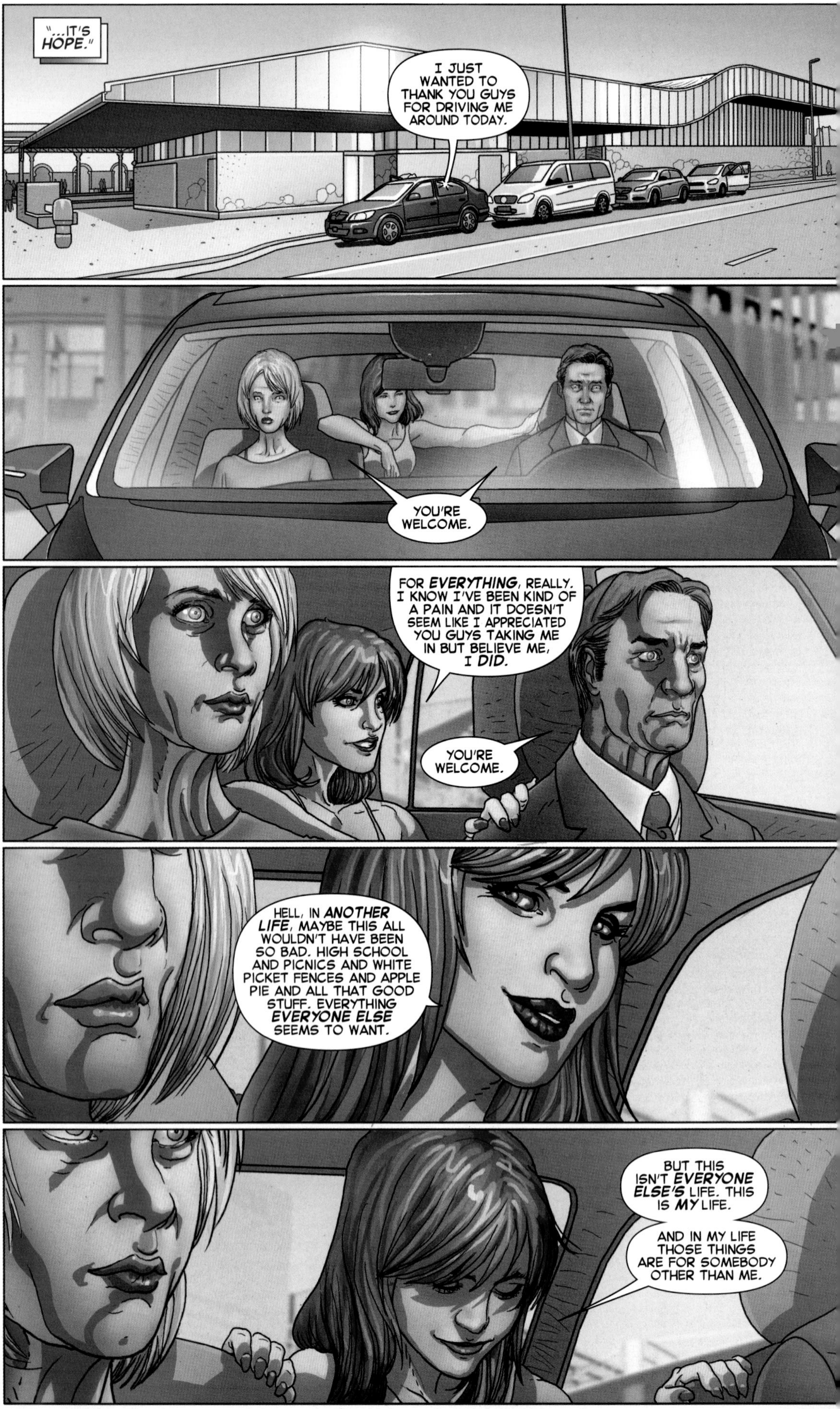
"...IT'S HOPE."
I JUST WANTED TO THANK YOU GUYS FOR DRIVING ME AROUND TODAY.
YOU'RE WELCOME.
FOR EVERYTHING, REALLY. I KNOW I'VE BEEN KIND OF A PAIN AND IT DOESN'T SEEM LIKE I APPRECIATED YOU GUYS TAKING ME IN BUT BELIEVE ME, I DID.
YOU'RE WELCOME.
HELL, IN ANOTHER LIFE, MAYBE THIS ALL WOULDN'T HAVE BEEN SO BAD. HIGH SCHOOL AND PICNICS AND WHITE PICKET FENCES AND APPLE PIE AND ALL THAT GOOD STUFF. EVERYTHING EVERYONE ELSE SEEMS TO WANT.
BUT THIS ISN'T EVERYONE ELSE'S LIFE. THIS IS MY LIFE.
AND IN MY LIFE THOSE THINGS ARE FOR SOMEBODY OTHER THAN ME.

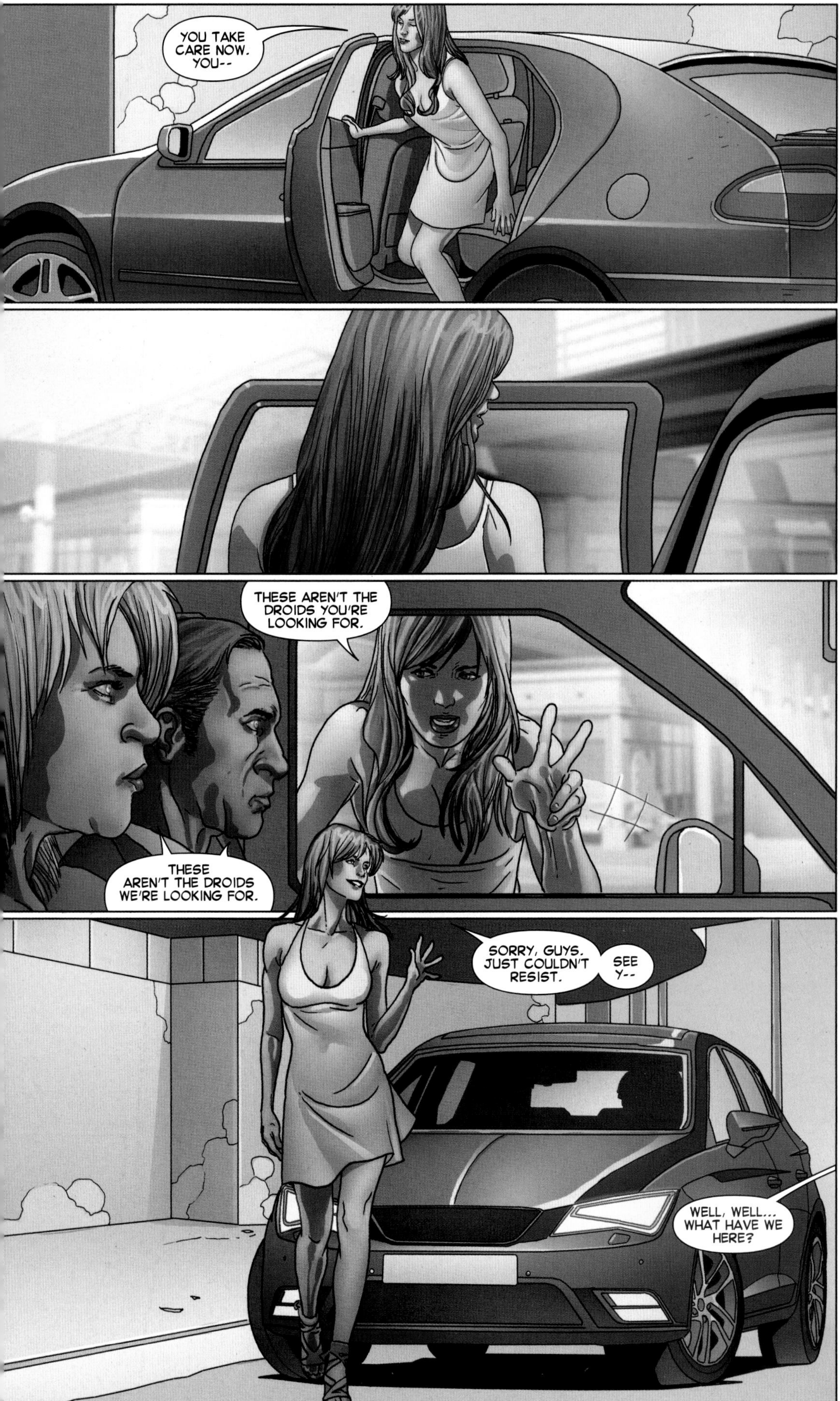
YOU TAKE CARE NOW. YOU--
THESE AREN'T THE DROIDS YOU'RE LOOKING FOR.
THESE AREN'T THE DROIDS WE'RE LOOKING FOR.
SORRY, GUYS. JUST COULDN'T RESIST.
SEE Y--
WELL, WELL... WHAT HAVE WE HERE?

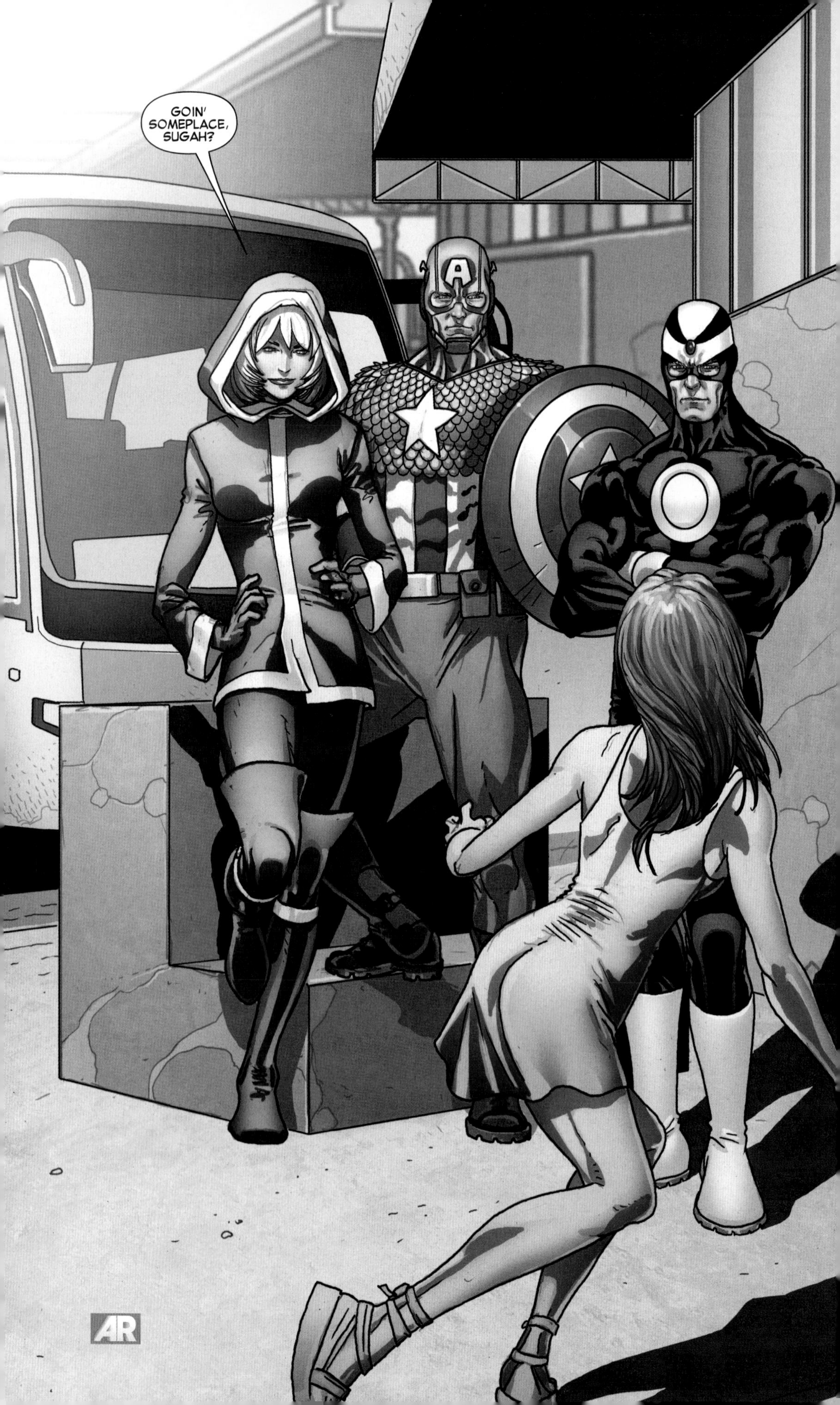
GOIN' SOMEPLACE, SUGAH?

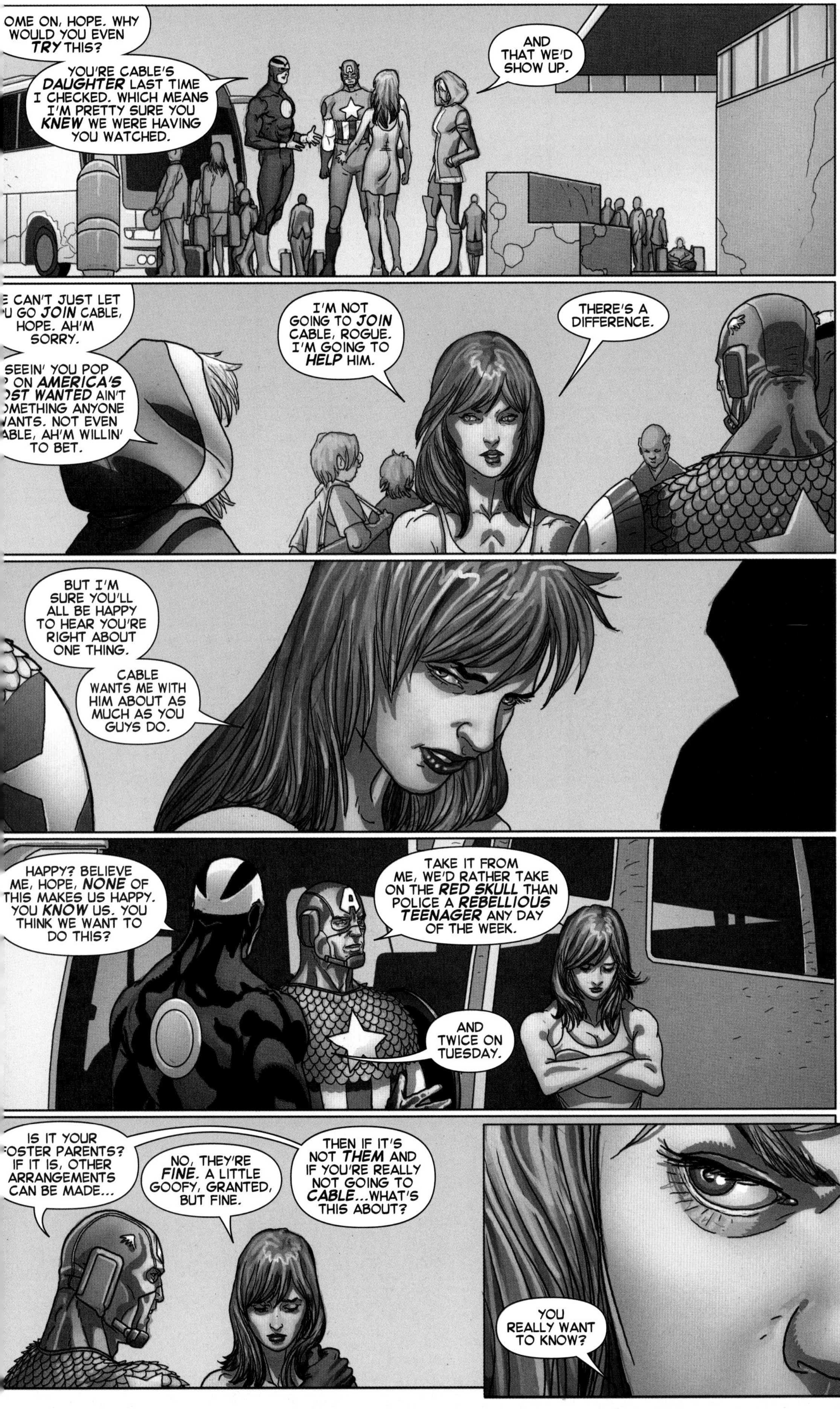
OME ON, HOPE. WHY WOULD YOU EVEN TRY THIS?
YOU'RE CABLE'S DAUGHTER LAST TIME I CHECKED. WHICH MEANS I'M PRETTY SURE YOU KNEW WE WERE HAVING YOU WATCHED.
AND THAT WE'D SHOW UP.
E CAN'T JUST LET U GO JOIN CABLE, HOPE. AH'M SORRY.
SEEIN' YOU POP P ON AMERICA'S OST WANTED AIN'T OMETHING ANYONE VANTS. NOT EVEN ABLE, AH'M WILLIN' TO BET.
I'M NOT GOING TO JOIN CABLE, ROGUE. I'M GOING TO HELP HIM.
THERE'S A DIFFERENCE.
BUT I'M SURE YOU'LL ALL BE HAPPY TO HEAR YOU'RE RIGHT ABOUT ONE THING.
CABLE WANTS ME WITH HIM ABOUT AS MUCH AS YOU GUYS DO.
HAPPY? BELIEVE ME, HOPE, NONE OF THIS MAKES US HAPPY. YOU KNOW US. YOU THINK WE WANT TO DO THIS?
TAKE IT FROM ME, WE'D RATHER TAKE ON THE RED SKULL THAN POLICE A REBELLIOUS TEENAGER ANY DAY OF THE WEEK.
AND TWICE ON TUESDAY.
IS IT YOUR FOSTER PARENTS? IF IT IS, OTHER ARRANGEMENTS CAN BE MADE...
NO, THEY'RE FINE. A LITTLE GOOFY, GRANTED, BUT FINE.
THEN IF IT'S NOT THEM AND IF YOU'RE REALLY NOT GOING TO CABLE...WHAT'S THIS ABOUT?
YOU REALLY WANT TO KNOW?

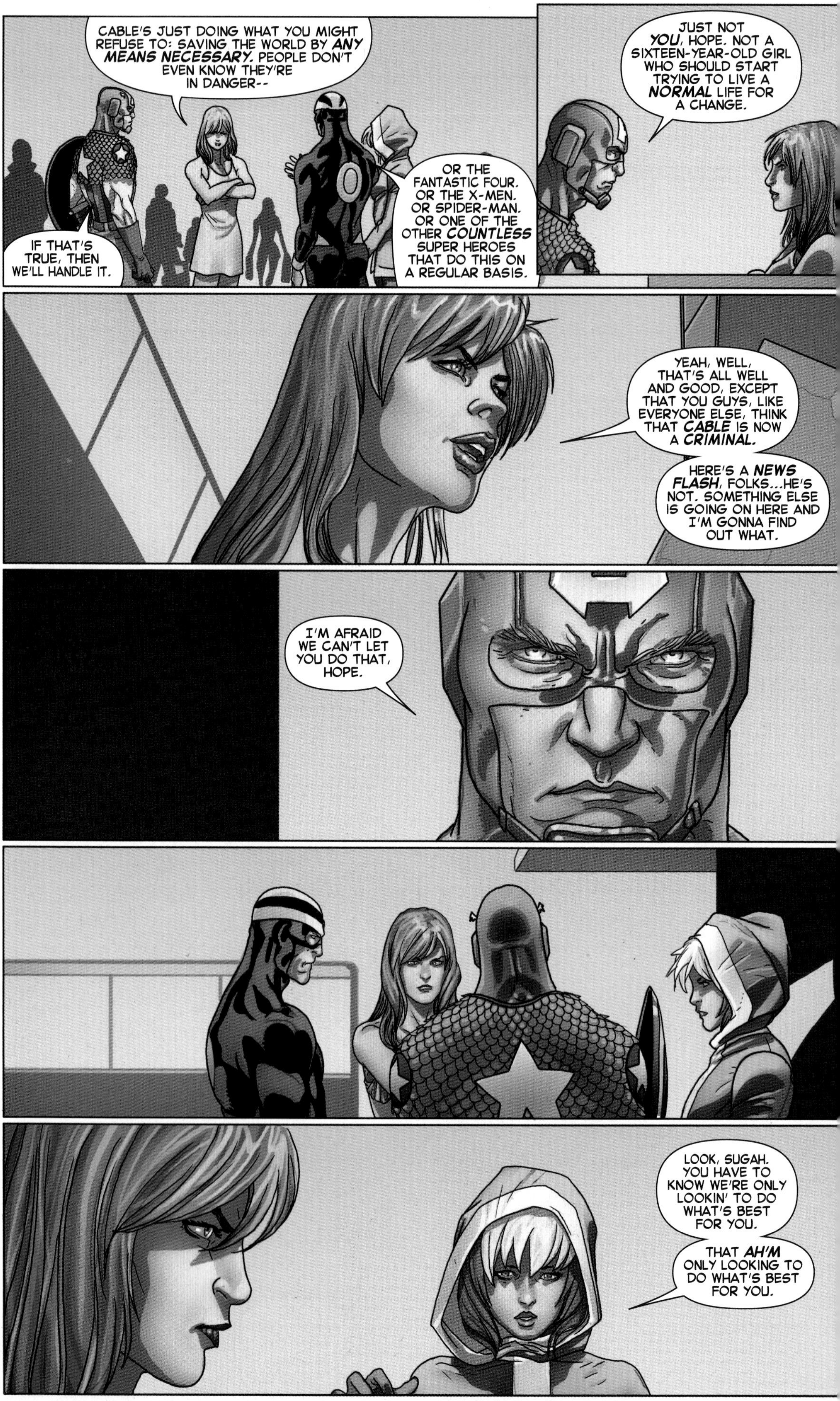

CABLE'S JUST DOING WHAT YOU MIGHT REFUSE TO: SAVING THE WORLD BY ANY MEANS NECESSARY. PEOPLE DON'T EVEN KNOW THEY'RE IN DANGER--
IF THAT'S TRUE, THEN WE'LL HANDLE IT.
OR THE FANTASTIC FOUR. OR THE X-MEN. OR SPIDER-MAN. OR ONE OF THE OTHER COUNTLESS SUPER HEROES THAT DO THIS ON A REGULAR BASIS.
JUST NOT YOU, HOPE. NOT A SIXTEEN-YEAR-OLD GIRL WHO SHOULD START TRYING TO LIVE A NORMAL LIFE FOR A CHANGE.
YEAH, WELL, THAT'S ALL WELL AND GOOD, EXCEPT THAT YOU GUYS, LIKE EVERYONE ELSE, THINK THAT CABLE IS NOW A CRIMINAL.
HERE'S A NEWS FLASH, FOLKS...HE'S NOT. SOMETHING ELSE IS GOING ON HERE AND I'M GONNA FIND OUT WHAT.
I'M AFRAID WE CAN'T LET YOU DO THAT, HOPE.
LOOK, SUGAH. YOU HAVE TO KNOW WE'RE ONLY LOOKIN' TO DO WHAT'S BEST FOR YOU.
THAT AH'M ONLY LOOKING TO DO WHAT'S BEST FOR YOU.

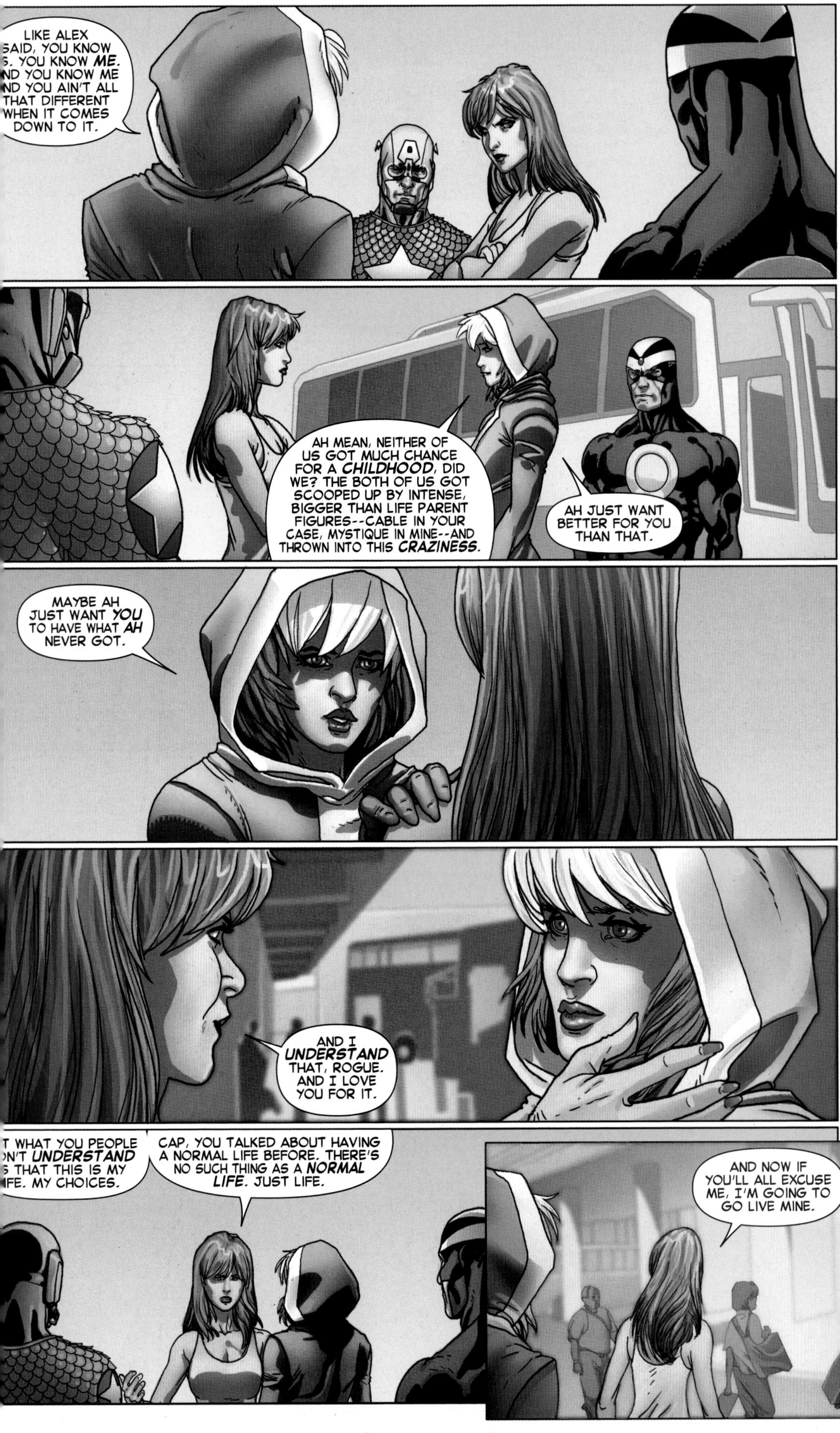

LIKE ALEX SAID, YOU KNOW S. YOU KNOW ME. ND YOU KNOW ME ND YOU AIN'T ALL THAT DIFFERENT WHEN IT COMES DOWN TO IT.
AH MEAN, NEITHER OF US GOT MUCH CHANCE FOR A CHILDHOOD, DID WE? THE BOTH OF US GOT SCOOPED UP BY INTENSE, BIGGER THAN LIFE PARENT FIGURES--CABLE IN YOUR CASE, MYSTIQUE IN MINE--AND THROWN INTO THIS CRAZINESS.
AH JUST WANT BETTER FOR YOU THAN THAT.
MAYBE AH JUST WANT YOU TO HAVE WHAT AH NEVER GOT.
AND I UNDERSTAND THAT, ROGUE. AND I LOVE YOU FOR IT.
T WHAT YOU PEOPLE N'T UNDERSTAND S THAT THIS IS MY IFE. MY CHOICES.
CAP, YOU TALKED ABOUT HAVING A NORMAL LIFE BEFORE. THERE'S NO SUCH THING AS A NORMAL LIFE. JUST LIFE.
AND NOW IF YOU'LL ALL EXCUSE ME, I'M GOING TO GO LIVE MINE.

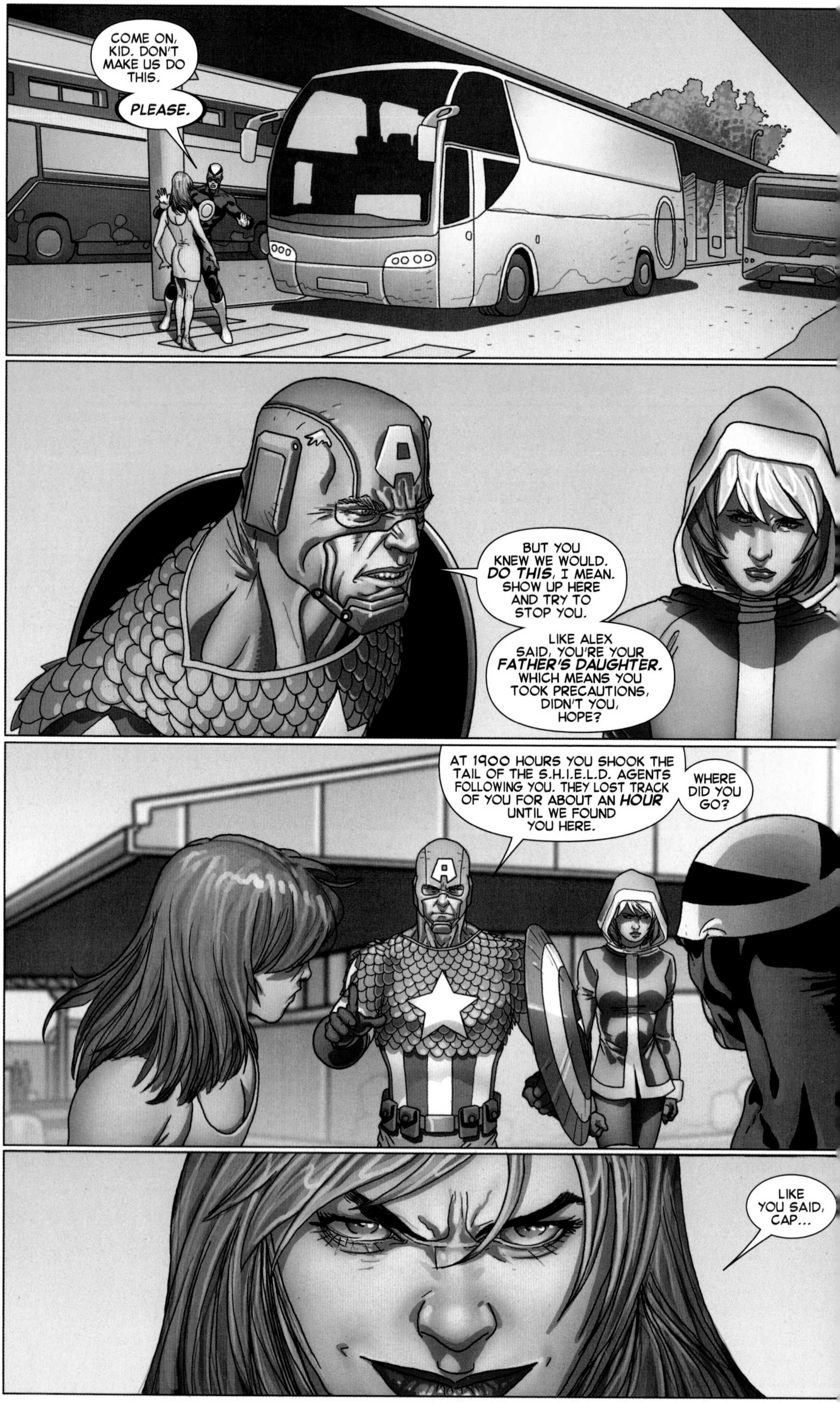
COME ON, KID. DON'T MAKE US DO THIS.
PLEASE.
BUT YOU KNEW WE WOULD. DO THIS, I MEAN. SHOW UP HERE AND TRY TO STOP YOU.
LIKE ALEX SAID, YOU'RE YOUR FATHER'S DAUGHTER. WHICH MEANS YOU TOOK PRECAUTIONS, DIDN'T YOU, HOPE?
AT 1900 HOURS YOU SHOOK THE TAIL OF THE S.H.I.E.L.D. AGENTS FOLLOWING YOU. THEY LOST TRACK OF YOU FOR ABOUT AN HOUR UNTIL WE FOUND YOU HERE.
WHERE DID YOU GO?
LIKE YOU SAID, CAP...

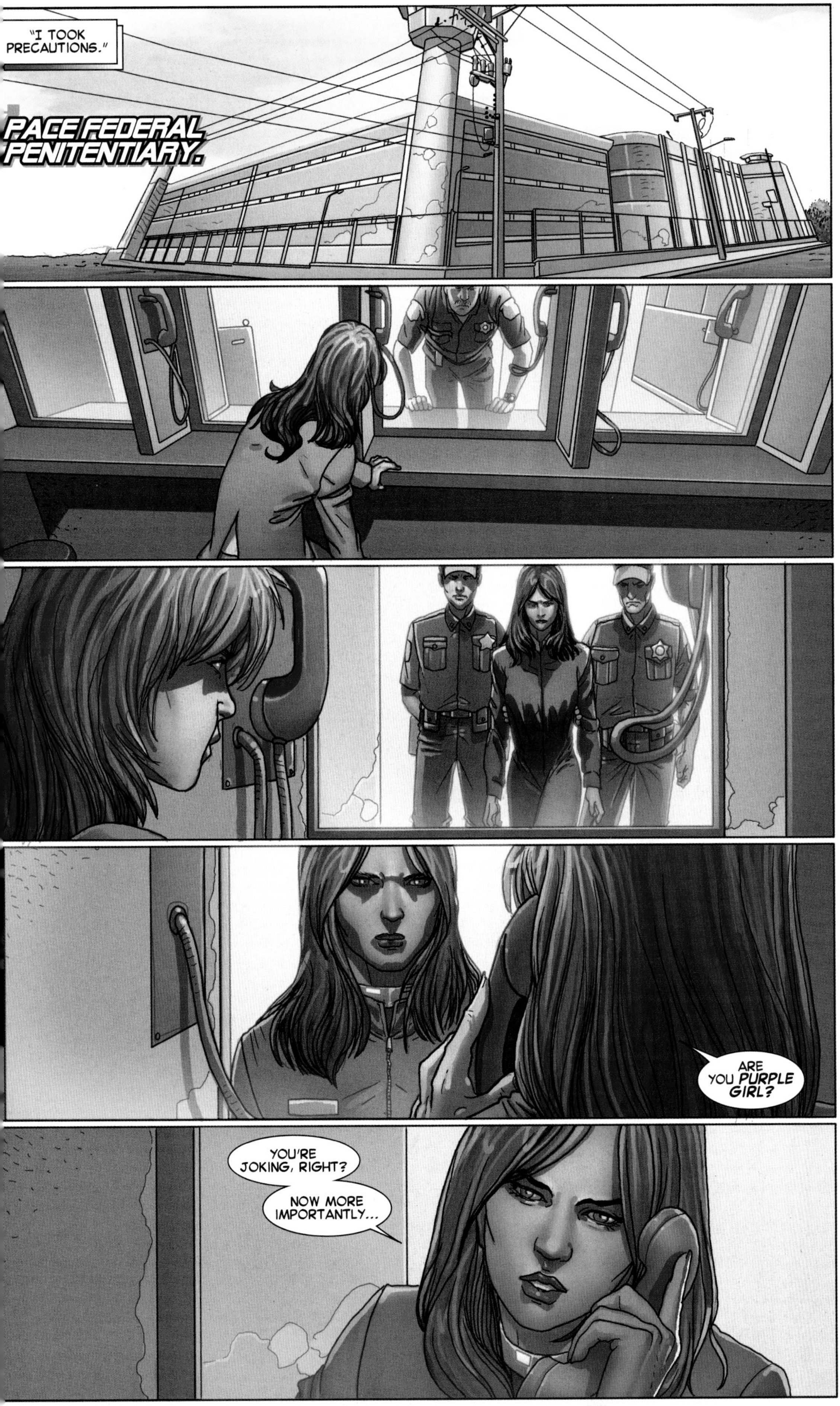
"I TOOK PRECAUTIONS."
PACE FEDERAL PENITENTIARY.
ARE YOU PURPLE GIRL?
YOU'RE JOKING, RIGHT?
NOW MORE IMPORTANTLY...

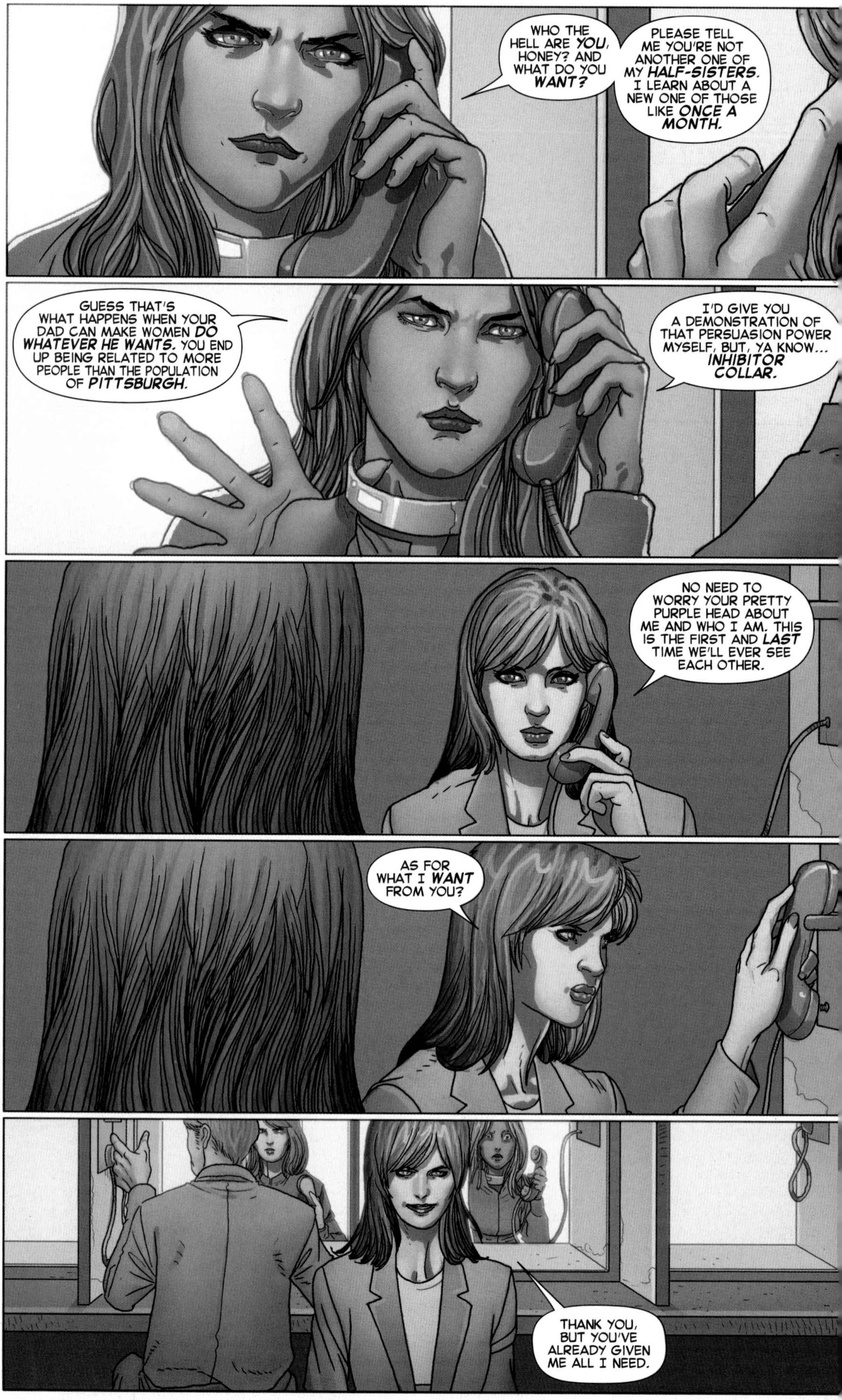
WHO THE HELL ARE YOU, HONEY? AND WHAT DO YOU WANT?
PLEASE TELL ME YOU'RE NOT ANOTHER ONE OF MY HALF-SISTERS. I LEARN ABOUT A NEW ONE OF THOSE LIKE ONCE A MONTH.
GUESS THAT'S WHAT HAPPENS WHEN YOUR DAD CAN MAKE WOMEN DO WHATEVER HE WANTS. YOU END UP BEING RELATED TO MORE PEOPLE THAN THE POPULATION OF PITTSBURGH.
I'D GIVE YOU A DEMONSTRATION OF THAT PERSUASION POWER MYSELF, BUT, YA KNOW... INHIBITOR COLLAR.
NO NEED TO WORRY YOUR PRETTY PURPLE HEAD ABOUT ME AND WHO I AM. THIS IS THE FIRST AND LAST TIME WE'LL EVER SEE EACH OTHER.
AS FOR WHAT I WANT FROM YOU?
THANK YOU, BUT YOU'VE ALREADY GIVEN ME ALL I NEED.

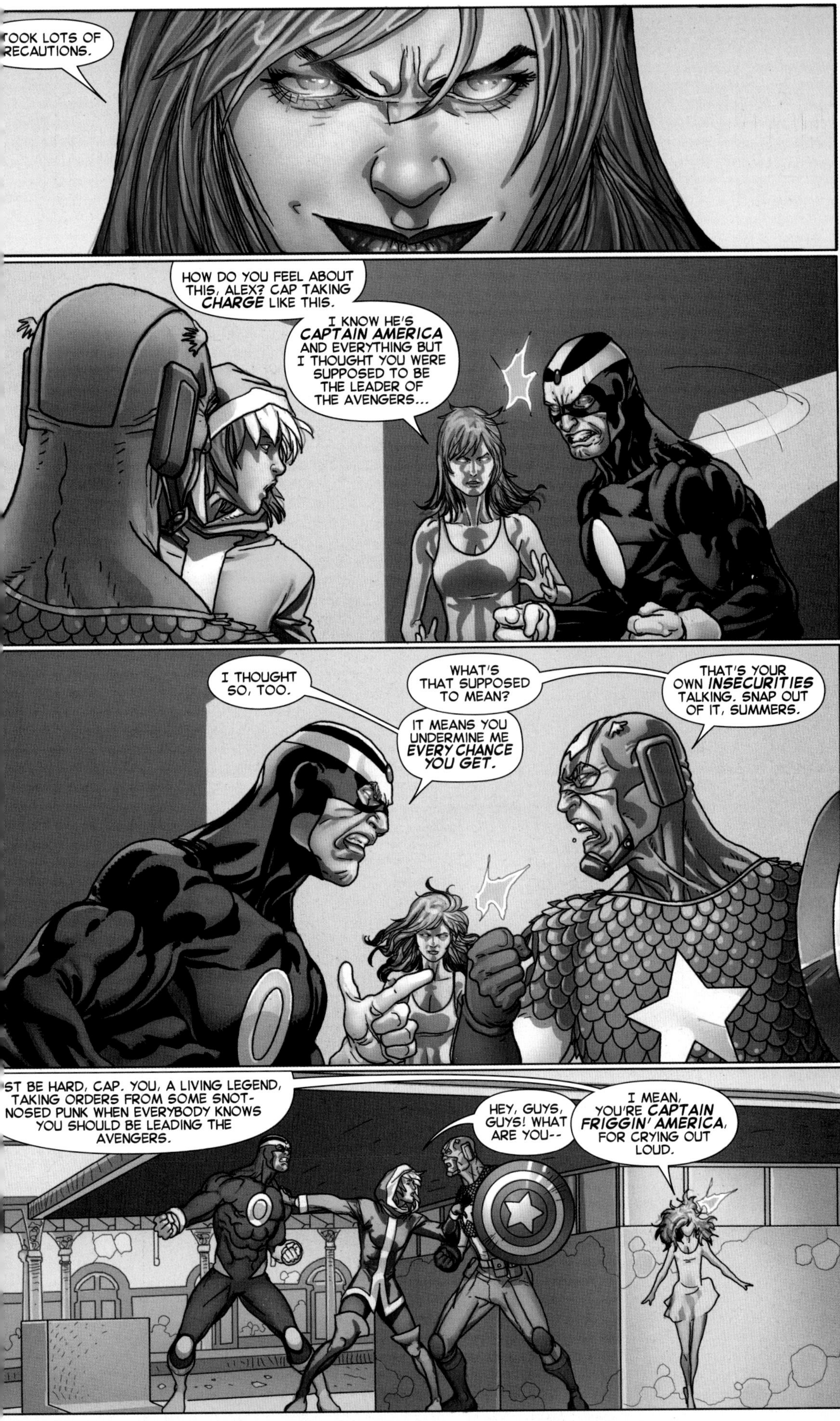
TOOK LOTS OF
RECAUTIONS.
HOW DO YOU FEEL ABOUT THIS, ALEX? CAP TAKING CHARGE LIKE THIS.
I KNOW HE'S CAPTAIN AMERICA AND EVERYTHING BUT I THOUGHT YOU WERE SUPPOSED TO BE THE LEADER OF THE AVENGERS...
I THOUGHT SO, TOO.
WHAT'S THAT SUPPOSED TO MEAN?
IT MEANS YOU UNDERMINE ME EVERY CHANCE YOU GET.
THAT'S YOUR OWN INSECURITIES TALKING. SNAP OUT OF IT, SUMMERS.
ST BE HARD, CAP. YOU, A LIVING LEGEND, TAKING ORDERS FROM SOME SNOT-NOSED PUNK WHEN EVERYBODY KNOWS YOU SHOULD BE LEADING THE AVENGERS.
HEY, GUYS, GUYS! WHAT ARE YOU--
I MEAN, YOU'RE CAPTAIN FRIGGIN' AMERICA, FOR CRYING OUT LOUD.

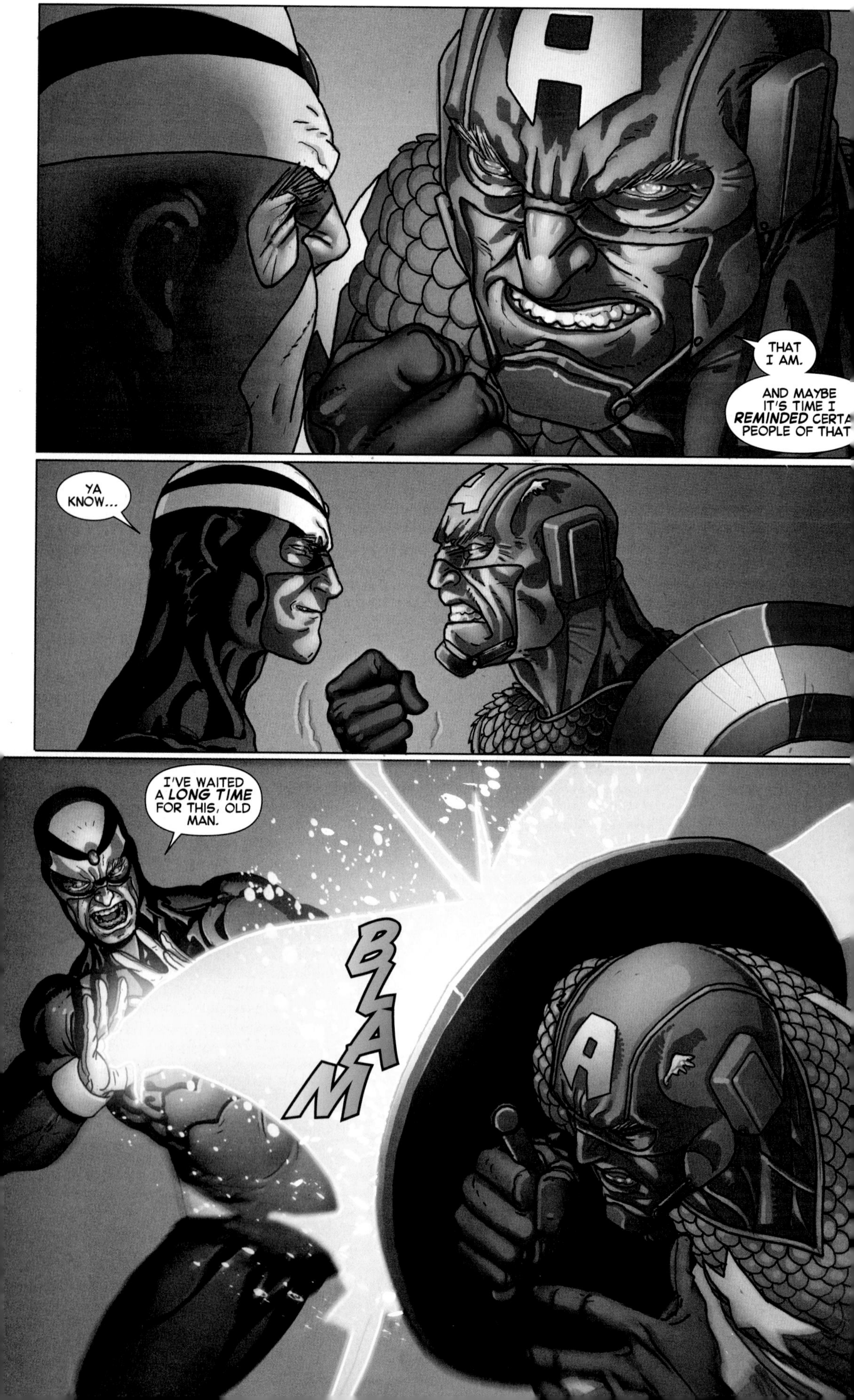

THAT I AM.
AND MAYBE IT'S TIME I *REMINDED* CERTA PEOPLE OF THAT
YA KNOW...
I'VE WAITED A *LONG TIME* FOR THIS, OLD MAN.
BLAM

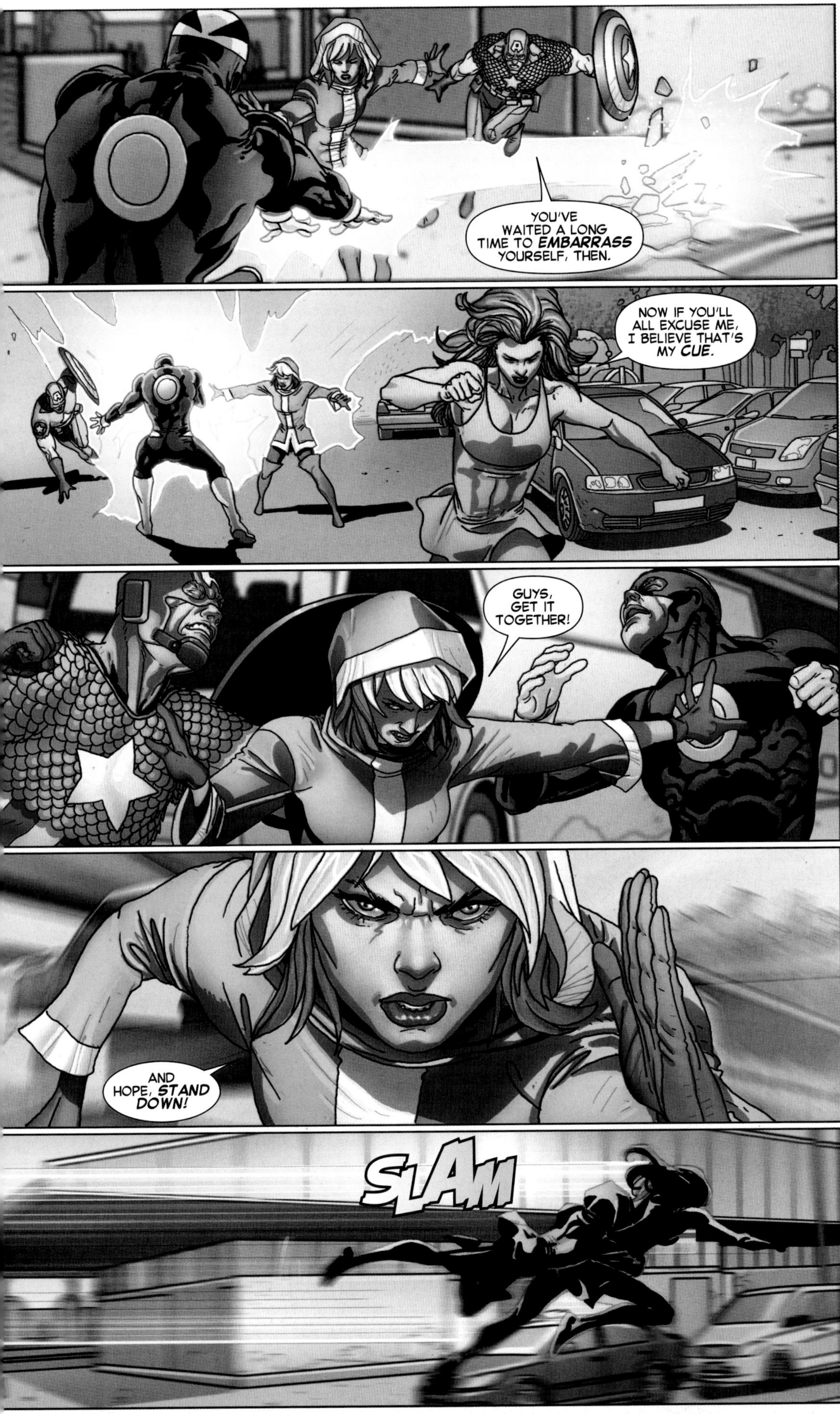
YOU'VE WAITED A LONG TIME TO EMBARRASS YOURSELF, THEN.
NOW IF YOU'LL ALL EXCUSE ME, I BELIEVE THAT'S MY CUE.
GUYS, GET IT TOGETHER!
AND HOPE, STAND DOWN!
SLAM

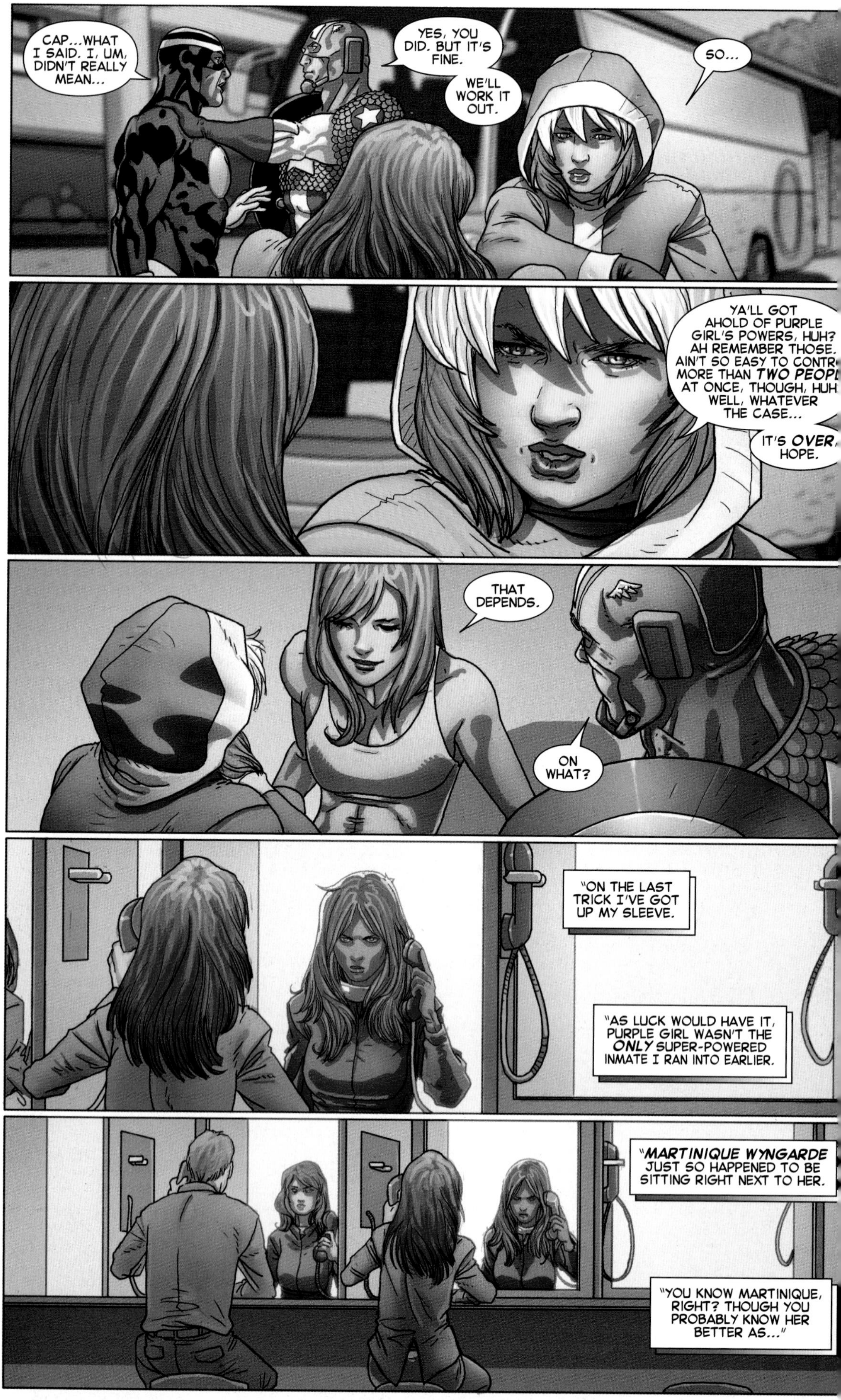

CAP... WHAT I SAID. I, UM, DIDN'T REALLY MEAN...
YES, YOU DID. BUT IT'S FINE.
WE'LL WORK IT OUT.
SO...
YA'LL GOT AHOLD OF PURPLE GIRL'S POWERS, HUH? AH REMEMBER THOSE. AIN'T SO EASY TO CONTR MORE THAN TWO PEOP AT ONCE, THOUGH, HUH WELL, WHATEVER THE CASE...
IT'S OVER, HOPE.
THAT DEPENDS.
ON WHAT?
"ON THE LAST TRICK I'VE GOT UP MY SLEEVE.
"AS LUCK WOULD HAVE IT, PURPLE GIRL WASN'T THE ONLY SUPER-POWERED INMATE I RAN INTO EARLIER.
"MARTINIQUE WYNGARDE JUST SO HAPPENED TO BE SITTING RIGHT NEXT TO HER.
"YOU KNOW MARTINIQUE, RIGHT? THOUGH YOU PROBABLY KNOW HER BETTER AS..."

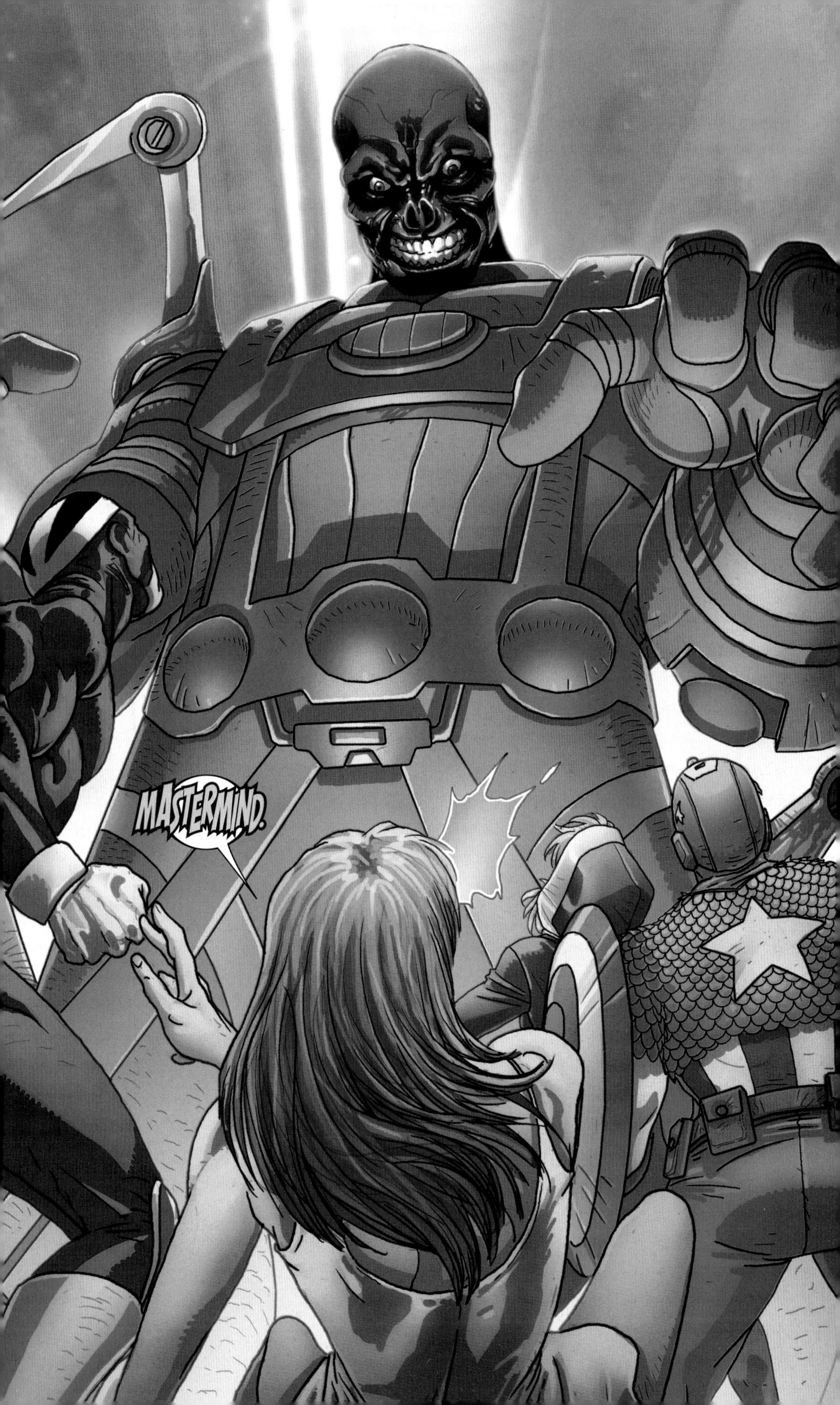
MASTERMIND.

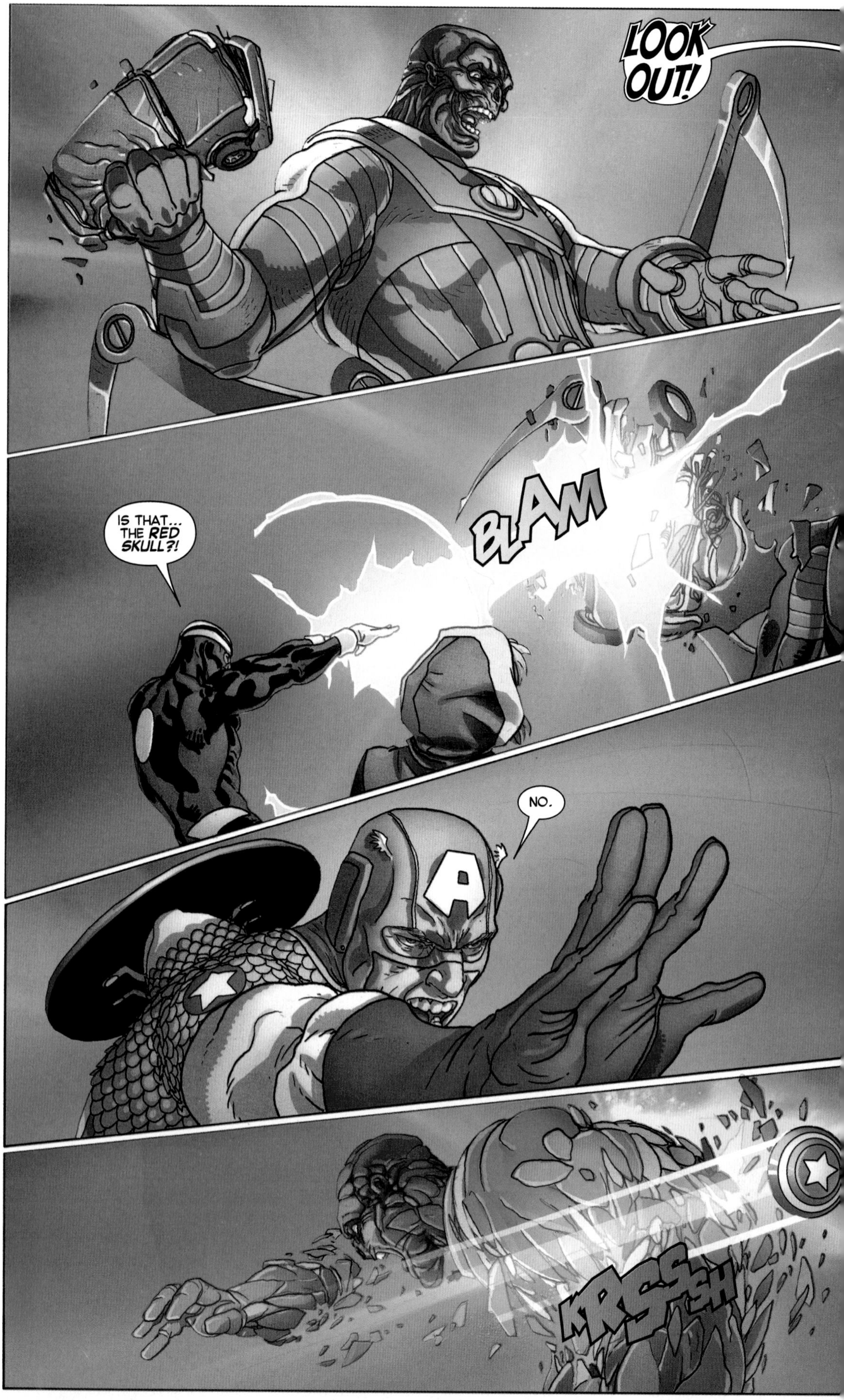
LOOK OUT!
BLAM
IS THAT... THE RED SKULL?!
NO.
KRSSSH

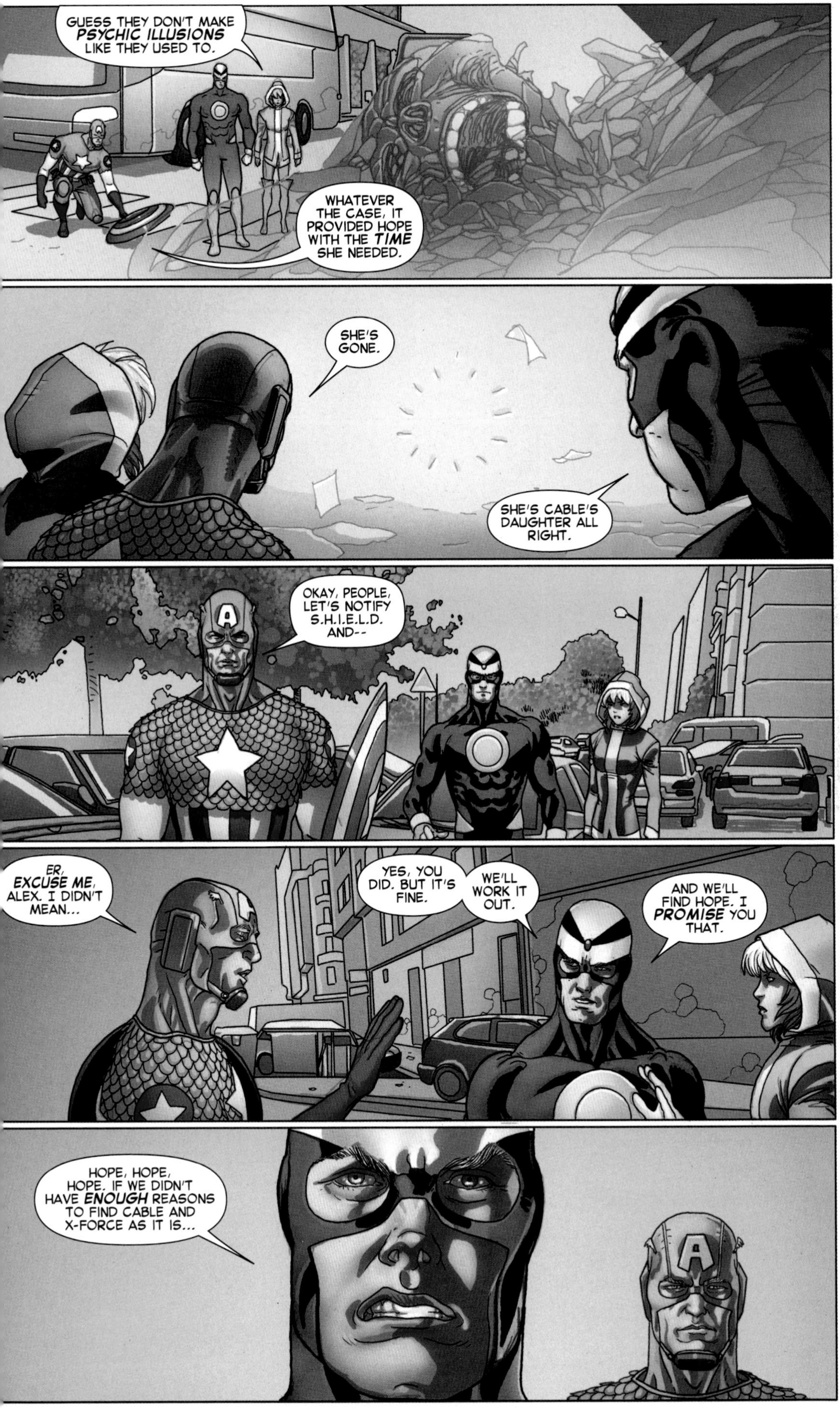

GUESS THEY DON'T MAKE PSYCHIC ILLUSIONS LIKE THEY USED TO.
WHATEVER THE CASE, IT PROVIDED HOPE WITH THE TIME SHE NEEDED.
SHE'S GONE.
SHE'S CABLE'S DAUGHTER ALL RIGHT.
OKAY, PEOPLE, LET'S NOTIFY S.H.I.E.L.D. AND--
ER, EXCUSE ME, ALEX. I DIDN'T MEAN...
YES, YOU DID. BUT IT'S FINE.
WE'LL WORK IT OUT.
AND WE'LL FIND HOPE. I PROMISE YOU THAT.
HOPE, HOPE, HOPE. IF WE DIDN'T HAVE ENOUGH REASONS TO FIND CABLE AND X-FORCE AS IT IS...

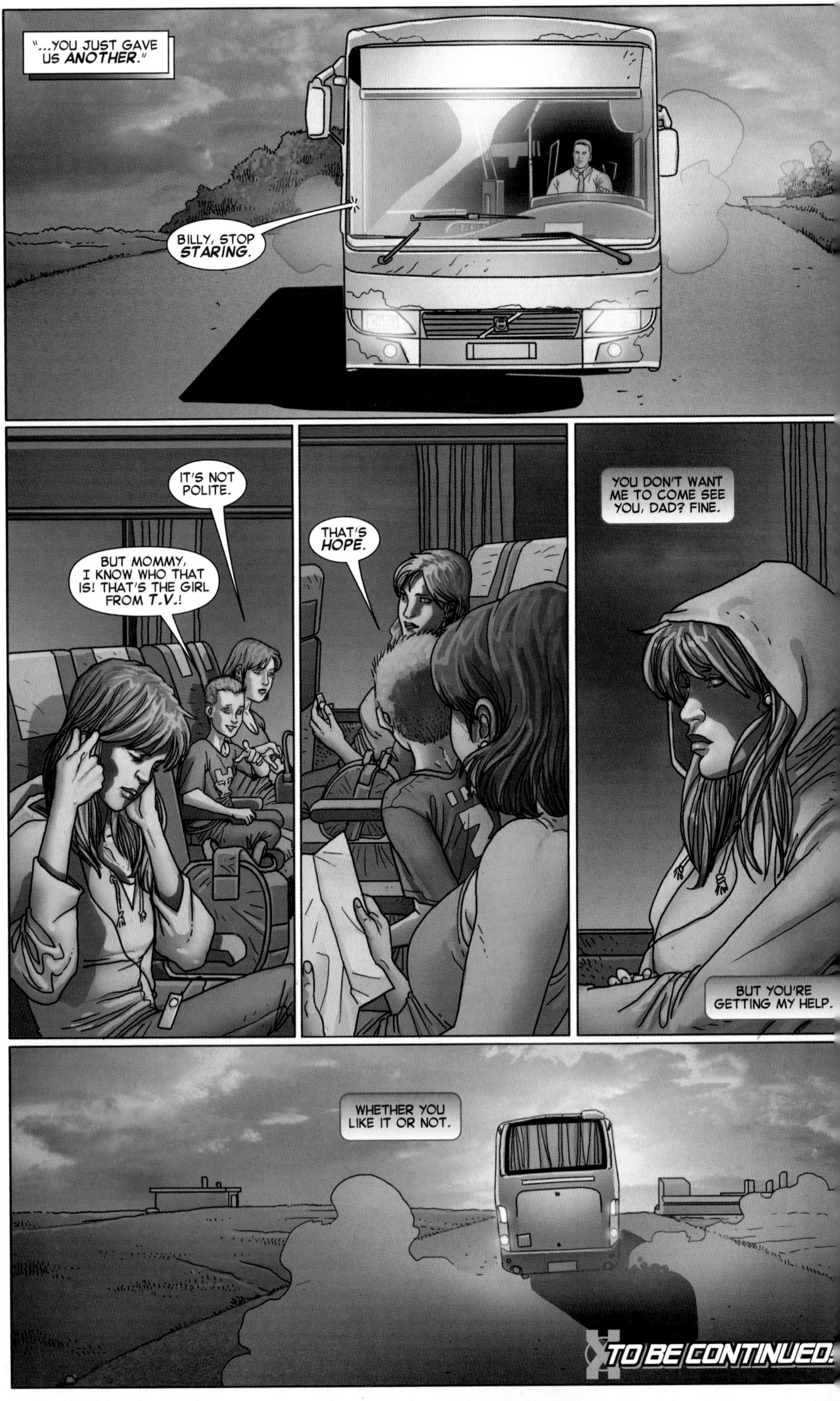
"...YOU JUST GAVE US ANOTHER."
BILLY, STOP STARING.
IT'S NOT POLITE.
BUT MOMMY, I KNOW WHO THAT IS! THAT'S THE GIRL FROM T.V.!
THAT'S HOPE.
YOU DON'T WANT ME TO COME SEE YOU, DAD? FINE.
BUT YOU'RE GETTING MY HELP.
WHETHER YOU LIKE IT OR NOT.
TO BE CONTINUED.

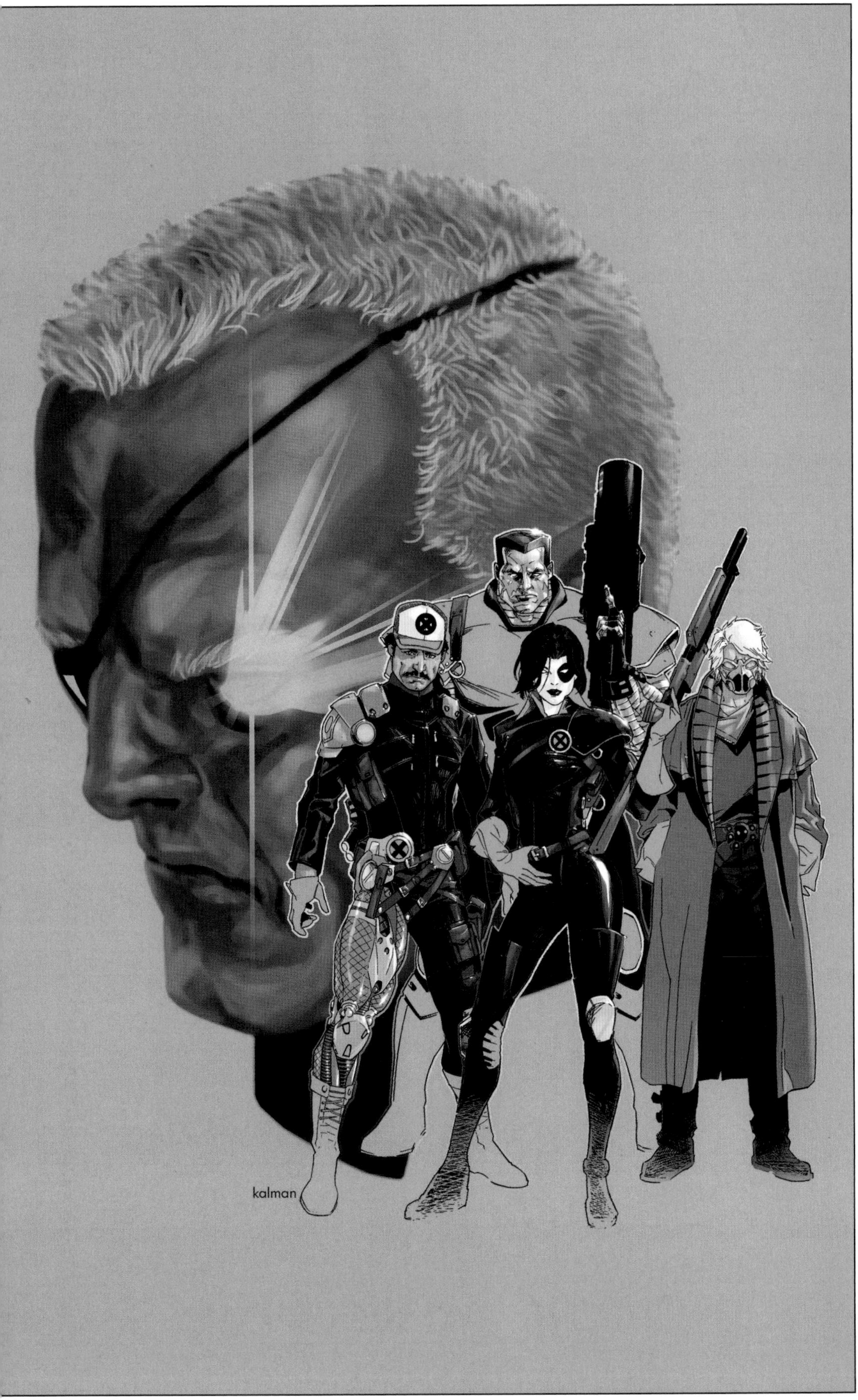
kalman

CABLE AND X-FORCE #6 VARIANT
BY KALMAN ANDRASOFSZKY

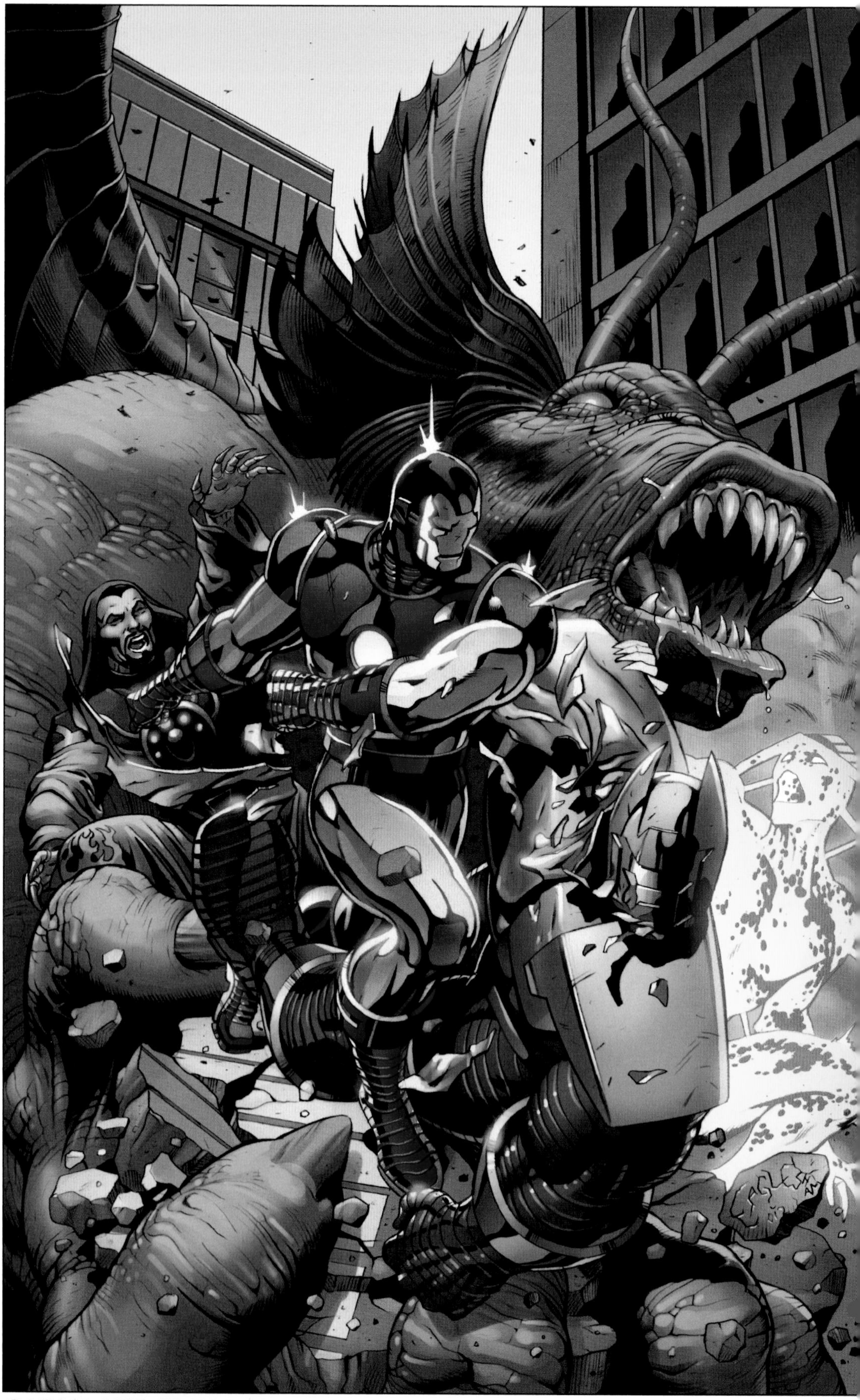

CABLE AND X-FORCE #7 MANY ARMORS OF IRON MAN VARIANT
BY DALE EAGLESHAM & VAL STAPLES

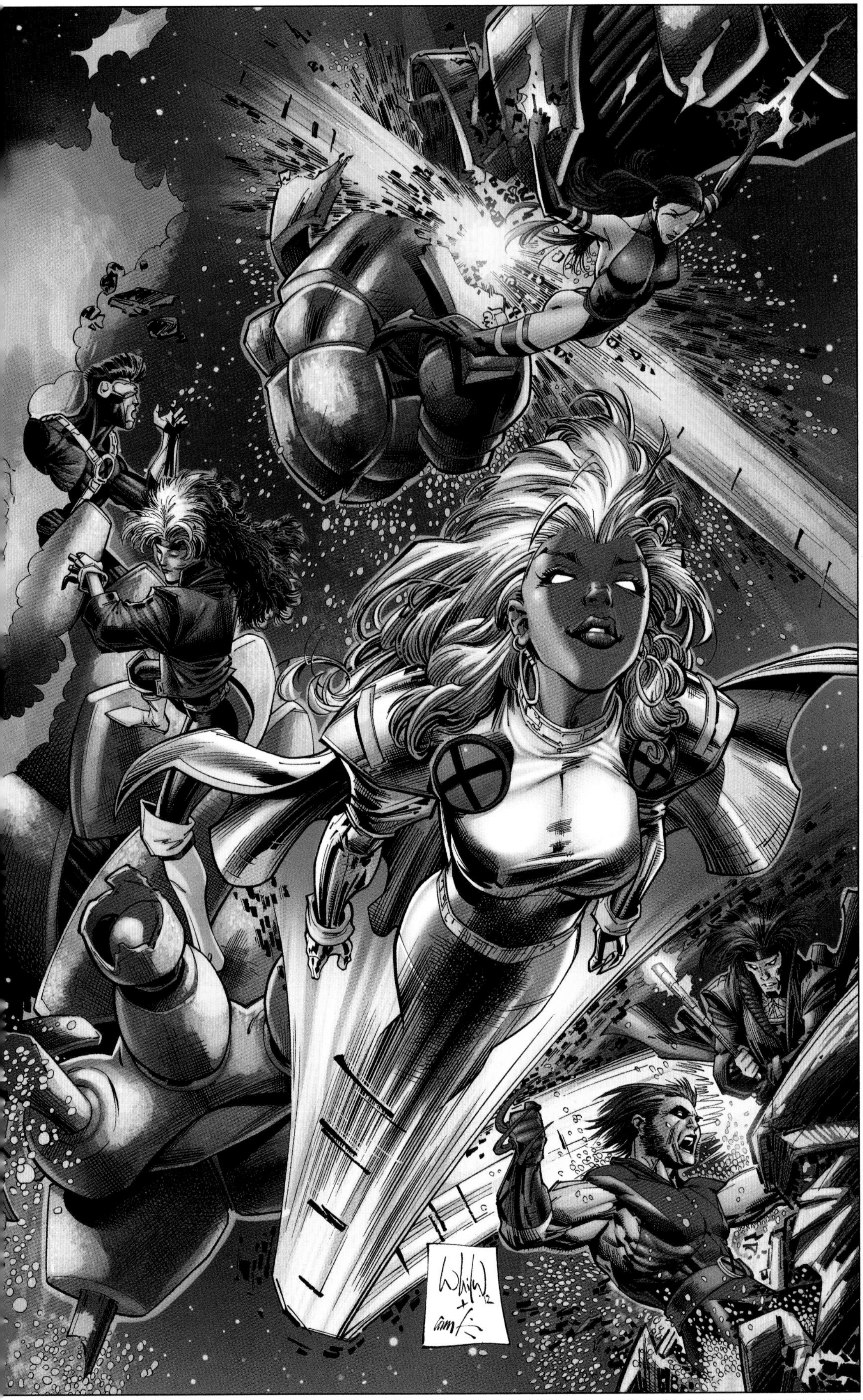

CABLE AND X-FORCE #8 X-MEN 50TH ANNIVERSARY VARIANT
BY WHILCE PORTACIO, CAM SMITH & ANDRES MOSSA

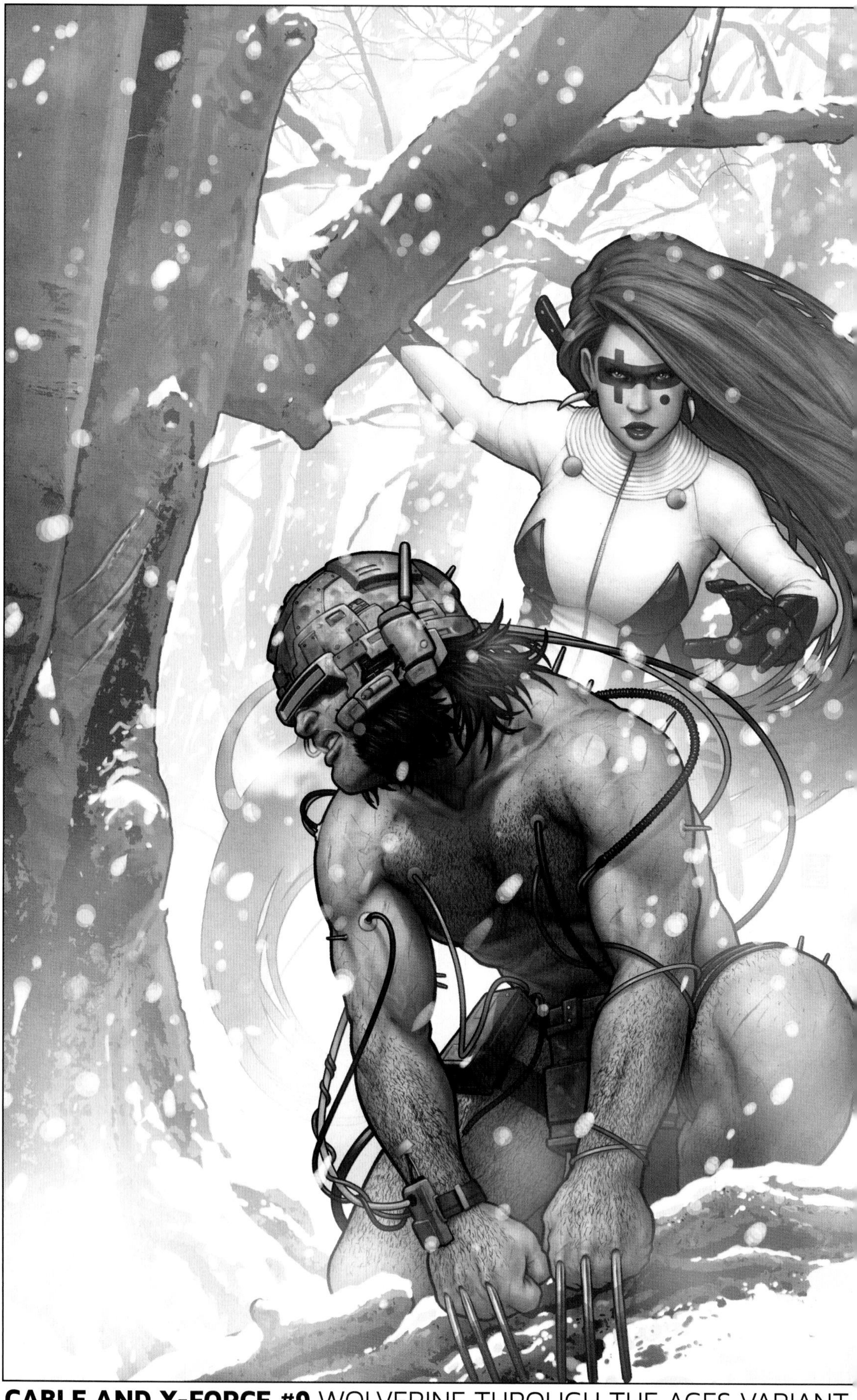

CABLE AND X-FORCE #9 WOLVERINE THROUGH THE AGES VARIANT
BY JOHN TYLER CHRISTOPHER

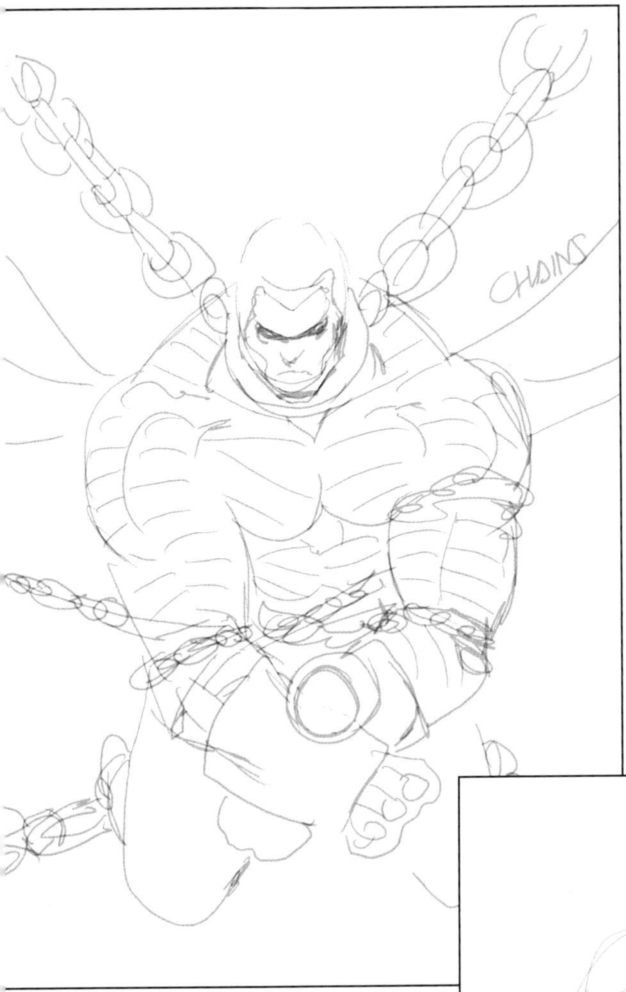
CHAINS

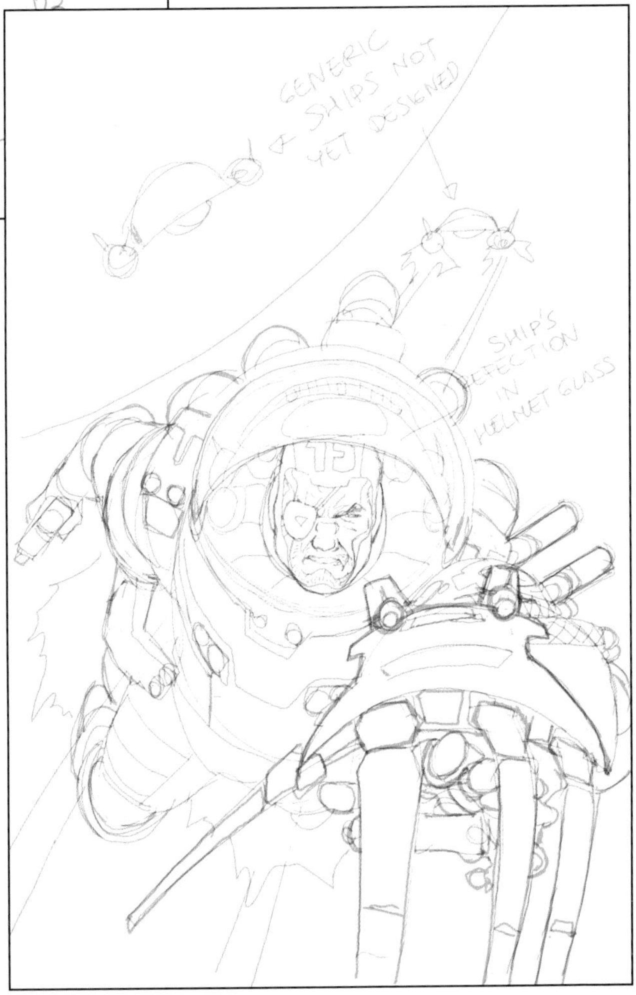
GENERIC
SHIPS NOT
YET DESIGNED
SHIP'S
REFLECTION
IN
HELMET GLASS

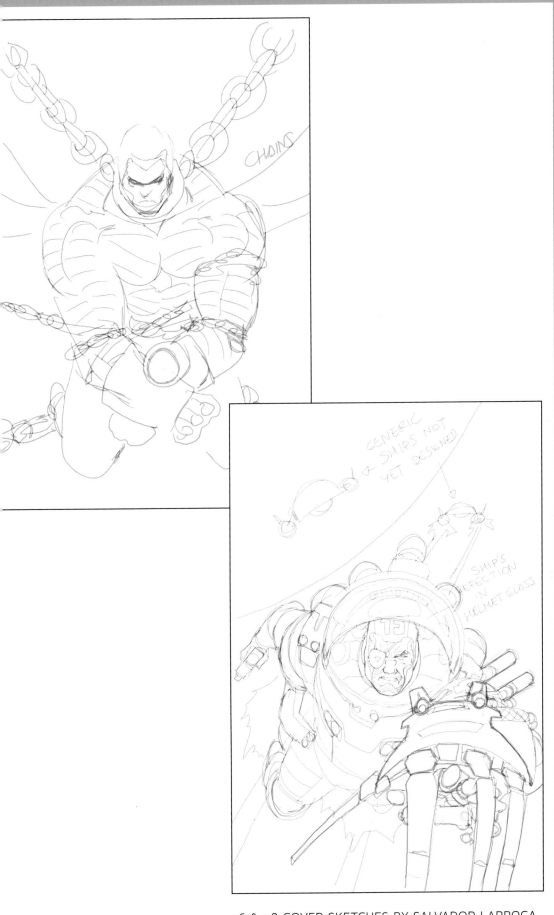

#6 & #8 COVER SKETCHES BY SALVADOR LARROCA

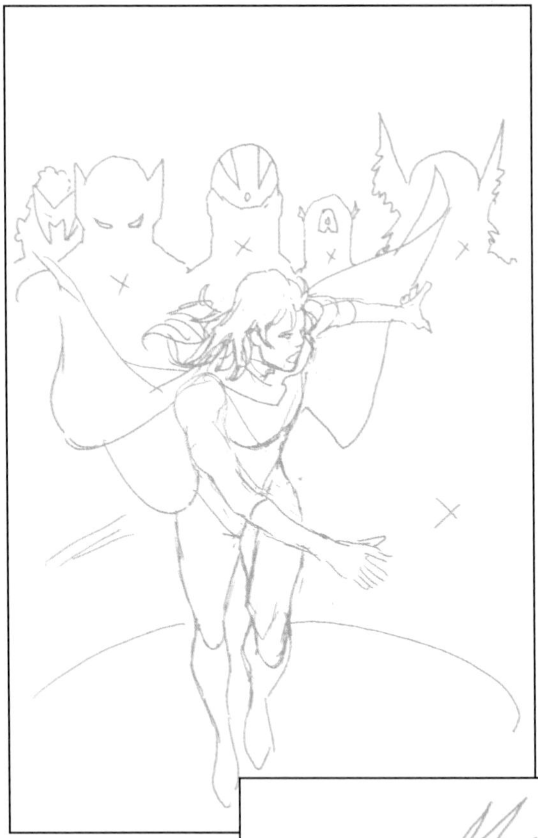
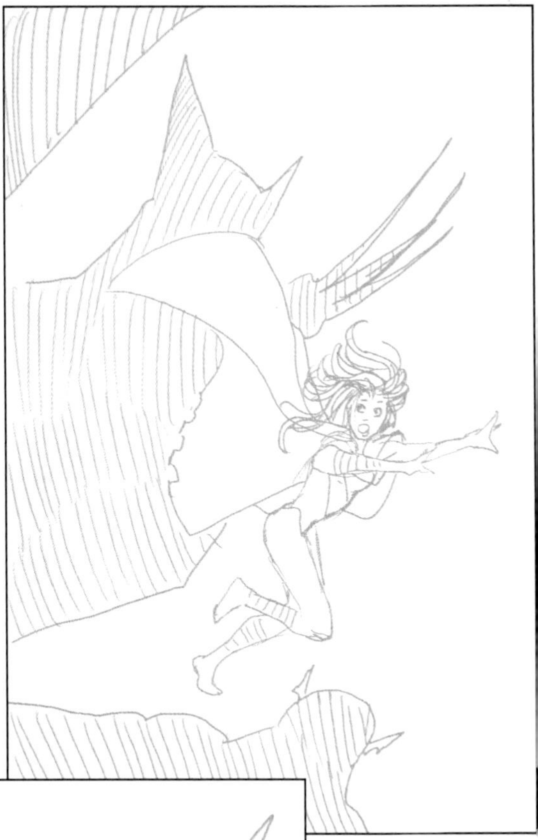
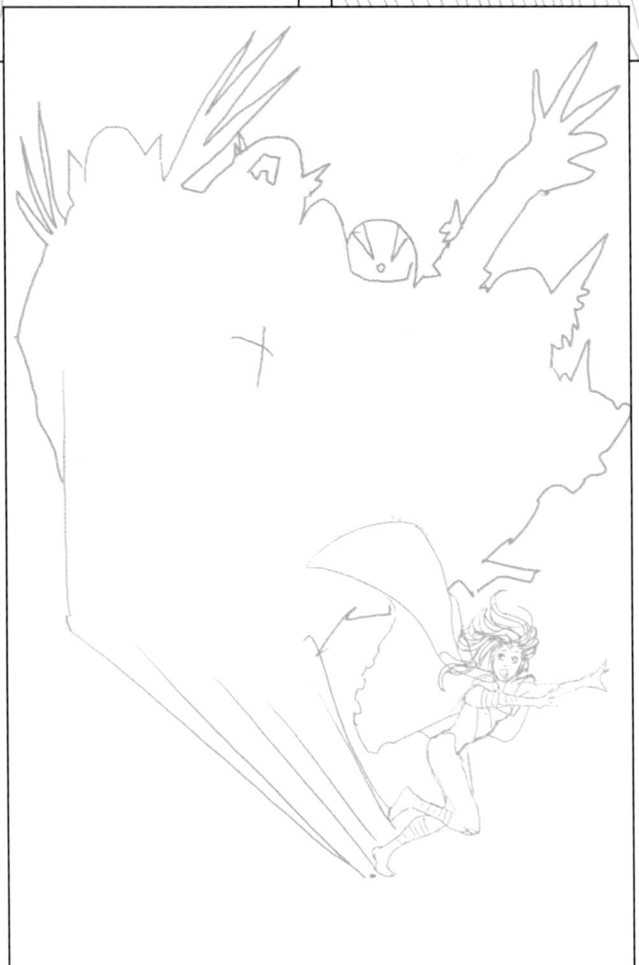

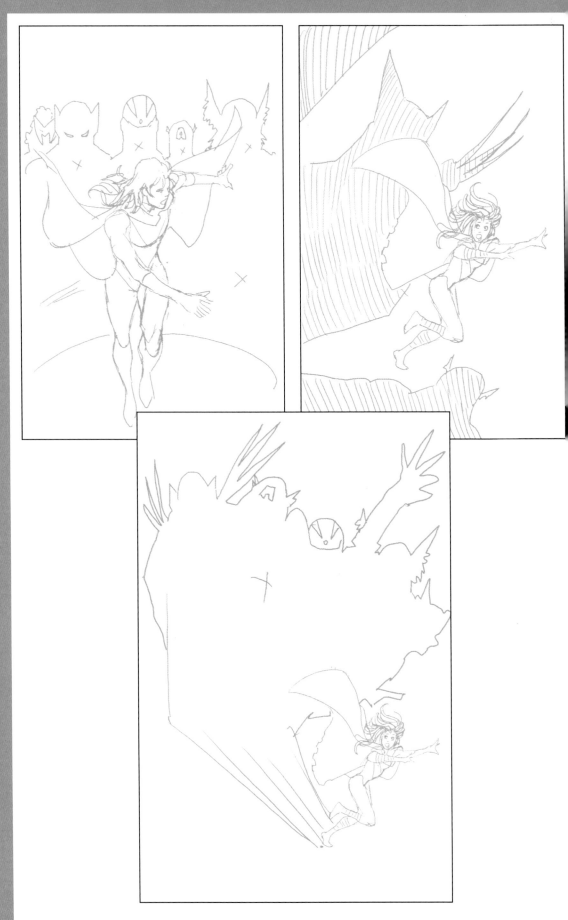

#9 COVER SKETCHES BY SALVADOR LARROCA

"MAD MAX MEETS OCEAN'S 11" – *SuperHeroHype*

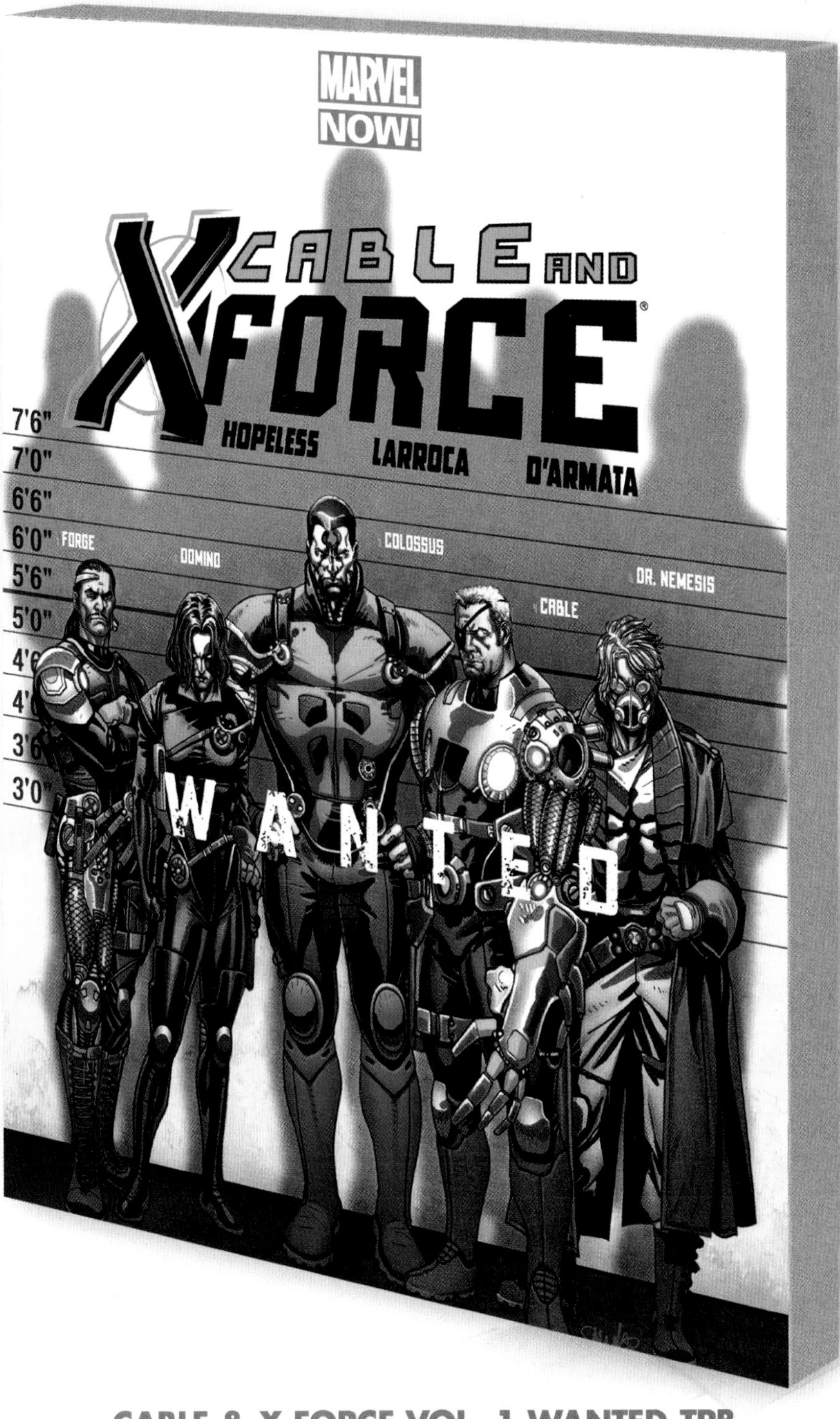
MARVEL NOW!
CABLE AND X-FORCE
HOPELESS
LARROCA
D'ARMATA
7'6"
7'0"
6'6"
6'0"
5'6"
5'0"
FORGE
DOMINO
COLOSSUS
CABLE
DR. NEMESIS
WANTED

CABLE & X-FORCE VOL. 1 WANTED TPB

978-0-7851-6690-0 • FEB130625

"VERY SOLID STUFF" – *CraveOnline*

MARVEL NOW!

TO ACCESS THE FREE *MARVEL AUGMENTED REALITY APP* THAT ENHANCES AND CHANGES THE WAY YOU EXPERIENCE COMIC

1. **Download the app for free via marvel.com/ARapp**
2. **Launch the app on your camera-enabled Apple iOS® or Android™ device***
3. **Hold your mobile device's camera ove any cover or panel with the AR grapł**
4. **Sit back and see the future of comics in action!**

***Available on most camera-enabled Apple iOS® and Android™ devices. Content subject to change and availability.**

CABLE AND X-FORCE AR INDEX

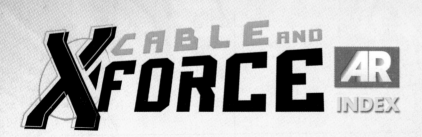

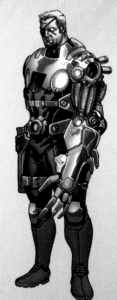